Beyond
Machiavelli

Beyond Machiavelli

Policy Analysis Reaches Midlife

Second Edition

Beryl A. Radin

Georgetown University Press
Washington, DC

Library of Congress Cataloging-in-Publication Data

Radin, Beryl.
  Beyond Machiavelli : policy analysis reaches midlife / Beryl A. Radin. —
2nd ed.
      p.   cm.
  Includes bibliographical reference and index.
  ISBN 978–1–58901–958–4 (pbk. : alk. paper)
  1. Policy sciences. I. Title.
  H97.R33 2012
  320.6—dc23

                                                    2012023482

∞ This book is printed on acid-free paper meeting the requirements of the
American National Standard for Permanence in Paper for Printed Library
Materials.

15 14 13   9 8 7 6 5 4 3 2   First printing

Contents

Preface to the Second Edition

More than a decade has passed since the first edition of this book was published. Although significant elements of that volume continue to be useful to students and scholars of policy analysis, much has changed during these years. These changes have occurred both in the field itself as well as in the environment where its practitioners work. Thus the field is constantly changing, and in some ways this book confronts a very different world than the original book did when it was published in 2000. As such, for the book to continue to be relevant to students and scholars, it had to be modified.

When I wrote the preface to the first edition, I noted that I had based it on many years of teaching, practicing, and talking about the policy analysis profession. Up to that point, most of my experience had been within the borders of the United States, and the field of policy analysis was assumed to be a set of activities that was largely limited to the United States. Since that time, however, the field has become globalized. This has happened in several ways. First, policy analysts are now found in many parts of the globe. Although they share some assumptions and methods, these shared activities take place in political structures that are quite different from that in the United States and in political cultures that approach analytic activities in diverse ways. Second, policy analysis has changed the way that US analysts think about the boundaries of the systems that define their tasks. Even a decade ago, there appeared to be a clear differentiation between domestic and international issues. Today, however, that differentiation is much less clear. Globalization has meant that policy issues transcend the boundaries of the United States in terms of both substantive policies as well as economic conditions. Both the economic crisis of the twenty-first century and concerns that emerged from the experience of the September 11, 2001, terrorist attacks indicate that decisions and problems have little respect for national boundaries.

Over the past decade an already messy decision-making world has become even more complex. In part this was a response to globalization but it is also an acknowledgment of the fuzzy boundary lines between public and private sectors and a movement away from a belief that decision making followed a hierarchical model. Traditional decision-making processes have often been replaced by decision making that involves networks and collaborative as well as conflictual processes. Networks increasingly draw on intergovernmental relationships (crossing bureaucratic lines) and, as well, involve both for-profit and nonprofit actors in hierarchical as well as horizontal relationships. It is extremely difficult to figure out who is the client for the analyst in these network situations.

Another major change that has taken place since 2000 involves the relationship between analysis and politics. When the original book was published, it did include a chapter titled "Dealing with Two Cultures: Politics and Analysis." That discussion largely focused on the differences between the two approaches, drawing on C. P. Snow's framework that describes the conflict between two very different cultures. But in the decade that has passed, it has become increasingly difficult for policy analysis to find a way to approach contemporary issues without succumbing to dramatic pressures that emerge from various forms of politics. It is often difficult to differentiate politics from analysis in a world where politics is entwined with the consequences of the fiscal crisis both in the United States and worldwide. What we now define as politics is a result of not only the formal structures of government and governance but also of the complexity from globalization and policy networks. It is difficult to determine whether analysis belongs to a long-term perspective and political realities always lead one to short-term approaches.

This book was written during a period when reliance on any form of analytic approach has become an act of hope. Thus the result of these changes has not always been positive to someone who had great expectations about the impact of analysis on the quality of decisions. Analysts too often face what many view as an unholy dilemma. They either buy into the political and ideological perspectives of their clients (the decision makers they seek to advise) or retreat into narrow and technical methodologies that are doomed to be ignored in the decision-making process.

Finally, as a result of these changes, there have been significant shifts in the way that the field has defined itself. Although there was never unanimous agreement on the dimensions of the paradigms, methodologies, and concepts of success in the policy analysis enterprise, there are even stronger disagreements in the field today. Increasingly, the difference between policy research and policy analysis is ignored even though the perspectives of the two seem to be quite different.[1] The list of skills and capabilities required for policy analysis grows longer and longer but there is disagreement about priorities to be emphasized between the items on that list. These conflicts are particularly important for those who are responsible for producing new entrants into the field and thus are found in the different assumptions that define the various academic institutions offering master's in public policy degrees. They also emerge from decreased reliance on strong communication between practicing policy analysts and the faculties and students in the academic world.

Although much has changed, this book continues to represent my attempt to synthesize and make some sense of the often-incomplete answers that I have given to the questions raised by public policy analysis students at the five universities where I have taught as they have envisioned their careers in this field. These students have pushed me to reflect on the practice of policy analysis and to attempt to sort out a range of issues that seem to be central to the profession.

I came to the policy analysis field as someone who, before becoming an academic, had already watched the policymaking process as both an activist and an individual working inside a bureaucracy. Indeed, I often describe my career as one of a "pracademic," someone who has spent time in both the academy and the world of practice. As one concerned about policy change, I was chagrined to watch the decision-making process close at hand. I certainly resonated to the saying, "If you like the product, don't watch the process of making either sausage or policy."

The process that I have watched continues to suffer from the absence of good policy advice. Both government decision makers and influential individuals outside government have been allowed to make (or influence) policy on the basis of cronyism or bad hunches or to rely on overly technical and narrowly specialized experts who have defined policy issues in very incomplete ways by focusing only on efficiency criteria and driving out other values. The policies that were a part of my own personal agenda suffered from the failure of those who made them to think about interrelationships between programs and policies, policy implementation difficulties, and the negative consequences experienced by individuals who were expected to benefit from the policies.

Thus, when I entered the world of the academy, I did not bring with me a set of favorite analytic techniques. In fact, I was skeptical about the appropriateness of attempts to turn the policy process into a highly rational and logical set of activities. Rather, I sought ways to improve what is a messy, fragmented decision-making process that in the United States always involves a wide range of actors both inside and outside government. I had no illusions that the process could become neat and tidy. I believed—and continue to believe—that all the actors involved in the process would benefit from the application of more systematic ways of assessing options and the consequences of both proposed and existing policies. It is clear that this task is more difficult today than it was in the field's early days. The process of providing policy advice involves not only those with official authority in the system (like Machiavelli's prince) but also those who are in positions to influence decisions. The developments that have taken place in the policy analysis profession over the years have moved us closer to the role that seems to me to be central: setting the activity in a pluralistic and fragmented policy world that operates in a society characterized by diversity. These developments have occurred despite the modifications that have taken place in American society as a result of political, economic, and social changes.

I had the opportunity to reflect on these issues in my presidential address to the Association of Policy Analysis and Management in November 1996. This address, titled "The Evolution of the Policy Analysis Field: From Conversation to Conversations," raised many of the questions that I seek to answer in the following pages.[2] It is my hope that this book as well as that article will help to stimulate a serious discussion in the policy analysis field about the changes that have taken place in the profession in its nearly forty years of practice. The literature today is much more substantial than it was in the late 1990s. I have no doubt that some people will disagree with my view of the profession's history and developments, but I believe that we will all benefit from careful reflection on our practice.[3]

I am indebted to many individuals who have contributed to my policy analysis education. In considering this topic, perhaps I have learned more from my students than from any other group. I benefited from the comments of a number of individuals who read the book's manuscript and made very useful suggestions. My first edition thanked Eugene Bardach, Thomas Birkland, Kathy Dalton, George Greenberg, Robert Nakamura, William Prosser, Carroll Seron, and the anonymous reviewers for Georgetown University Press. Others have joined them in this edition: Susannah Ali, Karen Baehler, Angela Evans, Elizabeth Hill, Nick Johnson, Iris Lav, Claudia Scott, and Mack Taylor. I was privileged to enjoy a month-long resident scholarship at the Rockefeller Foundation's incredibly beautiful Bellagio Study and Conference Center in Bellagio, Italy, during the summer of 1998. The first edition of the book would not have been completed without that jump start. I would also like to thank the staff members of the policy organizations described in chapter 4 who were willing to spend time with me and share their valuable experiences.

Finally, this book is dedicated to the memory of Aaron Wildavsky. As I wrote the original manuscript, I thought about the comments he might have made about it. Given the changes that have occurred since the book's first edition, I wish it were possible to discuss their impact with him. No one else in the field's short history has made a more substantive and substantial contribution to policy analysis. He continues to be missed.

Notes

1. See the discussion by Aidan R. Vining and David L. Weimer, "Policy Analysis," in *Foundations of Public Administration, Public Administration Review*, 2010.

2. Beryl A. Radin, "The Evolution of the Policy Analysis Field: From Conversation to Conversations," *Journal of Policy Analysis and Management* 16, no. 2 (1997).

3. Soon after the original edition of this book came out, I asked four individuals with extensive careers in policy analysis to reflect on their experience. I highly recommend that readers seek out this article to see a range of opinions and experiences: Beryl A. Radin, "Reflections on Careers in Policy Analysis," *Journal of Policy Analysis and Management* 22, no. 2 (2003): 299–312.

Introduction

What does it mean to be a policy analyst? Despite the growth of the field over the past several decades, this is not a profession that the general public understands. Indeed, as time has gone by since the profession took shape, there sometimes appears to be less agreement about the activity than there was in its earliest days. It is obvious that policy analysis has not gained a place in the world of professions equal to that of law, medicine, or engineering. Because many of the original policy analysts worked for the government, it was difficult for those outside the field to differentiate between public administrators and policy analysts. This became even more confusing when academic institutions offered both master's in public policy (MPP) and master's in public administration (MPA) degrees in the same school or department. My experience teaching in three academic programs that offered both MPP and MPA degrees indicates that it was not always clear how to differentiate between the two programs because both degrees shared the same faculty.

Both practitioners and students of the field are likely to confront blank stares from family members or casual acquaintances when, in response to the question "What do *you* do?" they answer, "I am a policy analyst." In fact, one individual noted that people think a policy analyst actually sells insurance. It is difficult to find the right words to describe the field of practice. One could choose terms such as *advice giver*, *personal counselor*, *creator of options*, *information broker*, *researcher*, or *evaluator*, but none of them quite captures the breadth and depth of the role and the field.

There are many reasons for this situation, but at least one of them is the field's inability to define itself in the context of a changing economic, political, and social environment and, at the same time, to find a way to describe and appreciate the contributions of the fluid profession. The answer to the question "What is a policy analyst?" is different today than it was in the 1960s, when the profession first defined itself.

This book seeks to do several things. First, it is designed to help policy analysis students, faculty, and practitioners explain who they are and how they got there. Its major arguments emphasize the changes that have taken place in the profession since its early days. The assumptions, work, and constraints experienced by policy analysts in the late 1990s were very different than they were in 1961, when the first policy analysis professionals began working at the Department of Defense to implement the Planning, Programming, and Budgeting System. And, as the twenty-first century began, even more changes occurred.

Although the book focuses on the practice of the profession, it also casts a wider lens on the field. In doing so, it is an example of the intellectual history of the development of a profession that—in its practice—must directly confront the broader changes in American society. All professions go through modifications as they operate in always-changing political, economic, social, and technological environments. Policy analysis, perhaps more than the traditional professions (e.g., law, medicine, and engineering), directly confronts the changing political values of the day. The America of the 1960s was characterized by a strong belief in progress, abundance, and the possibilities of public-sector change. The economic, political, and social fabric of society supported a reliance on expertise and experts. Soon afterward, however, the climate of opinion within society had shifted. Americans were less confident about the future, were more focused on the realities of scarcity, and had pulled back from public-sector responsibilities. And as many policy issues have confronted ideological and value differences, there has been an attempt to avoid them through reliance on technocratic solutions. Yet at the same time, many in society are much less willing to defer to so-called experts than they were in the past. According to one experienced practitioner, by the 1990s the terms "fear, paranoia, apprehension, and denial" described the life of a policy analyst.[1] But during the same period that this shift has occurred, the number and range of jobs in the field have markedly increased. The twenty-first century, however, has brought less clarity about what a policy analyst would or could do.

There are other ways to think about the changes that have taken place in the policy analysis field. Nearly fifty years of practice have inevitably changed the field; one would be surprised if there had been no shifts, given the normal life cycle of a profession. Whether one views this as the normal maturation of a profession, particularly an interdisciplinary one, some types of changes are quite predictable.[2] The uncertainty that is found in the contemporary practice of policy analysis suggests that the field is within its midlife.

There are those who bemoan the modifications in the profession and continue to point to a golden day when decision makers listen to experts and seem to take the work of policy analysts seriously. Walter Williams, for example, believed that federal agencies' social policy analysis "reached its peak in the first decade" of its practice.[3] Some others believe that the dimensions of the field in the 1990s were more appropriate to the institutions, values, and processes of American democracy than were the more elite practices of the world of the 1960s. These modifications, it could be argued, have produced a profession that has become classically American as it has become more pluralistic and open, whereas the earlier version of the field had more in common with societies that had traditions of elitism and secrecy. Yet as the twenty-first century has begun to unfold, it has sometimes appeared that pluralism and openness have led to increased conflict and an inability to deal with multiple perspectives.

Contrasting Three Eras

This book contrasts the realities of the policy analysis profession during three periods: the 1960s, the 1990s, and the 2010s. It does so by focusing on several knotty issues that confront the policy analysis practitioner: the conflict between the imperatives of analysis and the world of politics; the analytic tools that have been used, created, or discarded during the profession's fifty years; the changing relationships between decision makers and analysts as the field has proliferated; and the assumptions about the availability and appropriateness of information that can be used in the analytic task. It also emphasizes the shifts in society's attitudes toward public action, the availability of resources to meet public needs, and the dimensions of policymaking.

My approach of using only three periods to frame these contrasts does not capture the gradual changes that have taken place in the more than fifty years that have led to the contemporary situation. The book does, however, provide a way to emphasize the shifts that have occurred in the profession. This treatment thus is not a history but a portrayal of the contrast between two generations.

This book deals with a number of issues by providing both human and organizational examples that illustrate the world today. Three hypothetical individual policy analysts have been created to illustrate the issues discussed—one working in the 1960s, the second working in the 1990s, and the third working in the 2010s. They are presented as variants of the typical professional policy analyst of each era. There clearly were—and are—analysts who do not fit the mold presented for the period, because struggles and variation are always present in the field. Neither individual is based on an identifiable person, but each contains attributes based on those of actual individuals. The vignettes that are provided at the beginning of most of the chapters try to show how individuals have coped with the demands of the field. John Nelson, Rita Stone, and Veronica Lopez, the three prototypical policy analysts, are successively introduced in the first three chapters. Two of them meet in the last chapter and have a conversation about the developments in the field.

John Nelson—the fictional policy analyst of the 1960s—is an economist who moved into the field during its early stages, became an expert on the techniques of economic analysis, and learned to apply these techniques to a range of policy issues. He came to the federal government and stayed only for a few years. Though he was a specialist in analytic techniques, he was a generalist in terms of the substance of policy. By contrast, Rita Stone—the fictional policy analyst of the 1990s—focused her interest and experience in a specific policy area. She was trained in an interdisciplinary public policy academic program that acquainted her with a range of analytic approaches, and she became a career public servant in the federal government. The third policy analyst—Veronica Lopez—began her career as doctor of medicine and policy specialist on health inside the US federal government but became involved in international issues relatively early in her career. She moved from the US government first to the Pan American Health Organization and then to a staff position at the Bill & Melinda Gates Foundation. She stands as an example of someone who was trained as a specialist in a policy area and then moved into an analytical role, but who also moves back and forth between roles as a decision maker and an analyst.

In addition, chapter 4 offers profiles of nine quite diverse policy analysis organizations to illustrate the field's great variety of approaches and institutions.[4] Policy analysis organizations come in different forms—as think tanks or government agencies (in both the executive and legislative branches)—and are found at different levels of government. The nine organizations described here were selected as examples of groups currently doing policy analysis but do not represent the possible range of cases. The nine—the Heritage Foundation, the Center on Budget and Policy Priorities, the Twentieth Century Fund, the Congressional Research Service of the Library of Congress, the California Legislative Analyst's Office, the Office of the Assistant Secretary for Planning and Evaluation of the Department of Health and Human Services, the Danish National Centre for Social Research, the State Fiscal Analysis

Initiative, and the policy analysis unit of AARP (formerly the American Association for Retired Persons)—are very different from one another in clients/audiences, the roles of analysts, the skills used, and in their approaches to issues, history, and ideology. Yet the staff members of all these organizations can be legitimately described as policy analysts.

As both the hypothetical analysts and the organizational profiles indicate, policy analysts operate with quite different standards of success, which reflect the essentially normative character of the profession. For some, success comes when decision makers seek and accept their advice. For others, the reward is involvement—even tangentially—in the decision-making process. Some measure success as the ability to do interesting work and apply a range of analytical methodologies. Still others define their success in terms of their ability to advance substantive policy positions or at least to influence the views of others involved in the decision-making process. Some analysts believe that they must include all possible options and strive for a comprehensive approach to policy problems. Others, by contrast, begin with a set of values (or even a specific agenda) and define their roles as advocacy analysts.

Although policy analysts initially focused on the stage of the policy process when alternative approaches to issues were being formulated, it is clear that the scope of their role has widened. Analysts are now involved in bringing issues to the policy agenda; in working with decision makers, particularly at the legislative level, in the actual adoption of policy; in ascertaining the details of implementation; and in the evaluation process. In some instances it is difficult to disentangle the policy analyst role within the various stages of the policy process. Analysts are involved in putting issues on the table, in negotiating with decision makers during the adoption process, in working closely with managers in the implementation stage, and in conducting evaluations of the policy or program once it is in operation. The image of the policy analyst as someone operating in an ivory tower without getting his or her feet wet in the decision-making world continues to be challenged. Yet it is often not clear what analysts do, what their impact is on the process, and what the expectations are about their role.

Examining the Differences

It is not surprising that a field rooted in the world of practice has changed over the years. But the textbooks used for graduate courses in policy analysis tend to rely on the intellectual frameworks, experiences, and images of practice from the profession's early years and thus do not always reflect the many changes that have since taken place. In some cases the more recent textbooks have even moved back to follow the approaches of the texts used by the more traditional social sciences—political science and economics in particular. The disciplinary roots of individuals have reemerged, and there are few examples of approaches that represent a multidisciplinary perspective. As a result, students may complete their educational experiences without a clear sense of the contemporary dimensions of the profession they have chosen. However, when students focus on their possibilities in the job market, they often gain a more realistic view of the world than is held by their professors, who can be somewhat removed from contemporary developments in the profession. Unlike many of the original faculty members in MPP programs, it appears that fewer instructors and professors have had actual experience as policy analysts inside public organizations, consulting firms, or nonprofit/interest groups. Thus the faculty does not always have personal examples to bring to the classroom, something that is problematic for students seeking a practitioner degree.

There is a tendency for policy analysis students to be somewhat confused about the professional identity they are assuming. The range of assumptions about the field is illustrated in the array of answers that were given when the question "What is policy analysis?" was posed to an introductory master's-level class. The range of responses suggests that there are many ways to describe the field and that all the descriptions may be viewed as appropriate:

- Policy analysis is a multielement process of assessing and analyzing the components that make up the stated policy, or plan of action. The process should include viewing the players, environmental issues, and forces that influence and/or determine the policy.
- Policy analysis is not an exact science but rather an art. There are numerous approaches one can take within policy analysis. One is to establish an agenda and then formulate the issues, address alternatives, set the adoption and implementation plans, and establish a feedback vehicle. Policy analysis deals with both formal and informal policy. Formal policy covers laws and regulations, whereas informal policy addresses directives and standard operating procedures.
- Policy analysis sheds light on the components of an issue or problem. It provides insights as well as the data necessary to open minds to new alternatives, and it creates the basis for informed decision making and charting a course of action.
- Policy analysis is the process whereby governmental decision making can be explained and understood. It can help anticipate decisions

through the use of techniques that enable various factors and their relative influence to be identified. Various models are available that do this.

- Policy analysis is an exploration of values of the client and how they affect the impact, problems, deficiencies, and feasibility of a particular policy. It is done in many different ways, using a variety of techniques. It is dependent upon the environment, politics, actors, history, organizational culture, and clients.
- Policy analysis is rooted in the details of specific policy sectors and requires a detailed knowledge of the sector's history and construction.
- Policy analysis is the utilization of applied techniques, both formal and informal, to arrive at one recommendation for the benefit of a client based on a prescribed policy.
- Policy analysis is client-based. It entails looking at quantifiable and/or qualitative data through various methodologies so as to create a definition of the problem, assumptions, alternatives, a recognition of actors, and recommendations (observing political feasibility). It moves from agenda setting to formulation to operations to implementation to evaluation.
- Policy analysis is a process that employs qualitative and/or quantitative techniques to describe a problem, illustrate its effects, and present possible solutions.
- Policy analysis is the comprehensive, objective, and systematic assessment of political problems, possible solutions, and their means of implementation.
- Policy analysis is the study of numerous variables affecting an identified issue or problem and the alternative recommendations for solutions provided to decision makers. It produces an adequate range of alternatives to produce the best solution in light of foreseeable constraints.
- Policy analysis is the process of reviewing, evaluating, analyzing, and measuring a policy matter as a means of devising recommendations and policy alternatives for a particular client.
- Policy analysis is a process that seeks to generate viable solutions to public-sector (and often nongovernmental) problems.
- Policy analysis is a way or ways whereby we can examine, evaluate, and provide advice.

The Future

In the more than fifty years since the early days of policy analysis, this profession has changed dramatically. Many of the changes described in this book are set in the contemporary environment. Thus it is not always clear whether these shifts are idiosyncratic to this era or illustrative of broader changes. One would, however, assume that further change is likely. The book ends with the attempt to think about the dimensions of the policy analysis field and profession in the future. The field struggles with the consequences of several major forces. It must respond to the allegations about elitism and the role of policy analysis in a democracy. It must somehow deal with the critiques of the rational actor model—which assumes that action is based on the explicit choices and aims of actors—particularly by those critical theorists who argue that policy analysis is part of the problem, not the solution. And it must confront the concerns of those who believe that the diffusion within the field has actually led to a loss of professional identity. In addition, it is important to consider the impact of globalization, technology, and continual value clashes. Chapter 9 thus focuses on the implications of these changes and uncertainties for the education of policy analysts.

Organization of the Book

This book is organized in nine chapters. Because it is written for a diverse readership—including students, faculty members, and practitioners—some chapters may be of more interest to one group than another. Chapter 1 reviews the origins of the field, harking back to the ancient practice of advising the "prince," to use Machiavelli's term, and to the early stages of the practice of policy analysis in the 1960s. Chapter 2 highlights the expansion of the field both inside and outside government, the impact of a changing environment on the effort, and the process of the maturation of analytic activity. Chapter 3 describes the movement of the field across the globe and the response within the field to changes in the decision-making process. Chapter 4, as was explained above, provides profiles of nine organizations that practice policy analysis and contrasts their approaches to clients, skills, staffs, roles, information, and ideology. Chapter 5 contrasts the assumptions made about politics during the field's early stages with those made today. It also discusses the challenges to these assumptions and the concepts of neutrality and objectivity. Chapter 6 reviews the various methodologies and analytic techniques that are viewed as the tools of the analyst's trade. It emphasizes the alternative formulations that have entered the field in recent years. Chapter 7 discusses and contrasts the optimistic views about the availability and appropriateness of information with current perspectives on the utilization of and investment in information. It includes attention to the impact of technology on the availability of information. Chapter 8 details the shifts that have occurred in the policymaking task, moving from analysis focused on the creation of new programs to fine-tuning existing programs or analyzing cutbacks. It emphasizes the relationship between policy analysis and the budget process. Finally, chapter 9 focuses on the questions "Where are we now?" and "Where are we going?" It examines a series of developments that have already had or can be expected to have an impact on the field.

Some readers will find this book frustrating because it does not set forth a single, clear vision of good policy analysis. This is by design. I have drawn on a wide variety of sources and perspectives to illustrate the many views about the profession. This breadth of sources also reflects the reality that there is no agreement in either the academic wing of the discipline or in its applied side about the seminal books in the field.

As the field developed and became more closely linked to the contours of the US decision-making process, it came to support a relativist and eclectic approach to the practice. The globalization of the field increases this tendency. No single model adequately fits all the players now engaged in something called *policy analysis*. The chapters in this book deal with questions that must be answered by all types of policy analysts. As they struggle with these issues, they learn that what is appropriate in one setting is ineffective or even destructive in another. The diffusion of the practice thus creates both opportunities and constraints.

Notes

1. Quoted by David R. Beam, "If Public Ideas Are So Important Now, Why Are Policy Analysts So Depressed?" *Journal of Policy Analysis and Management* 15, no. 3 (1996).

2. The literature on professionalism suggests that fields go through fairly predictable processes as they attempt to establish a monopoly on expertise, turn toward formal professional training, and seek to establish a monopoly on who may practice in the field. However, policy analysis has not secured a way to establish a monopoly on practice, nor has it achieved agreement on the attributes of the expertise that make up the field.

3. Walter Williams, *Honest Numbers and Democracy* (Washington, DC: Georgetown University Press, 1998).

4. The first edition included only six organizations.

Chapter 1

A Portrait of the Past

John Nelson began his career as a policy analyst soon after he completed his PhD in economics at Stanford in 1959. His dissertation used cost-benefit analysis as a method of examining and recommending efficiencies in procurement of defense weapon systems. He was recruited by the RAND Corporation in Santa Monica, California, to work on a project for the US Department of Defense (DoD). RAND was one of several nonprofit think-tank organizations created specifically to do work for the federal government. Through that experience, he broadened his analytic focus and became proficient in other related disciplines, particularly systems analysis and operations research.

When John Kennedy was elected president and former Ford Motor Company president Robert McNamara was appointed secretary of defense, Nelson became intrigued by the possibility of spending a few years inside government. His contacts in the DoD were delighted to hear of his interest, and when the first staff was assembled to put the Planning, Programming, and Budgeting System (PPBS) in place, he became a federal official. His previous experience with the cost-benefit technique was extremely valuable to the DoD staff, and he soon became one of the resident experts in the use of the PPBS approach. Though he missed California, he believed that his experience inside DoD would serve him well in the future.

Before he knew it, Nelson found that his PPBS expertise was being sought by other federal agencies. President Lyndon Johnson had mandated the use of the PPBS approach throughout the government, and there was a short supply of individuals in Washington who understood the process and were able to use the technique. In 1965 Nelson was asked to join the first policy analysis staff in the Department of Health, Education, and Welfare (HEW), where he worked with William Gorham and Alice Rivlin.

Though Nelson had expected to return to California after two or three years, he was intrigued by the possibilities inside HEW. The three years he spent there were characterized by an incredible growth in federal domestic programs. His assignments were diverse, and he was able to work on several major initiatives in education, health, and social services. He couldn't imagine a career opportunity that was more challenging. Legislative proposals were spun out almost daily; interesting ideas were grabbed from many different sources, just as if they were low-hanging fruit on a tree.

He learned that it was a lot easier to compare weapons systems within the various DoD services than it was to compare and analyze opportunities and costs of programs for the elderly, children, and poor women. The differences among client groups and programs made it difficult to define trade-offs and opportunity costs across HEW. Although he recognized that many of the programs that were being proposed would require implementation by state, local, or nonprofit groups, the pace of change was too rapid to allow much attention to these issues. He also learned that what he saw as analytically irrational behavior within the department was viewed as highly rational behavior by HEW career staff members.

By 1968, however, he decided that it was time to return to California. Though he felt that his years in Washington had provided him with unparalleled experiences, he believed that his long-term career path was outside, not inside, government. Together with two other former RAND staff members who had also spent time in Washington, he created what became a very successful consulting group in Los Angeles that specialized in work for DoD and the aerospace industry. Up until 2000 his firm had been involved in analytic work on the effects of military base closings, a set of projects conducted for DoD and required by the Base Closing Commission. As the twenty-first century began, he decided that it was time to retire.

Although policy analysis as a distinct field and emerging profession is relatively recent, the practice of providing policy advice to decision makers is an ancient art. This chapter discusses the profession in terms of its antecedents and its early years; it provides examples of the first policy analysis offices in the federal government during the 1960s and details the early assumptions made by policy analysis practitioners about their craft. The title of this book, *Beyond Machiavelli*, underscores the origins of the policy analysis profession and its reliance on the heritage of Machiavelli as an important adviser to a ruler. During the most recent period of the field's life, the relationship between the analyst and the client appears to have lost some of the traditional imperative for the analyst to serve as an adviser to decision makers. This is particularly true in the academic expression of the profession.

Antecedents

Herbert Goldhamer's book on the subject of policy analysis, *The Adviser*, begins by noting, "The political adviser appears in man's earliest surviving documents and has never disappeared from the political stage since that time."[1] Indeed, although Western political thought has tended to emphasize the role that Machiavelli played as adviser to the prince above all others, Goldhamer notes that others—namely, early Chinese, Indian, and Greek writers—have also reflected on their experiences as counselors to rulers and other decision makers. Although Ibn Khaldun, Kautilya, and Han Fei Tzu are not individuals whose names are familiar to most contemporary policy analysts, these individuals nonetheless performed the timeless functions of friend, educator, conscience, eyes and ears, executor, and adviser to often isolated and lonely rulers.[2]

Our tendencies to focus on the uniqueness of the contemporary American environment have often evoked approaches that ignore the lessons of history. A field that seeks to create its own special identity works hard to differentiate itself from the past. Yet some universal functions involved in the art of advising are worth discussing. Goldhamer has noted, "The profession of adviser and the development of political skills as a fine art or practical science were most notable precisely where a multiplicity of small states lived in close proximity in a condition of continual rivalry, intrigue, and warfare."[3] In this sense, feudal Europe shared many attributes with contemporary American federalism or the demands of the new European Union. Similarly, Goldhamer comments that the emergence of the adviser role requires a belief "that human will, effort, and intelligence count for something in human affairs, that an implacable destiny or fate does not rule over men."[4] A belief in progress is not a uniquely American phenomenon or a conviction that emerged full blown during the eighteenth-century Age of Enlightenment.

Machiavelli's comments on the importance of advisers seem almost timeless: "The first thing one does to evaluate the wisdom of a ruler is to examine the men that he has around him; and when they are capable and faithful one can always consider him wise, for he has known how to recognize their ability and to keep them loyal; but when they are otherwise one can always form a low impression of him; for the first error he makes is made in this choice of advisers."[5]

There are other lessons from the past that can help us understand the attributes of the policy analysis field that took shape in the early 1960s. Goldhamer emphasizes the use of history and experience as a major source of wisdom, and he describes the replacement of clergy by jurists/lawyers.[6] He notes the skepticism through the years about the ability of youthful—rather than elderly—advisers to provide effective counsel, citing Aristotle's observation that "youths do extremely well in mathematics but that young men of practice wisdom are difficult to find."[7] He also accentuates what he calls "wandering scholars," professional wandering political experts who were able to find employment in lands other than those of their birth.[8] According to Goldhamer, "The individual who moves from one society to another—the 'marginal man'—often has his wits sharpened and his knowledge broadened by the great variety of experiences that his travels provide and by his increased detachment from his own society."[9]

Though the ruler may be motivated to seek additional sources of information, Goldhamer suggests that one must limit the number of advisers who provide counsel. He quotes the advice of Kautilya, the tutor and first minister of Chandragupta, founder of the fourth-century-BC Maurya Dynasty in India:

> This kind of seeking for advice is infinite and endless. The king should consult three or four ministers. Consultation with a single minister may not lead to any definite consultation in cases of complicated issues. A single minister proceeds willfully and without restraint. In deliberating with two ministers, the king may be overpowered by their combined action, or imperiled by their mutual dissension. But with three or four ministers he will not come to any serious grief, but will arrive at satisfactory results. With ministers more than four in number, he will come to a decision [only] after a good deal of trouble; nor will secrecy of counsel be maintained without much trouble.[10]

The conflicts between the cultures of science and politics also are not unique to our own time. Goldhamer writes that the "conflict between the rival claims of what Pascal in the mid–seventeenth century called *l'esprit de geometrie* and *l'esprit de finesse*, that is, between the mathematical or analytic mind and the intuitive mind, between the claims of calculation and those of wisdom and experience, is as old as discussions of the political process, and still continues today."[11] Yet few advisers of the past had to contend with the institutions of democracy with attention to accountability and transparency.

Creating a Profession

Let us fast-forward in history to the end of World War II. Although advice giving and advice seeking were hardly new, American society had experienced a significant change. During the Progressive Era and especially during the New Deal, lawyers played a very important role as advisers in the US governmental system. The shifts that had taken place in the legal profession (especially at Harvard Law School) broadened the legal field, formalized it, and provided a way for lawyers to think of ways to use data and scientific information in their work. And their status within governmental agencies made their advising role very important.

But in the post–World War II period, social scientists began to play a role in the decision-making process. The imperatives of war had stimulated new analytic techniques—among them systems analysis and operations research—whose users sought to apply principles of rationality to strategic decision making. The precepts developed in the natural sciences found expression in the social sciences in two modes: positivism, which means using the concept of laboratory experimentation to seek to differentiate the true from the false; and normative economic reasoning, which means using the concept of a market made up of individual rational actors as the basis for prescription.[12] Although still in an embryonic form, the computer technology of that period did allow individuals to manipulate what were then considered large data sets in ways that had been unthinkable in the past.

In a sense the techniques that were available in the late 1950s cried out for new forms of use. The energy of Americans that had been concentrated on making war in a more rational manner now sought new directions.

Yehezkel Dror, one of the earliest advocates for the creation of policy analysis as a new profession, described the early phases of this search for new expressions as "an invasion of public decision making by economics."[13] Further, he wrote, "Going far beyond the domain of economic policymaking, the economic approach to decision making views every decision as an allocation of resources between alternatives, that is, as an economic problem."[14]

Hugh Heclo also noted that the analytic and conceptual sophistication of the economic approach "is far in advance of any other approach in policy studies, with the result that a mood is created in which the analysis of rational program choice is taken as the one legitimate arbiter of policy analysis. In this mood, policy studies are politically deodorized—politics is taken out of policymaking."[15]

All this took form in the components of the Planning, Programming, and Budgeting System (PPBS), a decision allocation process that was established in the Department of Defense (DoD) in 1961 and eventually extended by President Lyndon Johnson to other parts of the federal government. This analytic approach would always be closely associated with the style and interests of President John Kennedy's secretary of defense, Robert McNamara. A graduate of the Harvard Business School and former president of the Ford

Motor Company, McNamara had great confidence in analytic skills and the rational framework that would produce data.[16]

PPBS itself had antecedents in the work of the RAND Corporation in Santa Monica, California, the nonprofit organization created in 1948, just after World War II was over, to do analytic work for the government, especially the DoD. RAND separated itself from the Douglas Aircraft Company and became an independent, nonprofit organization dedicated "to furthering and promoting scientific, educational, and charitable purposes for the public welfare of the United States."[17]

The link to the RAND experience was obvious when McNamara asked former RAND staff member Charles Hitch to establish the DoD Systems Analysis Unit with responsibility for the PPBS process. Today, more than fifty years since its initial implementation, PPBS continues to have both advocates and detractors. But it is clear that its roots are in microeconomic theory and welfare economics as well as quantitative decision theory, and it uses techniques of operations research, cost-effectiveness and cost-benefit analysis, and program budgeting and systems analysis.[18]

The PPBS process itself required an analyst to identify the objectives of the agency being analyzed, to relate costs and budgetary decisions to these objectives, and to assess the cost-effectiveness of current and proposed programs. This analytic planning process was linked to the budget process (Hitch was actually named comptroller of DoD, with responsibility for the budget), which provided a way to translate what might have been academic exercises to the actual allocation of resources. It represented the first serious effort to link strategic management processes to the budget.

The PPBS process that was put in place had at least three different goals. First, it sought to create opportunities for control by top agency officials over fragmented and diffuse organizational and program units. Despite the organization chart, the DoD was clearly a federal department that operated more like a feudal system than a tight bureaucratic hierarchy. The separate services—army, navy, and air force—were distinct and separate units with their own programs, cultures, and constituencies. The secretary of defense had limited ways of reining in the services to operate as a single department. The PPBS process sought to look at DoD as a unity and to provide advice to the secretary; it represented a way for the secretary to establish control over hitherto-decentralized operations. The analytic categories that were used provided a way for the secretary to identify crosscutting programs and issues within the highly fragmented department.

Second, the PPBS process was an attempt to improve efficiency in the way that resources were allocated and implemented. When DoD was examined from a centralized vantage point and functional categories across the department were defined, it was obvious that there were overlaps and redundancies within the multiple units, particularly in the procurement process. For example, economic efficiencies were not served by processes that could not define areas of economies of scale.

Third, the PPBS process rested on a belief that an increased use of knowledge and information would produce better decisions. The experience of World War II was a heady one; advances in the availability and production of information gave the PPBS proponents the sense that it was possible to differentiate the false from the true and that the conceptual models on which they relied would produce accurate and appropriate information.[19]

DoD: Organizing a Policy Analysis Office

The office that was established at DoD to carry out McNamara's analytical agenda became the model for future analytic activity throughout the federal government. As the office developed, its goal of providing systematic, rational, and science-based counsel to decision makers included what has become the classic policy analysis litany: problem identification, the development of options or alternatives, the delineation of objectives and criteria, evaluation of the effects of these options, estimates of future effects, and—of course—recommendations for action.

In many ways the establishment of this office represented a top-level strategy to avoid what were viewed as the pitfalls of traditional bureaucratic behavior. Rather than move through a complex chain of command, the analysts in this office—regardless of their rank—had direct access to DoD's top officials. Their loyalty was to the DoD secretary, the individual at the top of the organization (the ruler, in Machiavelli's formulation) who sought control and efficiencies in running the huge department. In addition to PPBS, they introduced a range of analytic methods to the federal government, including cost-benefit analysis, operations and systems research, and linear programming.

This office was viewed as an autonomous unit, made up of individuals with well-hewn skills who were not likely to have detailed knowledge of the substance of the policy assignments given them. Their specializations were in the techniques of analysis, not in the details of their application. Though these staff members thought of themselves as specialists, their specializations were not a part of the areas of expertise found within the traditional bureaucracy. As would become clearer as the field developed, these staff members were viewed as individuals who had much more in common with short-term political appointees than with career public servants.

Several other patterns emerged that had a dramatic impact on the field. There was an assumption that the policy analysts who were assembled would constitute a small, elite corps, made up of individuals who would be expected to spend only a few years in the federal government. Most of the individuals hired had been trained as economists or operations researchers and had received their PhDs fairly recently; a significant number of them had come to Washington from RAND, where they had worked on similar assignments. Their frame of reference and support system were atypical for a federal employee—many brought their past relationships with think tanks, consultants, universities, and other analytical organizations with them as they did their work.

Sometimes called the "Whiz Kids," these staff members were highly visible; both their PPBS activity and their general expertise came to the attention of President Lyndon Johnson.[20] In October 1965 the Bureau of the Budget issued a directive to all federal departments and agencies, calling on them to establish central analytic offices that would apply the PPBS approach to all their budget submissions. Staff members were sent to various educational institutions to learn about the PPBS demands.

According to a report in the *New York Times*, Johnson met with the members of his cabinet and instructed them "to immediately begin to introduce a very new and very revolutionary system of planning and programming and budgeting through the vast Federal government, so that through the tools of modern management the full promise of a finer life can be brought to each American at the lowest possible cost."[21] Johnson argued that the use of "the most modern methods of program analysis" would "insure a much sounder judgment through more accurate information, pinpointing those things that we ought to do more, spotlighting those things that we ought to do less."[22]

Even during these days, however, there were those who were skeptical about the fit between the PPBS demands and the developing field of policy analysis. In what has become a classic article, Aaron Wildavsky argued in *Public Administration Review* in 1969 that PPBS had damaged the prospects for encouraging policy analysis in America's national government.[23]

Spreading the Word

Most of the policy analysis offices that became a part of the federal government landscape were created as a result of Johnson's PPBS directive. The development of three such offices—in the now-defunct Office of Economic Opportunity (OEO), the Department of Health and Human Services (HHS) (formerly the Department of Health, Education, and Welfare—HEW), and the Department of Interior—provides a glimpse of the early days of the field as it moved beyond DoD. In addition, it is instructive to describe the development of the policy office within the Department of State, which actually preceded the office in DoD but developed in a different fashion.

OEO: The Office of Research, Plans, Programs, and Evaluation

Even before the Bureau of the Budget issued its directive to create PPBS processes across the federal government, in 1965 OEO had established a small office that was engaged in the functions of planning and program examination, advice, and research management.[24] The office also included the budget function, which, according to Walter Williams, was "clearly subordinate to policy analysis."[25] Following the DoD model, the office was found in OEO's top reaches, and its early directors had the direct ear of the agency's head.

At no time was the office staff larger than fifty individuals. Staff members did not expect to make a career of this task; Williams has described this staff as follows: "The archetypal analysts came to government armed with an economics PhD, had worked in a think tank or a university, and saw themselves as markedly different from the BoB [Bureau of the Budget] mandarins."[26] Several staff members had actually come to OEO from DoD, bringing their analytical skills to a new setting.

Williams has summarized the experience of the OEO office as follows:

> The OEO analytic office quickly emerged as a major power within the agency policy process and became a central actor in shaping social policy analysis and research as we know it. First, RPP&E [the Office of Research, Plans, Programs, and Evaluation] dominated the OEO planning effort, and later its second head, Robert Levine, ranked as the agency director's closest policy adviser. Second, facing a shortage of information on the circumstances and behavior of the poor, RPP&E supported major survey research projects that included a two-year picture of the poor. . . . Third, RPP&E generally fostered poverty research and more specifically provided the funds to start the University of Wisconsin's Institute for Research on Poverty, which became the nation's top research organization on poverty issues. Fourth, RPP&E funded the first major social program evaluation and the initial large-scale field experiment to investigate a new social policy idea in a field setting.[27]

Unlike the other examples in this discussion, it is important to note that OEO itself was created to focus on poverty issues that could be seen to cut across the operational cabinet departments. Unlike that of the DoD, however, the change strategy was not a managerial approach but was, rather, an effort to create programs that paralleled those of the existing agencies. The OEO was a very small agency and did not survive through the Nixon administration. Many of its responsibilities were distributed across the federal government, especially to HEW and the Department of Labor. Its major policy analysis activities were moved to HEW. But in its heyday, OEO was an agency that was committed to change and saw itself as an antibureaucratic body. In this sense the policy office had many fewer internal problems to deal with as it went about its business.

HEW/HHS: The Office of the Assistant Secretary for Planning and Evaluation

The policy analysis office that was established in the Department of Health, Education, and Welfare in response to Johnson's directive had clear linkages to the DoD office.[28] The office that was created was called the Office of Program Coordination, and its first director, William Gorham, had been one of McNamara's Whiz Kids at DoD. A staff of eight people reported to an assistant secretary, who in turn reported to HEW's undersecretary. The original functions of the small staff were defined in response to the PPBS demands and were linked to a multiyear planning process. The office was renamed the Office of the Assistant Secretary for Planning and Evaluation (ASPE) during the Nixon administration.

Recalling the experience of those early days, Alice Rivlin, who joined the original staff in 1965 as one of two deputies to Gorham, emphasized the environment of change and energy that created incredible demands on this staff. Lyndon Johnson's agenda for social program change seemed insatiable and unstoppable. Speaking at the dedication of the Alice Mitchell Rivlin Conference Room at HHS in February 1998, she commented:

> Presidents dream of such successes, but they and their staffs forget how rarely it happens. . . . In HEW, in early 1966, such an extraordinary atypical series of legislative events had just happened, affecting virtually all parts of the Department, which then included the Social Security Administration and what is now the Department of Education. Most of the burden of implementing this legislation fell on HEW and on the Office of Economic

Opportunity, which was set up separately to manage the War on Poverty. The bureaucracy was both energized and overwhelmed by the magnitude of the new challenges. The job of our fledgling ASPE office was to bring analysis and systematic thinking to bear on planning and priority setting and to try to evaluate the new programs so as to make them work as effectively as possible. . . . We thought we were pioneers, crusaders for a cause. The ideas of quantifying, measuring, evaluating and systematically analyzing the cost-effectiveness of alternative policies were relatively new and quite threatening. We were young and brash and hopeful—and to many of the seasoned bureaucrats in the Department we must have sounded pretty naive and silly.[29]

Like the staff at DoD, this policy analysis unit was drawn from individuals with strong quantitative skills, many of whom had little if any knowledge of the programs in HEW's portfolio and did not expect to make public service their lifetime career. Gorham's staff (and a number of subsequent staffs) had access to the top officials at HEW/HHS. At that time both Secretary John Gardner and Undersecretary Wilbur Cohen were active participants in the process of churning out new program initiatives. Their strategy for change involved efforts to create some level of centralization and coherence of programs that had been historically autonomous. Again, as at DoD, the policy analysis activity was part of an agenda to establish some semblance of control over programs that had their own separate cultures, constituencies, and modes of operation. It was separate from the budget office and was not aggressively managerial in its approach.

The Department of the Interior: The Office of Policy Analysis

Efforts to create a centralized analytic office in the Department of the Interior actually predated the PPBS efforts in 1965. As early as the New Deal, Secretary Harold Ickes had attempted to build up an office that would provide staff resources to the secretary.[30] Subsequent efforts were made over the years to use analytic capability as a way to increase the secretary's ability to exert influence over strong, independent units. When he assumed office in 1961, Secretary Stewart Udall had support from staff members (called the Resources Program Staff) who were able to perform cost-benefit analyses in several program areas. The head of this office was very close to Udall and actually worked with him in writing his book, *The Quiet Crisis*.[31] The development of the cost-benefit field was closely tied to decisions about water products; indeed, legislation as early as 1936 had required cost-benefit analyses of these projects.

When the PPBS requirements were imposed by the White House, the Interior Department created a separate unit to fulfill this obligation. The Office of Program Analysis was created within the Office of the Secretary. This unit lasted only as long as the PPBS requirements were alive. According to Robert Nelson, its relationships with program agencies became strained, and in 1971 a reorganization was accomplished to create the Office of Policy Analysis under its own assistant secretary. Five offices were created within this unit with responsibilities for program development and coordination, regional planning, environment and project review, international activities, and economic analysis.

Nelson, a longtime staff member in the office, has commented that the office was called on in several ways when a high-profile issue was before the secretary: "The secretary wanted his own staff assistance, partly because he lacked confidence in the line agencies involved. The secretary also preferred to have a second opinion for an important policy matter in which he had a large personal stake. [The office] has been most likely to be brought into the picture when these circumstances were combined with a third factor—the issue was amenable to economic analysis."[32]

The Department of State: The Policy Planning Staff

Unlike that of DoD, OEO, HHS, or the Interior Department, the formation of the policy analysis staff within the Department of State had very little direct relationship to the PPBS requirements of the Johnson administration. Though constructed around analytical capacities, the Policy Planning Staff focused on substantive foreign policy issues and consisted of highly experienced career individuals.

The first staff was actually established in 1947, when Secretary of State George Marshall asked George Kennan, who had been trained as a Russian specialist, to create a unit that would be able to respond to a Soviet ability to plan its foreign policy objectives.[33] Thus the first assignment given to this office was to develop a long-range plan for American foreign policy.

Although Kennan's office was successful on a number of important policy issues, Kennan himself was frustrated by his inability to deal with the functional and geographic bureaus in the department. He wrote in 1949:

I recognized that my Planning Staff, started nearly three years ago, has simply been a failure, like all previous attempts to bring order and foresight into the designing of foreign policy by special institutional arrangements within the department. . . . The reason for this seems to lie largely in the impossibility of having the planning function performed outside of the line of command. But when it comes to any formalized staff effort, anything that has to be put down in writing and is designed to serve as a major guide for action, the operating units—the geographic and functional units—will not take interference from any unit outside the line of command. They insist on an effective voice in policy determination; if one of them cannot make its voice alone valid, it insists on the right to water down any recommendation going to the Secretary to a point where it may be meaningless but at least not counter to its own views.[34]

During the Johnson administration, Secretary of State Dean Rusk assigned the office responsibility for the coordination and development of national strategy or policy papers. This office was headed by Walter Rostow, and it had more to do with the operations within the department, and more attention was given to economic issues. During this period the office was heavily involved in the budgeting of foreign affairs programs; Lucien Pugliaresi and Diane Berliner have written about Rostow's attempt to institute the Comprehensive Country Programming System, a variant of the PPBS process.[35]

The policy staff in the State Department was—and continues to be—a small group composed of individuals drawn from the senior ranks of the Civil Service and Foreign Service, other agencies, academia, and the private sector. Most serve for a limited number of years, and most have at least ten years of experience in their field of specialization. According to Pugliaresi and Berliner, there is a tendency "to rely largely on experienced analysts, which does deprive the office of some of the enthusiasm and fresh ideas that younger analysts can often contribute to the policy process."[36]

Creating a New Profession

As these examples suggest, the policy analysis institutions of the early 1960s shared many of the problems and characteristics of those who practiced the ancient art of providing advice to decision makers—but though the functions contained similarities, something new *had* occurred. What had been a relatively informal set of relationships and behaviors in the past had moved into a formalized, institutionalized world. Although the process began with responsibility for the PPBS process, it became obvious very quickly that the policy analysis task moved beyond a single analytic technique. Other management or budgetary requirements had been imposed in the past, but none seem to have had the breadth of possibility and impact of requirements that stemmed from the initial PPBS activity.[37] Much still depended on the personal relationships between the analyst/adviser and the decision maker/ruler, but these organizations took their place in public, open, and legally constituted organizations. As a result, a new field or profession was emerging. And many of the policy analysis activities inside the federal government continued to have a close linkage to the decisions related to the budget.

This field was conceptualized as integral to the formulation stage of the policy process—the stage of the process where analysts would explore alternative approaches to "solve" a policy problem that had gained the attention of decision makers and had reached the policy agenda. Both decision makers and analysts saw this early stage as one that was separable from other aspects of policymaking. It did not focus on the imperatives of adopting the preferred alternative (particularly in the legislative branch) or on the details of implementing an enacted policy inside an administrative agency on a day-to-day basis rather than as a demonstration experiment. Instead, it focused on the collection of as much information and data as were available to help decision makers address the substantive aspects of the problem at hand.

Laurence Lynn, an individual with leadership experience in several policy organizations within federal agencies, sought to assess the unique contribution of the early days of the policy analysis field. He wrote: "What seemed to be new a quarter of a century ago was the self-conscious incorporation of policy analysis and policy analysts as a matter of principle into the central direction of large, complex government organizations. A new group of staff officers—policy analysts—answerable only to the organization's senior executive, were given privileged access to that executive and were empowered to speak for that executive in a variety of forums. Almost overnight, the views of young, professionally trained analysts came to matter, and to matter visibly and decisively, in important affairs of state."[38]

Less than two years after the diffusion of PPBS throughout the federal government, in September 1967, Yehezkel Dror sounded a clarion call for a new profession, in what has become a classic article in *Public Administration Review*: "Policy Analysts: A New Professional Role in Government." In this definitive article Dror sought to differentiate policy analysis from systems analysis and to delineate the characteristics of policy analysts as government staff members.[39] He called upon his colleagues to "develop institutional arrangements, professional training, and job definitions which will provide the desired outputs with good, and hopefully very good, but not always out-standing, personnel."[40]

Dror argued for "a more advanced type of professional knowledge, which can be used with significant benefits for the improvement of public decision making. . . . The term *policy analysis* seems to be suitable for the proposed professional discipline, as it combines affinity with systems analysis with the concept of policy in the broadest sense."[41] He outlined the characteristics of policy analysts as government staff officers—what he described as "an important new professional role in government service."[42] He called for the establishment of these offices in all government agencies, as close to the senior policy positions as possible.

Though Dror used the PPBS experience as his point of departure, he advocated a somewhat broader approach: "The aim of policy analysis is to permit improvements in decision making and policymaking by allowing fuller consideration of a broader set of alternatives, within a wider context, with the help of more systematic tools."[43] Comparing policy analysis with systems analysis, he called for paying attention to the political aspects of public decision making, a conception of decision making that is broader than a resources allocation effort, reliance on tacit understanding, emphasis on futures, and a search for new policy alternatives.

In a later article Dror spelled out some other characteristics of the staff of the policy analysis units.[44] He noted that the offices should have significant autonomy in their operations and that the staff members should be highly qualified professionals who were not selected solely because of their personal or political acceptability to the decision maker. He suggested that the half-life of the staff should approximate three to five years but that changeovers of most of the staff were appropriate when the top staff of the agency also changed.

Dror called for "strict secrecy in respect to all work" that emphasized the confidential relationship between the decision makers and the analyst.[45] He envisioned a relatively small staff, with a minimum of between ten and fifteen persons but a preference for between twenty-five and thirty individuals. He saw the government analysts as a part of an infrastructure of policy research, including think tanks, consultants, brain trusts and resources persons, ad hoc study groups, university institutes, institutions for advanced study, and similar policy analysis and policy thinking capacities within society. Such a network would, he argued, not only help in data collection and analysis of problems but also provide a way for staff members to handle problems that would require distance from day-to-day pressures and emotions.

Dror did not expect policy analysis institutions to focus on the details of policy implementation. Indeed, he wrote, policy analysts should not move into issues dealing with administrative reforms, implementation management, and similarly detailed organizational matters: "To move into such items cannot but ruin the essence of policy analysis as focusing on policymaking."[46]

By the early 1970s the field of policy analysis began to assume both visibility and self-definition. Through support from private foundations, between 1967 and 1970, graduate programs in public policy were begun at Harvard University; the University of California, Berkeley; Carnegie-Mellon University; the RAND Graduate Institute; the University of Michigan; the University of Pennsylvania; the University of Minnesota; and the University of Texas at Austin.[47] Almost all these programs were at the master's degree level, focused on training professionals to enter the policy analysis field.

There were sufficient examples of the new breed within federal agencies for Arnold Meltsner to begin a study of their experiences in the early 1970s. His work, *Policy Analysts in the Bureaucracy*, suggested that the model assumed by Dror had already become a somewhat more variegated species than originally envisioned.[48] Meltsner found that policy analysts used two different types of skills—technical and political. He described the worlds of those who accentuated these two different skills.

The individual who emphasizes technical skills has a "desk and shelves . . . cluttered with papers. His books will be the same as those of academic social scientists."[49] The individual who highlights technical skills "is convinced that he is objective, a scientist of sorts."[50] This individual sees the policy analyst as someone who can do high-quality, usually quantitative, policy-oriented research that satisfies him and his peers, sees his command of details and knowledge as his main resources, views his impact in relation to the long term, and defines policy analysis as an end in itself.

By contrast the individual who emphasizes political skills is, in many ways, more like a traditional bureaucrat. But this individual wants to be able to work on the major problems facing the agency. "They want to be where the action is."[51] Concern about timeliness and ability to write and talk well are essential. Meltsner notes that this type of individual "makes the complex simple."[52] This individual sees the policy analyst as someone who defines opportunities for self-advancement and personal influence that also satisfy the immediate client. Communication and coordination skills are the main resources, impact is viewed in the short term, and analysis is a means for personal influence.

Meltsner created an analytic model that described four types of analysts: the entrepreneur, the politician, the technician, and the pretender. This book looks at Meltsner's four types of analysts but does not reproduce his model; see table 1.1.

Table 1.1   **Meltsner's Four Different Types of Policy Analysts and Their Traits**

Type of Analyst	Political Skills	Technical Skills
Technician	Low	High
Entrepreneur	High	High
Politician	High	Low
Pretender	Low	Low

Source: Adapted from Arnold J. Meltsner, *Policy Analysts in the Bureaucracy* (Berkeley: University of California Press, 1976), 16.

Meltsner's work indicates that a number of attributes contribute to the variety of behaviors. Some have to do with the analyst's own skill level and personal comfort with various approaches. Others have to do with clients' expectations. Meltsner describes the world of the policy analyst as one composed of concentric circles. The analyst is in the center, immediately surrounded by the client; the client is surrounded by the organization; and, finally, the organization is surrounded by the attributes of the policy issue or sector.

Despite Dror's attempt to broaden the scope of the policy analyst's task beyond the use of technical skills, it appears that the technician role is the one most frequently adopted. In the rush to staff the new offices, technical skills seem to be those most highly valued. An individual who does not have any experience with the organizational or political realities of a particular policy but, rather, is able to design and conduct cost-benefit analyses or exhibit skill in linear programming is likely to be most comfortable in the technician's role.

The Profession after a Decade

By the mid-1970s the policy analysis field did seem to be moving toward a professional identity. It had its own journals, a range of university-based professional schools, and individual practitioners (largely in government agencies) who identified themselves as policy analysts.

Yet many issues remained unresolved that would surface as problems for the future. It appeared that policy analysis functions legitimately included planning, evaluation, and research. But the relationship between policy analysis and budgeting was not clear. Some agencies had followed the PPBS path and directly linked the analytical activity to fiscal decision making. Others separated the two functions. When the zero-based budgeting requirements were imposed on agencies during the 1970s, they were again pushed to link the two aspects.[53]

Many policy analysis shops consciously separated their responsibilities from those of the operating divisions in the department or agency, following Dror's advice. Even those analysts who exerted political skills did not focus on the implementation stage of the policy process. If they accentuated politics at all, they highlighted the political realities of the agenda-setting stage of the process, looking to the agenda of their political masters and to the political intrigue involved in achieving passage of a proposal. It was the rare analyst who believed that effectiveness was related to the ability to raise implementation issues in the analysis, requiring interaction with the operating units.

Some policy analysts found that they were assuming two quite different roles in their activities. Not only were they the neutral analysts, laying out all possible options, but they were also advocates for their preferred positions that they believed best represented the "national interest." Unlike advisers in other societies, American policy analysts often described their role as including concern about the best policy option that was in the "public interest." Despite the difficulty of defining a single "public interest" in the diverse American society, this language was often used by analysts. This created a tension that was not easy to manage.[54] In a related dilemma, analysts who were trained as academics were likely to approach their task with a high degree of skepticism and hesitancy about their own advice. Yet when they were on the line, asked to make recommendations, they had to assume a posture of certainty.

Finally, as the field took shape, the definition of success in the practice of policy analysis was not always obvious or agreed on. Was success the ability to convince the client–decision maker to adopt your recommendation? Was an analyst successful when he or she helped the client understand the complexity and dimensions of a policy choice situation? Or was the analyst successful when the work that was performed was of a quality that was publishable and was well received by one's peers within the profession? These problems continued to challenge the profession in the coming years.

Notes

1. Herbert Goldhamer, *The Adviser* (New York: Elsevier, 1978), ix.

2. Ibid., 8.

3. Ibid., 22.

4. Ibid., 23.

5. Peter Bondanella and Mark Musa, eds., *The Portable Machiavelli* (New York: Penguin Books, 1979), 154.

6. Goldhamer, *The Adviser*, 42, 63.

7. Ibid., 69.

8. Ibid., 76.

9. Ibid., 82.

10. Ibid., 94–95.

11. Ibid., 129.

12. Hugh Heclo suggests that developments in political science did not always support an enthusiastic move toward policy advising. Hugh Heclo, "Modes and Moods of Policy Analysis," *British Journal of Political Science* 2, no. 1 (January 1972): 117.

13. Yehezkel Dror, *Ventures in Policy Sciences* (New York: Elsevier, 1971), 226.

14. Ibid.

15. Heclo, "Modes and Moods," 131.

16. McNamara's confidence in numbers would later haunt him during the Vietnam War.

17. RAND Corporation home page, www.rand.org.

18. Dror, *Ventures*, 225.

19. For an examination of the continued interest in the PPBS effort, see William F. West, *Program Budgeting and the Performance Movement: The Elusive Quest for Efficiency in Government* (Washington, DC: Georgetown University Press, 2011).

20. The advisers to Roosevelt during the New Deal had some of the attributes of these Whiz Kids in terms of their status within the government.

21. Quoted by Walter Williams, *Honest Numbers and Democracy* (Washington, DC: Georgetown University Press, 1998), 61.

22. Ibid.

23. Aaron Wildavsky, "Rescuing Policy Analysis from PPBS," *Public Administration Review* 29 (1969): 189–202.

24. This discussion relies on the description of the activities given by Williams, *Honest Numbers*.

25. Ibid., 80.

26. Ibid., 5.

27. Ibid., 7.

28. Much of this discussion is drawn from Beryl A. Radin, "Policy Analysis in the Office of the Assistant Secretary for Planning and Evaluation in HEW / HHS: Institutionalization and the Second Generation," in *Organizations for Policy Analysis: Helping Government Think*, edited by Carol H. Weiss (Newbury Park, CA: Sage, 1991), 144–60.

29. Alice M. Rivlin, "Does Good Policy Analysis Matter?" Remarks at the Dedication of the Alice Mitchell Rivlin Conference Room, Office of the Assistant Secretary for Planning and Evaluation, Department of Health and Human Services, Washington, February 17, 1998.

30. Robert H. Nelson, "The Office of Policy Analysis in the Department of the Interior," *Journal of Policy Analysis and Management* 8, no. 3 (1989): 395–410.

31. Ibid., 396.

32. Ibid., 398.

33. Lucien Pugliaresi and Diane T. Berliner, "Policy Analysis at the Department of State: The Policy Planning Staff," *Journal of Policy Analysis and Management* 8, no. 3 (1989): 379–94.

34. Quoted in ibid., 384.

35. Ibid., 387.

36. Ibid., 381.

37. For a discussion of the survival of PPBS in the Department of Defense for more than fifty years, see West, *Program Budgeting*.

38. Laurence E. Lynn Jr., "Policy Analysis in the Bureaucracy: How New? How Effective?" *Journal of Policy Analysis and Management* 8, no. 3 (1989): 374–75.

39. Reprinted by Dror, *Ventures*, 225–34.

40. Ibid., 226–27.

41. Ibid., 229–30.

42. Ibid., 231.

43. Ibid., 232.

44. Yehezkel Dror, "Policy Analysis for Advising Rulers," in *Rethinking the Process of Operational Research and Systems Analysis*, edited by Rolfe Tomlinson and Istvan Kiss (Oxford: Pergamon Press, 1984), 79–123.

45. Ibid., 90.

46. Ibid., 107.

47. Aaron Wildavsky, "Rescuing Policy Analysis from PPBS," in *Classics of Public Administration* (Fort Worth: Harcourt Brace College, 1997), 275–88. This is as described by Robert A. Heineman, William T. Bluhm, Steven A. Peterson, and Edward N. Kearny, *The World of the Policy Analyst: Rationality, Values, and Politics* (Chatham, NJ: Chatham House, 1990).

48. Arnold J. Meltsner, *Policy Analysts in the Bureaucracy* (Berkeley: University of California Press, 1976).

49. Ibid., 19–20.

50. Ibid., 23.

51. Ibid., 32.

52. Ibid., 35.

53. The performance measurement activities of the late 1990s and early twenty-first century also combined analysis and budgeting.

54. See Nelson, "Office of Policy Analysis," 401.

.

Chapter 2

Policy Analysis by the 1990s

Dueling Swords

Rita Stone knew that she was concerned about child care policy when she completed her undergraduate work at Duke University in 1989. Her senior thesis in recent American history had focused on the creation and early implementation of the Head Start program in the 1960s, an interest that clearly was affected by hearing of her mother's experience as a Head Start program director in Philadelphia.

Although she knew that she would eventually go to graduate school, she wasn't sure about either the field of study she would pursue or what career path made the most sense for her. In the spring before her graduation from Duke, she accompanied her mother to a Children's Defense Fund (CDF) conference in Washington and was excited by the work done by that organization. At one of the receptions during the conference, she met the CDF research director and learned about the availability of a two-year internship in that organization. She applied for the internship and was selected to begin in the fall of 1989.

Stone's experience at CDF was eye-opening for her. She had been assigned to a project that elicited information from various child care programs across the country. The project's goal was to identify federal policy directives that acted as impediments to effective child care programs. Through telephone interviews and a few field visits, she began to see a rather depressing pattern. She learned that federal programs that sought to create opportunities in some areas (e.g., income maintenance) could actually create problems for the child care efforts. She began to see interrelationships between a range of domestic social programs and realized the importance of taking a broad approach to issues such as child care.

At the end of her first year at CDF, Stone met a friend of a friend who told her about master's programs in public policy. She scrutinized the catalogues of a number of schools and decided that the University of Chicago's program made the most sense. The program would provide her with a range of core courses on analytic approaches; yet at the same time, she would be able to focus on the issue of child care by taking elective courses at the university's School of Social Administration.

Stone was accepted by the University of Chicago and began her course-work in the fall of 1991. She found the program both challenging and terrifying. Although she had avoided economics and mathematics in her undergraduate years, she recognized the importance of economists' logic and the rigor of quantitative analysis. Though the curriculum emphasized generic approaches to policy issues, for course projects she focused on child care policy and re-lated issues. She was able to arrange an internship in the Office of the Assis-tant Secretary for Planning and Evaluation (ASPE) at the Department of Health and Human Services (HHS) during the summer between her first and second years in the graduate program.

Although Stone had not envisioned a career for herself as a bureaucrat, she met a number of young people that summer who had entered the federal gov-ernment as Presidential Management Interns (PMIs). This competitive program gave its participants a fast-track opportunity to have a variety of experiences in the federal government and to move to a permanent position in a government agency. Her interest in the PMI program was reinforced in November 1992, when Bill Clinton was elected president; she thought that this would be an auspicious time to enter the federal service. Though she recognized that much had changed in the world since the 1960s, she was taken with the possibility that this era might mark the renewal of social policy activity.

In the spring of 1993, Stone came to Washington to interview for possible PMI placements. She was fairly sure that she wanted to return to HHS but was not sure whether she wanted to return to ASPE. She received an offer from the Office of the Assistant Secretary for Management and Budget (ASMB), which she decided would allow her to be an effective policy analyst working on child care issues. And to gain more of a global and high-level policy view of child care issues, she used the PMI program's rotation opportunities to spend three months in Paris at the Organization for Economic Cooperation and Develop-ment and another three months with a congressional committee.

When she completed her two-year PMI assignment, she became a per-manent ASMB staff member with major responsibility for the child care block grant program. In 1997 she played an important role in crafting the program's expansion, a policy initiative that emanated from the White House. In 1998 she attended a CDF conference as a speaker and was struck by the changes that had taken place in her career life since she had attended a similar meeting with her mother in 1989. She had moved up rapidly in the bureaucracy and expected to have a range of interesting assignments at HHS in the future. She continued to work at ASMB until 2003, when she took a leave of absence to stay home with her children. When the administration changed in 2009, she received a political appointment in the Office of Human Development Services and became responsible for running the child care programs.

The federal government's early policy analysts faced a world that was very different from that confronting policy analysts in the 1990s. This chapter deals with the proliferation of policy analysis offices and activities in federal agencies, legislative settings, think tanks, and interest groups. It also discusses the process of institutionalizing the policy analysis function and redefining the concept of client in the changed environment. The growth of evaluation, interest in implementation, and the creation of an academic identity are also considered.

The years that elapsed since policy analysis activity began in the 1960s have been characterized by dramatic economic, social, and political changes in American society. The environment of possibility and optimism of the early 1960s was replaced by a mood of scarcity and skepticism. Indeed, by the end of the 1960s, the experience of the Vietnam War and demands for equality within the society forced many to acknowledge that there were large cleavages among groups within the nation. And as the century came to an end, public policy within the United States was distinguished by strong value conflicts and issues that transcended the country's geographic boundaries. Globalization has meant that few policy issues could be easily defined as clear domestic or international concerns. Technological innovations—particularly those involving computers and the internet—meant that decision processes were often greatly sped up, which in turn minimized whatever chance there had been to take time to accomplish analytic activity.

When it became clear that policy analysis was becoming a part of the decision-making process and language, multiple actors within the policy environment began to use its forms and sometimes its substance. As a result, policy analysis has become a field with many voices, approaches, and interests. As it has matured, the profession has taken on the complex structure and diverse culture of American democracy instead of the quite limited practice found only in the top reaches of government bureaucracies that characterized its early stages.

The impact of these macro-level changes was not always obvious to policy analysis practitioners in the government. Perhaps the most direct effect of the modifications was in the range of practitioners' possibilities for policy changes. As Alice Rivlin noted, the crusading spirit attached to the early days of the field was closely linked to the large number of new programs that were being created.[1] Soon, however, the agenda for many analysts focused mainly on changes in existing policies, not on the creation of new policies and programs.

Policy analysts did experience other shifts in their world. In the early 1960s—beginning with the Planning, Program, and Budgeting System activity in the Department of Defense—it was assumed that policy analysis units would be established at the highest levels of organizations, and that these units would look to the top executives and senior line staff members as the clients for their analyses.[2] These clients would define the perspective, values, and agenda for the analytic activity. Once completed, policy analysis would become an additional resource for decision makers and thus help improve policymaking. The focus of the analytic activity was thus upward, and the separate nature of the policy analysis units minimized concern about the organizational setting in which analysis took place. Whether or not these individuals were as influential as they hoped to be, this conceptualization of their role became the point of departure for the field.

By the mid-1970s policy analysis activities had dramatically increased throughout the federal government. Most units began in the top reaches of departments or agencies. But as time went on, policy analysis offices appeared throughout federal agencies, attached to specific program units as well as middle-level structures. As it became clear that the terms of policy discourse would be conducted (at least superficially) in analytic terms, those who had responsibility for subunits within departments or agencies were not willing to allow policy shops attached to the highest level of the organization to maintain a monopoly on analytic activity. Their creation of their own policy units was often triggered by a reluctance to defer to the centralized unit in the offices of the cabinet department's secretary or agency head. By the mid-1980s any respectable program unit had its own policy staff—individuals who were not overwhelmed by the techniques and language of the staff of the original policy units and who could engage in debate with them or even convince them of other ways of approaching issues. Both budget and legislative development processes were the locations of competing policy advice, often packaged in the language and form of policy analysis.

As a result, staff members appeared to become increasingly socialized to the policy cultures and political structures with which they were dealing. Those members who stayed in a particular office for significant periods of their careers became attached to and identified with specific program areas and took on the characteristics of policy area specialists, and they sometimes even served as the department's institutional memory.[3]

The institutionalization and proliferation of policy analysis throughout federal departments—not simply at the tops of their structures—also contributed to changes in the behavior of the managers of the centralized policy analysis units, who became highly interactive in their dealings with analysts and managers in other parts of the departments. Increasingly, policy development took on the quality of debate or bargaining between policy analysts working in different parts of the agency. In addition, policy analysis staff members found that they shared an interest in activities performed by other offices; in many ways, they behaved more like career bureaucrats than the in-and-out analysts envisioned in the early writings on the field. Longevity and specialization combined to create organizational units made up of staff members with commitments to specific policy areas (and sometimes to particular approaches to those policies). In some of the larger federal agencies, the centralized policy shops grew in size and structure—from small, almost intimate work groups to compartmentalized and specialized bureaucracies. Recruitment patterns over the years broadened the methodological approach, and the early reliance on economics was complemented by other approaches. Staff members were drawn from political science, public administration, and—increasingly—from the public policy graduate schools.

As a result of the spread of the policy analysis function, analysts implicitly redefined the concept of a "client." Though there had always been some tension over the definition of a client—it could be your boss, the secretary, the president, the society, or the profession—the proliferation of the profession made this even more complicated. In part this was understandable as analysts developed predictable relationships with programs and program managers over time. Not only were clients the individuals (or groups) who occupied top-level positions within the organization, but clients for analysis often became those involved in the institutional processes within the agency as well as the maintenance of the organization itself. Institutional processes included the standard operating decision procedures in federal agencies (e.g., planning, budgeting, regulation drafting, and legislative drafting), which are predictable and defined by law, internal decision rules, and externally imposed calendars.[4] Organizational maintenance as the "client" for analysis developed in the 1980s as the imperative for some analysts became the survival of the agency and maintenance of its programs.

Analysts, not their clients, became the first-line conduit for policy bargaining. The relationships among policy analysts became even more important by the late 1970s, when the reality of limited resources meant that the policy debate was frequently focused on the modification of existing programs, not on the creation of new policies. Analysts were likely to be working on issues where they already had a track record, either in substantive policy approaches or in relationships with others within the organization. Stories are told about policy analysts who completed analyses that were ignored by one set of decision makers. In more than one case, that work simply went into the bottom drawer of the analyst's desk, and when a new set of decision makers arrived, the analyst elicited interest from this new cast of characters and pulled out the analytic work that had been ignored earlier. This process was sometimes called shopping for clients.

By the mid-1980s, policy analysis activities across the federal government took on the coloration of the agencies and policy issues with which they worked. For instance, the policy office in HHS had an approach and organizational culture that was distinct from that of the policy office in the Department of Labor or in the Environmental Protection Agency (EPA). Thus agencies with highly specialized and separate subunits invested more resources in the development of policy analysis activities in these subunits than in the offices in centralized locations. EPA's responsibilities in water, air, and other environmental problems were different enough to make such an approach effective. Some policy offices were organized around substantive policy areas (e.g., HHS had units for health, Social Security, social services, and welfare), whereas others were created around functional approaches to analysis. For example, the Office of the Assistant Secretary for Policy Development and Research—the centralized policy office within the Department of Housing and Urban Development—had subunits focused on long-term research, evaluation, short-term evaluation, and "quick and dirty" analysis (efforts that responded to the secretary's immediate needs). Other units, such as those in inspectors general offices, actually performed short-term evaluations.[5]

Despite these developments, in many instances the role definitions of the policy analyst continued to be expressed in the language and rhetoric of earlier years. One new policy deputy assistant secretary said that his staff members told him that their role was to advise the secretary—yet when queried further, they admitted that none of them had ever had direct contact with the secretary, and what was perceived as giving advice to the secretary actually took place through multiple layers of the bureaucracy. Indeed, some have suggested that policy analysts operate with a set of myths about decision makers; among these are the myths that decision makers operate like monarchs and that all decisions made by "big people" are always important.[6]

Policy Analysis beyond the Bureaucracy

As the policy analysis function proliferated within the federal government, it also spread outside the government to include the variety of actors engaged in the policy process. Aaron Wildavsky described this growth in his characteristically straightforward way: "It takes one to beat one, if only to counter those who are everywhere else—in the interest groups, the congressional committees, the departments, the universities, the think tanks—ensconced in institutions mandated by law to evaluate everything and accept responsibility for nothing."[7]

The dynamic that spawned this proliferation of policy units within the bureaucracy similarly stimulated the developments outside it. If the policy discourse was going to be conducted in the language of analysis, then one needed to have appropriate resources available to fully participate in this discussion.

David Weimer and Aidan Vining's account of policy analysis as an emerging profession describes the variety of organizational settings where policy analysts work—multiple types of agencies in the executive branch of the federal government, the legislative branch, state governments (including both executive and legislative organizations), local executive agencies, think tanks and policy research organizations, and profit-seeking firms in industries affected by government action.[8] The policy analysts who worked in each of these types of organizations engaged in their activity in ways that were quite different from the tasks and roles envisioned in the early 1960s.

Policy Analysis in the Legislative Branch: The US Congress

According to Michael Malbin, a student of congressional staffs, one could find a discernible increase in interest in policy analysis in the US Congress by the 1970s.[9] The 1970 amendments to the Legislative Reorganization Act indicated that members of Congress were seeking to develop their own analytic capacity. Indeed, one observer noted that these amendments "constitute[d] the congressional declaration of analytical independence from the executive branch," and in some cases actually exceeded the capacity of the executive branch.[10] These amendments created a number of new institutions—such as the Congressional Budget Office and the Office of Technology Assessment—and refocused evaluation activities within the General Accounting Office (since renamed the Government Accountability Office) as well as the analytic branch of the Library of Congress (renamed the Congressional Research Service).[11]

Despite the interest in policy analysis, the expectations of legislative institutions are different from those of executive branch policy analysts. Carol Weiss has noted that at least some congressional staff members treat analysts "less as bearers of truth and clarity than as just another interest group beating on the door."[12] She has suggested that Congress's Byzantine structure—with its tangled committee jurisdictions, the often-tenuous tenure of committee chairs and members, a shortage of time, the oral tradition, staff fragmentation, and, of course, the dynamics of decision making in a legislative body—does act as a deterrent to the use of analysis. Yet she found that analysis is nonetheless valued because congressional committees' staff members bring with them respect for analytic procedures. In addition, the assistants to representatives and senators find that they must be in a position to evaluate the work of others; thus, they must be at least somewhat familiar with the analytic work produced by pertinent agencies so they can help their bosses avoid surprises.

William Robinson has argued that the capacity to anticipate issues is the key to effectiveness of the legislative policy analyst.[13] He emphasizes the importance of timeliness of work and views policy analysts who do not directly serve on committee staffs as brokers between decision makers and researchers. He writes: "A realistic view of the appropriate role of policy analysis starts from the premise that the most important issues facing Congress depend on values choices, not technical concerns. Analysis may or may not have much to add to the elected representatives' intuitive grasp of what ought to be. At best, analysis may enlighten such choices and trace possible effects; it cannot make the choice."[14]

Other observers have noted that policy analysis work is of limited utility when ideology has taken over policy debate. Congressional staff members who were participants in the welfare reform debate during the past decade have suggested that analysis and research are effective only at the margins; policy debates about "big issues" rarely are affected by so-called neutral information (or at least information that is not pointedly focused on the values of the decision makers).[15] Though the analysts may not have played a major role in crafting the broad dimensions of the welfare reform effort, their work did make a difference in how details were designed.[16]

Policy Analysis and Think Tanks

Although their numbers have increased in recent decades, think tanks have been influential in American society throughout the entire twentieth century. As James Allen Smith, a student of think tanks, has noted, this institutional form is "one of the most distinctive ways in which Americans have sought to link knowledge and power."[17] He suggests that these organizations reflect the American system of separation of powers, nonideological politics, and a civil service that is directed by political appointees. He also notes that think tanks are shaped by philanthropic individuals and foundations, intellectual developments in the social sciences, modifications in graduate and professional education, and "energetic intellectual entrepreneurs."[18] Smith submits that Socrates was perhaps the first to inspire a think tank but that the American variety dates back to the Progressive Era and the scientific management movement of the pre–World War I period.[19]

Smith believes that there are more than one thousand private, not-for-profit think tanks in the United States, and that approximately one hundred of them operate in and around Washington. These include the traditional think tanks such as the Brookings Institution and the Urban Institute, but also the newer think tanks that have proliferated around the country.[20] Many of these institutions have research (policy) agendas; these agendas make these groups unlike an organization that is based on academic norms, where staff members follow their own intellectual agendas).[21] Though originally an American form, think tanks have proliferated around the globe. Diane Stone's study of think tanks in Australia, the United Kingdom, and the United States indicates how extensive this form has become. She notes that these organizations "have been involved in political activity and public policy in a variety of ways. They move ideas into politics. . . . Think tanks are an organisational expression of the blending of ideas, politics and policy *outside* formal political arenas."[22] Although the think tanks do differ from country to country, they are now not a uniquely American phenomenon.[23]

Smith's account of the development of the US think tank emphasizes its development as "an elemental urge to bring social science and technical skills to bear on policymaking, and our politics has been shaped and reshaped by a yearning to govern ourselves more intelligently—even if doing so means escaping the political process."[24] However, he argues, many changes have occurred in this institution over the years:

> The market metaphor, however deficient as a way of understanding the impact of think tanks, has taken on a reality of its own; it is a strategy not merely for promoting books, but for selling an institution. Over the past fifteen years, marketing and promotion have done more to change the think tanks' definition of their role (and the public's perception of them) than has any other phenomenon. The metaphors of science and disinterested research that informed the creation and development of the first think

tanks, naive as they sometimes were, have now given way to the metaphor of the market and its corollaries of promotion, advocacy, and intellectual combat.[25]

Smith is concerned that such an approach leads to "persuasion of the most superficial sort, not understanding or reflection."[26] This behavior, he argues, has made it difficult to draw a line between a scholar wrestling with predictable biases and preconceptions and an advocate who marshals evidence to bolster a political position.[27]

Think tanks do vary in the degree to which they take positions. When they do take positions, they behave much like interest groups with an advocacy posture. Some groups are identified with a general policy direction, but the work that is produced by individuals within the organization may still not fall into a clear or predictable approach. Some think tanks have actually become, in effect, extensions of government agencies because these agencies now depend on them to do their essential work. In an era of government staff reductions, outside groups have increasingly been used as surrogates by federal officials who rely on procurement mechanisms such as standing-task-order agreements to carry out these relationships. Such agreements allow an agency to develop fairly open contracts with outside organizations, so that it can call on these groups on demand to perform analytic work. It is sometimes difficult to differentiate between the outside group and the agency when these kinds of relationships play out over a number of years.[28]

Policy Analysis and Interest Groups

Because policy debate does often deal with analytical findings, it is not surprising that many interest groups established their own in-house policy analysis capabilities. To help carry out their well-known policy agendas, these groups have found it useful to have staff members who are comfortable with analytical techniques, methodologies, and research findings. Some interest groups have made investments in staff members who are able to critique the work of others, particularly emphasizing areas where so-called objective analysis actually reflects differences in values or where methodological determinations skew the recommendations or findings. Other groups have actually conducted their own analyses, even encouraging original data collection to support their positions or, at the least, to show that there is an alternative to the official analysis that has been performed. Wendell Primus, a policy analyst who has served on congressional legislative staffs, in government offices, and on the staff of the Center on Budget and Policy Priorities, has indicated that interest groups are sometimes able to use the results of models developed by official sources to support their own positions.[29]

Groups that represent those organizations or individuals that are involved in the implementation of policies (e.g., groups of state officials) may have access to extremely valuable and detailed information about implementation, which sometimes is not available from any other source. Although the organization collecting the data may have an ax to grind (and thus the data are clearly not objective), it is the only information available to decision makers who are unable to collect their own data because of authority or resource constraints.

Ironically, although analysts who work for interest groups are thought to be far from the image of the policy analyst without an agenda, they still may be valuable sources of information to others in society. But it is not always easy to define the boundaries between advocacy and fairness, or between objectivity and fairness. For some, policy analysts—no matter where they work—must fairly consider all alternative policies and then, after analyzing the options, recommend a position.

The value or policy perspectives of interest group analysts are often much clearer than are those of either government or think tanks. In the latter, values may be embedded in the analytic techniques that are used or in how problems are framed. For instance, groups such as the Center on Budget and Policy Priorities stake their reputations on the quality of information they produce and often become sources of information for decision makers as well as members of the press.[30] Their experience—focusing on the production of rigorous, high-quality work that is organized on the basis of a commitment to low-income citizens—suggests that it is possible to exhibit both commitment and rigor. Other organizations, such as AARP (formerly the American Association of Retired People), are membership groups whose policy analysts are concerned about the interests of their members.

The spread of the policy analyst role across government and nongovernmental locations has created new opportunities that were unthought of in the early 1960s. Students who have graduated from the policy schools have found jobs in the field and have learned that they are, indeed, a part of a new profession. Some of these new settings, however, call on staff members to do their work in ways that do not follow the norms of the classic policy analysis curriculum. It is not always easy for an individual who has been trained to think of himself or herself as a neutral analyst to move into such advocacy positions.

During the past several decades, shifts in many domestic policy areas have devolved new authority and responsibility to players at the state and local levels. Thus we can expect there to be demand for analytic activity outside Washington. Some state and local agencies are willing to invest in the policy analysis function, but others are not.[31] Similarly, policy analyst positions have been created in international organizations, such as the World Bank and the Organization for Economic Cooperation and Development, and thus analysts have been pushed to think of policy experience in a comparative fashion, across national boundary lines.

A Response to Complexity: Institutionalizing the Policy Analysis Function

As the years progressed, there were major changes in several of the attributes that were associated with the early stages of the policy analysis field. As fiscal scarcity and limited budgets became the reality in many policy areas, changes occurred in the availability of funds for new or enlarged programs. Ideological shifts demanded changes in the assumptions of policy analysts working inside government. Experience with analysis that was both positive and negative contributed to a growing sophistication both inside and outside government. At the same time, staffing in a number of policy analysis offices was reduced. One analysis suggested that the size of eight federal offices declined from 746 individuals in 1980 to 426 in 1988.[32]

Redefining the Concept of the Client

As has been suggested, the bureaucratization and spread of the government policy analysis function created a reality that was quite different from that envisioned by Dror and the field's early practitioners. The personal relationship between an organization's top official and a middle-level policy analyst has become tenuous, if it exists at all. An analyst is much more likely to provide advice to another analyst, who in turn provides it to another analyst. Rarely does an analyst assume the role of personal counselor to the top decision maker.

These changes suggest a broader range of clients than that described by Meltsner.[33] Clients are not only decision makers; the client relationship may also be defined by the institutional processes of governing (planning, budgeting, regulation development, legislative drafting), maintenance of the organization, and—perhaps as a result of strong attacks on the programs of some domestic agencies—the analyst himself or herself.

In addition, the work of the analyst demands a broader range of skills than those described by Meltsner.[34] The technical and political skills that he described continue to be required, but so too are skills in organizational analysis, specific knowledge of the program area, and evaluation techniques. A modified perspective on the roles and skills of policy analysts dealing with various types of clients is found in table 2.1.

Table 2.1   A Modified Perspective on the Roles and Skills of Policy Analysts vis-à-vis Types of Clients, circa 1990

| | *Type of Client* | | | |
Roles and Skills	*Decision Maker*	*Institutional Processes*	*Organizational Maintenance*	*Self*
Technical Statistics Research design Cost-benefit analysis Microeconomics	Technician	Technician	Researcher	Researcher/ entrepreneur
Political Legal analysis Political analysis Public speaking	Politician	Negotiator	Conflict manager	Entrepreneur
Organizational Implementation analysis Historical analysis Organizational analysis	Broker	Traffic cop	Coordinator	Entrepreneur
Issue-specific Specific program knowledge	Expert	Expert	Institutional memory	Conscience
Evaluation Survey research Evaluation techniques Case studies	Evaluator	Evaluator	Evaluator	Evaluator

The Growth of Evaluation

The early practitioners of policy analysis emphasized analytic functions that were *prospective* (i.e., they analyzed new program possibilities that were being considered). The evaluations conducted during the early years of the profession (especially in the Office of Economic Opportunity) were devised as evaluations of experiments that created new ways to deliver or define programs. But shifts in the policy environment during the 1970s and 1980s diminished the number and size of new programs that were created and instead concentrated on fine-tuning existing programs. Thus it is not surprising that subsequent analytic shops would also be concerned about employing *retrospective* analytic techniques (examining the effects of program interventions through various evaluation techniques).

Some evaluation activities, however, were found within federal agencies during the field's early years. Carol Weiss dates the beginning of large-scale government-funded evaluation to the War on Poverty in the mid-1960s.[35] Indeed, the Elementary and Secondary Education Act of 1965 required systematic evaluation of the program, information that would be accessible to parents of children in the programs as well as to program managers.

By the 1970s, however, evaluation activities became more commonplace in the policy analysis units, although some agencies did create offices for evaluation that were separate from the policy analysis shops. Evaluation activities were also found in other settings; for example, several federal offices of inspectors general created units that did undertake evaluations. Though these evaluations did not follow the classic social science approach, they emphasized the production of information that would be of direct use to decision makers. At HHS, for example, the inspector general's office conducts short-term evaluations to provide service-level information to both Congress and the department. Penny Thompson and Mark Yessian have noted that the HHS Office of Evaluation and Inspections seeks to document the dimensions of implementation problems and utilize the techniques of the applied researcher who draws on a variety of analytic and reporting techniques.[36]

During this period, significant resources were available to think tanks, research centers, and consulting firms to undertake federally financed evaluations. A series of social experiments were conducted to test policy and program possibilities before their enactment. Large investments were made involving welfare, housing, health insurance, and education. Weiss has noted that in "these experiments pilot programs were implemented on a large enough scale to stimulate actual operating conditions, and experimental results were expected to help policymakers decide whether to move ahead with the policies nationwide."[37] But because the experiments had fairly long time requirements, their results were usually not available in a timely fashion, at least for the decision makers who had commissioned the studies.

By the 1980s many evaluation studies were much more modest in scale and usually sought to produce findings that would be timely for decision makers. Congress mandated a series of evaluation projects in the education field that sought to provide information that would be useful to the reauthorization process (the decision cycle that required Congress to renew, revise, or eliminate programs with a finite life cycle). Evaluations were conducted to examine different approaches to welfare reform. Though specifying a user of the evaluation did not avoid all the problems common to the evaluation enterprise, the information produced by several of these efforts did play a role in the decision-making process.[38]

The kind of evaluation that was undertaken often reflected the bureaucratic location of the office commissioning the work. The department-wide policy analysis shops were likely to be interested in *summative evaluations*, which sought to examine the effectiveness or impact of a program or policy. Evaluations that were commissioned by program-level units highlighted *formative evaluations*, which sought information that could be used to improve the program. Increasingly, resources within the policy analysis shops shifted from large-scale research efforts to more modest evaluation activities.

Moving toward Implementation

As has been noted, the policy analysts of the 1960s emphasized the early stages of the policy process. Some analysts focused on work that would bring issues to the policy agenda; most, however, moved into action when they were confronted with a policy problem and sought to formulate alternatives that would advise the decision maker. By the 1980s policy analysts were found in later stages of the policy process. Some—particularly analysts in the legislative branch and in interest groups—sought to produce analyses that could be used by decision makers.

Others began to pay more attention to issues related to implementation and to raise these concerns when policies were being devised. By the mid-1970s both academics and practitioners in the field had realized that a significant number of problems (or what some viewed as failures) associated with the Great Society programs had occurred because program designers had not considered the implementation of these efforts when they developed new programs or policies.[39]

As a result, there was an increased sensitivity to the relationship between program ends and means. This usually required a policy analyst to have fairly detailed knowledge of the actual operation of program units and good relationships with those in the agency who had responsibility for those operations. Analysts located inside program units were likely to emphasize the details of implementation and to be concerned with the *how*, not the *what*, of policies. They might raise questions such as those that deal with levels of resources, detailed rules and regulations, staffing, and organizational structure. According to Lucian Pugliaresi and Diane Berliner, policy offices may be influential in the implementation process only when they are heavily involved in operations.[40]

However, some costs result from the collapsing of the analysis functions and actual operations within an agency. Analysts may find themselves in a situation where there is a blurring of the decision-making and analysis roles. For instance, evaluation activities involving the Head Start program were located in the program unit of HHS rather than in its centralized policy analysis office. Though the questions asked may have been useful to the program's managers, the answers provided by the evaluation were always suspect to those who were skeptical about the program's effectiveness.

Oliver North's role in the White House during the Reagan presidency provided an extreme example of this problem. North was supposed to be performing the role of national security adviser to the president, but by becoming embroiled in the details of implementing his recommended course of action, he redefined that key official position. The report of the Tower Commission (the body that investigated the Iran-Contra affair) described the importance of the role of the national security adviser as an "honest broker"—an individual who assures that issues and options are presented to the president with an analysis of their disadvantages and risks but is not a part of the decision-making chain.[41]

Creating an Academic Identity

Aaron Wildavsky's essay "Principles for a Graduate School of Public Policy," which was written in 1976, describes the academic dimensions of the policy analysis field. As he depicted the process of organizing the Graduate School of Public Policy (now the Goldman School) at the University of California, Berkeley, he highlighted the importance of problem solving "rather than fact grubbing" in the creation process.[42] The Berkeley school was one of the first ones created specifically to train students to become policy analysts. The school's original concept emphasized a number of dimensions: interdisciplinary approaches, faculty chosen specifically to work in that setting, a curriculum that acknowledged multiple analytic perspectives and techniques, and an approach to pedagogy that combined theory and practice. Wildavsky's advice to others highlighted several issues related to the faculty and the curriculum:

- Faculty should include people who have had practical experience in doing policy analysis. There should be an active policy of giving the faculty frequent leaves to perform policy research.
- Choose economists who are interested in politics, political scientists who are interested in economics, and sociologists, lawyers, historians, philosophers, and so on who are interested in both.
- Modeling is an art; hire an artist.
- Core courses are school courses; they belong to the school as an institution and not to the individual instructor.
- Courses should stress not passive appreciation but active manipulation.
- One cannot overemphasize political and organizational factors.[43]

The Berkeley school and the others created before the 1980s were usually institutions with a limited number of students, close working relationships between students and faculty as well as between faculty from different disciplines, and a self-consciousness about defining the dimensions of a new profession and field. During this early period, leaders of the field sought to differentiate it from past approaches, particularly from public administration.[44]

As the schools aged through the 1980s and into the 1990s, however, they found it difficult to sustain their spirit of experimentation.[45] Faculty tended to be drawn from the same age cohort, and at least some schools went through a period when very few new faculty members were hired. It was not unusual for members to argue that it was exhausting to continue to define and refine the program's curriculum year after year. There was some tendency for the faculty members to revert to the academic disciplines from which they had come. The balance of the curricular offerings tended to accentuate quantitative analysis and economics, sometimes at the expense of courses dealing with organizational and political issues. It became more common to have a faculty without experience either inside government or as staff employed by other organizations.

Students, however, were more rather than less diverse in their interests and backgrounds. Many had worked for a few years before returning to graduate school. Their interests were broad, and they saw career paths that could include the nonprofit and the corporate sector as well as government agencies and think tanks. Many were clear that they were engaged in professional education and valued opportunities to apply their analytical skills to real-life situations.

In 1978 the Association for Public Policy Analysis and Management (APPAM) was created, originally as an organization made up of the limited number of schools of public policy around the country as well as individuals working for think tanks such as the RAND Corporation, the Brookings Institution, and the Urban Institute. Two forms of membership were available—institutional and individual. Even combined, APPAM's total membership was small, and its annual research conference was an intimate meeting of several hundred people drawn from multiple academic disciplines. Its structure reflected a growing trend—an interdisciplinary approach to issues, but with specialization about specific policy topics. Donald Stokes characterized APPAM as "an association of professionals" that drew on "individuals from the academic world, the free-standing policy research institutes, and the practitioner community who thought of themselves as policy analysts or identified with this craft."[46]

By the 1990s APPAM's growth and development mirrored the growth in the field. Its institutional membership encompassed more than seventy groups, reaching beyond the initial policy schools and think tanks to include academic departments of public administration, political science, or other traditional fields that had moved into the public policy area, as well as several government agencies, consulting firms, and a few others. And its individual membership totaled more than eighteen hundred, and its annual research conference regularly had more than one thousand attendees. In addition, it moved from having a part-time, quasi-professional staff housed by one of its academic institutional members to a Washington-based staff office with a full-time professional staff.

During the early 1990s, APPAM articulated its vision and principles:

Vision Statement
The Association for Public Policy Analysis and Management (APPAM) aspires to be the leading professional organization dedicated to blending the talents of researchers, educators and practitioners in the production, dissemination and application of analysis bearing on public concerns. The Association is and aims to remain much more than an interdisciplinary umbrella. Through APPAM, public policy analysis and management will continue evolving toward an integrated field of study that supports the applied professions that address societal problems and opportunities.

APPAM's guiding principles are:

1. To aspire to excellence in every sphere of the organization's activity.

2. To maintain an atmosphere of collegiality that encourages and facilitates mutual professional development.

3. To foster diversity of participation across race, gender, ethnicity, and region.

4. To seek balance in the representation of researchers, educators, and practitioners while maintaining the organization's core emphasis on analysis of policy and management.

The Creation of Professional Elites?

For some observers, the development of the policy analysis field was a cause for concern. Guy Benveniste, for example, has noted that individuals with specialized knowledge of public policy have turned into a professional elite. He writes:

Professional elites in public policy transform the policy process by controlling its language. We conceive of them as a class of individuals who can assert more than personal preferences. As they dominate the language of policy decisions, they acquire leverage on these decisions. If expertise is not equally distributed in the polity, power is shifted. . . . Professional elites can pursue their own private interests. Since they do not apply a code of ethics vis-à-vis policy process, or more important, since the lay community does not know how to enforce a code of ethics, we do not know if they serve those who hire them or simply pursue their own personal interests. Given access to specialized knowledge, professional elites do not have to stand passively. They can invent problems and thus provide both the problems and the solutions.[47]

Despite his concerns about the developments of the professional elites, Benveniste sets forth a more optimistic future scenario:

Professional elites become aware that they are losing legitimacy. Informal networking becomes far more important. Self-interest of the profession results in calls for greater self-policing. The search for professional consensus takes on new importance. Discussions of codes of ethics for professional elites in policy lead some professions to adopt the first ones. A new institutional framework is elaborated. Truth speaks to power. Conflicts continue but professional elites begin to define areas of consensus where knowledge is considered more important than politics. This would correspond to a "future" period, one that does not yet correspond to our current experience.[48]

Others do not have Benveniste's optimism and have expressed their concern in somewhat different ways. Edward Banfield portrayed the field as "metaphysical madness" and viewed the development of the field as a substitution of social science and expertise for politics.[49] Banfield characterized the field as "one in a long series of efforts by the Progressive Movement and its heirs to change the character of the American political system—to transfer power from the corrupt, the ignorant, and the self-serving to the virtuous, the educated, and the public-spirited; and to enhance the capacity of the executive to make and carry out internally consistent, comprehensive plans for implementing the public interest."[50] He concluded his critique of the field by arguing that "it is a dangerous delusion to think that the policy scientist can supplant successfully the politician or statesman."[51] For some observers the policy analysis profession seemed to be increasingly composed of technocrats whose interest was in more academic work rather than application to the world of decision making.

Though a strong advocate for the field, Laurence Lynn issued a different kind of warning. He wrote that there is a danger that "policy analysts can become just another parochial interest: priests with their rituals, rather than searchers for a just and comprehensive view, who pay no attention to anything but realities and who counteth the cost."[52]

Speaking Truth to Power—or Speaking Truths to Powers?

In 1979 Aaron Wildavsky published a series of essays on policy analysis titled *Speaking Truth to Power*.[53] The book continues to be viewed as an important contribution in the field because it discusses such fundamental issues as resources versus objectives, social interaction versus intellectual cognition, dogma versus skepticism, and various aspects of the policy analysis process. Though many of these essays were prescient about future developments in the field, Wildavsky still held onto the original view of policy analysis as a process of advising the prince or ruler—of a two-person relationship in which an analyst advises the decision maker.

By the end of the twentieth century, the situation had become much more complex. We are members of a field with multiple languages, values, and forms, and the analyst has multiple individuals and groups as clients. We confront conflict between analysts who strive for objectivity and those who begin with an advocacy posture. Often our work involves dueling between analysts. Our conversations take place across a very broad policy landscape. We operate with many different definitions of success. Some of our efforts meet these expectations, and others do not—but policy analysis today has taken its place in the contemporary world of decision making.

Notes

1. Alice M. Rivlin, "Does Good Policy Analysis Matter?" Remarks at the Dedication of the Alice Mitchell Rivlin Conference Room, Office of the Assistant Secretary for Planning and Evaluation, Department of Health and Human Services, Washington, February 17, 1998.

2. Much of this discussion is drawn from Beryl A. Radin, "Presidential Address: The Evolution of the Policy Analysis Field: From Conversation to Conversations," *Journal of Policy Analysis and Management* 16, no. 2 (1997): 204–18.

3. Martin Rein and Sheldon H. White, "Policy Research: Belief and Doubt," *Policy Analysis* 21, no. 1 (winter 1977): 239–71.

4. See Robert H. Nelson, "The Office of Policy Analysis in the Department of the Interior," *Journal of Policy Analysis and Management* 8, no. 3 (1989): 395–410.

5. Penny R. Thompson and Mark R. Yessian, "Policy Analysis in the Office of Inspector General, US Department of Health and Human Services," in *Organizations for Policy Analysis: Helping Government Think*, edited by Carol H. Weiss (Newbury Park, CA: Sage, 1992), 161–77.

6. Peter W. House, *The Art of Public Policy Analysis* (Beverly Hills, CA: Sage, 1982), 36.

7. Aaron Wildavsky, *Speaking Truth to Power: The Art and Craft of Policy Analysis* (Boston: Little, Brown, 1979).

8. David L. Weimer and Aidan R. Vining, *Policy Analysis: Concepts and Practice*, 2nd ed. (Englewood Cliffs, NJ: Prentice Hall, 1989), 9–12.

9. Michael J. Malbin, *Unelected Representatives: Congressional Staff and the Future of Representative Government* (New York: Basic Books, 1980).

10. William H. Robinson, "The Congressional Research Service: Policy Consultant, Think Tank, and Information Factory," in *Organizations for Policy Analysis*, ed. Weiss, 184; William H. Robinson, "Policy Analysis for Congress: Lengthening the Time Horizon," *Journal of Policy Analysis and Management* 8, no. 1 (1989): 2.

11. The Office of Technology Assessment was eliminated by the Congress in 1995 as part of a budget-cutting effort. See chapter 4 for a profile of the Congressional Research Service.

12. Carol H. Weiss, "Congressional Committees as Users of Analysis," *Journal of Policy Analysis and Management,* 8 no. 3 (1989): 411.

13. Robinson, "Policy Analysis," 3.

14. Ibid., 6.

15. Ronald Hoskins and Paul Offner, both senior staff members for the Republicans and Democrats involved in welfare reform legislative development, agreed with this

characterization during a panel titled "Do Clients Use Policy Analysis?" Annual Research Conference, Association for Public Policy Analysis and Management, November 1997.

16. Ibid.

17. James Allen Smith, *The Idea Brokers: Think Tanks and the Rise of the New Policy Elite* (New York: Free Press, 1991), xv.

18. Ibid.

19. See chapter 4 for a profile of the Century Foundation (formerly the Twentieth Century Fund), a think tank that was formed during the early part of the century.

20. Also see James G. McGann, *The Competition for Dollars, Scholars, and Influence in the Public Policy Research Industry* (Latham, MD: University Press of America, 1995); and Weiss, ed., *Organizations for Policy Analysis*.

21. Nelson W. Polsby, "Tanks but No Tanks," *Public Opinion* 6 (April–May 1983): 15.

22. Diane Stone, *Capturing the Political Imagination: Think Tanks and the Policy Process* (London: Frank Cass, 1996), 1–2.

23. Ibid.

24. Smith, *Idea Brokers*, 3.

25. Ibid., 194.

26. Ibid., 237.

27. Ibid., 231. And see chapter 4 for a profile of the Heritage Foundation.

28. See Charles E. Metcalf, "Presidential Address: Research Ownership, Communication of Results, and Threats to Objectivity in Client-Driven Research," *Journal of Policy Analysis and Management*, 17, no. 2 (1998): 153–63.

29. See Wendell E. Primus, "Children in Poverty: A Committee Prepares for an Informed Debate," *Journal of Policy Analysis and Management* 8, no. 1 (1989): 23–34.

30. See chapter 4 for a profile of the Center on Budget and Policy Priorities.

31. See chapter 4 for a profile of the California Legislative Analyst's Office.

32. See Peter J. May, "Policy Analysis: Past, Present, and Future," *International Journal of Public Administration* 21, nos. 6–8 (1998): 1098.

33. Arnold J. Meltsner, *Policy Analysts in the Bureaucracy* (Berkeley: University of California Press, 1976).

34. See Beryl A. Radin, "Policy Analysis in the Office of the Assistant Secretary for Planning and Evaluation in HEW/HHS: Institutionalization and the Second Generation," in *Organizations for Policy Analysis*, ed. Weiss, 144–60.

35. See Carol H. Weiss, *Evaluation: Methods for Studying Programs and Policies*, 2nd ed. (Upper Saddle River, NJ: Prentice Hall, 1998), 12.

36. Thompson and Yessian, "Policy Analysis."

37. Weiss, *Evaluation*, 13.

38. See Beryl A. Radin, "Evaluation on Demand: Two Congressionally Mandated Education Evaluations," in *Making and Managing Policy*, edited by Ron Gilbert (New York: Marcel Dekker, 1984), 239–56.

39. See, e.g., Robert T. Nakamura and Frank Smallwood, *The Politics of Policy Implementation* (New York: St. Martin's Press, 1980).

40. Lucian Pugliaresi and Diane T. Berliner, "Policy Analysis at the Department of State: The Policy Planning Staff," *Journal of Policy Analysis and Management* 8, no. 3 (1989): 392.

41. John Tower et al., *The Tower Commission Report: The Full Text of the President's Special Review Board* (New York: Bantam Books/Times Books, 1987), 9.

42. Aaron Wildavsky, "Principles for a Graduate School of Public Policy," *Journal of Urban Analysis* 3 (January 1976). Reprinted by Wildavsky, *Speaking Truth to Power*, 407–19; ibid., 408.

43. Ibid., 411–13.

44. See, e.g., Richard F. Elmore, "Graduate Education in Public Management: Working the Seams of Government," *Journal of Policy Analysis and Management* 6 (1986): 69–83.

45. Over the years various policy schools have engaged in curriculum reform efforts that often involve faculty, students, and graduates in the process.

46. See Donald Stokes, "Strategic Choices for APPAM," report to the APPAM Policy Council, n.d., 2.

47. Guy Benveniste, "Some Functions and Dysfunctions of Using Professional Elites in Public Policy," *Research in Public Policy Analysis and Management* 4 (1987): 112.

48. Ibid., 118–19.

49. Edward C. Banfield, "Policy Science as Metaphysical Madness," in *Bureaucrats, Policy Analysts, Statesman: Who Leads?* edited by Robert A. Goldwin (Washington, DC: American Enterprise Institute for Public Policy Research, 1980), 1–19.

50. Ibid., 5.

51. Ibid., 18.

52. Laurence E. Lynn Jr., 1989, "Policy Analysis in the Bureaucracy: How New? How Effective?" *Journal of Policy Analysis and Management* 8, no. 3 (1989): 376.

53. Wildavsky, *Speaking Truth to Power*.

Chapter 3

Policy Analysis in the Twenty-First Century

Veronica Lopez began her career as a medical doctor. She grew up in southern Texas and from childhood on she realized how important it was for children— especially poor children—to have access to medical services. Though her own family was not poor, she was a part of a Hispanic community where health services were actually rationed because of the limited availability of doctors and other health professionals.

After completing her undergraduate education as a pre-med student, she received a fellowship to attend medical school. Her personal experience led her to specialize in infectious diseases involving children. During her residency she realized that this field required that a medical practitioner should have some knowledge of the patterns of illness; thus, after practicing in a group for two years, she began studying for a master's in public health, focusing on epidemiology—the study of health events and patterns within the population.

Her training and concerns drew her to accept a job at the federal Centers for Disease Control and Prevention (CDC), located in Atlanta. She joined the medical staff dealing with pediatric infectious diseases just at the time when the federal government was investing both money and expertise in HIV/AIDS issues affecting children. Although she did not always consider herself someone who focused on policy (rather than direct service delivery), it became clearer to her that the issues that were a part of her personal agenda required decision makers to think about those problems in more systematic ways than would be possible for a single medical practitioner to achieve. Her academic work involving epidemiology made her comfortable with a range of data sources both in the United States and around the globe. Her CDC experience in a range of

countries gave her the ability to communicate in Spanish and made her an un-
usually helpful resource in a number of Latin American countries.

As a result, when the Pan American Health Organization (PAHO) was look-
ing for a staff member to work on pediatric infectious diseases, she was drawn
to that position. She was familiar with many of PAHO's staff members located
in Washington, as well as health officials in many of the countries in both Cen-
tral and South America. She continued her work on HIV/AIDS but also spent
considerable time searching for ways to assure that children—particularly
those in poor communities—would be immunized against diseases that made
life chances for them very difficult.

When the Bill & Melinda Gates Foundation expanded its work in Latin Amer-
ica, Dr. Lopez's skills became of interest to them. She was offered the position
of director for Latin American health programs, and she was able to use the
contacts and expertise that she had developed at both the CDC and PAHO to
increase programs for children across Latin America. She became a visible and
influential individual who understood both the domestic American aspects of
these issues and their international components.

The field of policy analysis that exists in the twenty-first century is quite
different from that found in the field's two earlier phases. The world of the
1960s that gave rise to this field in the United States often seems unrelated
to the world we experience today. These shifts have occurred as a result of
a range of developments—technological changes, changes in the structure
and processes of government both internally and globally, new expectations
about accountability and transparency, economic and fiscal problems, and increased political and ideological conflict. It is interesting that policy observers
have been increasingly using the phrase "wicked problem" to describe problems that are difficult or impossible to solve.[1] But at the same time that these
developments require shifts in how the field operates, it also continues many
of the expectations from the past. Indeed, it is not unusual to find reading
lists in the field continuing some of the earlier literature, such as the technical
approach of Stokey and Zeckhauser's book in 1978, Arnold Meltsner's study
in 1976, the multiple editions of Weimer and Vining's textbook, and Harold
Laswell's vision of policy sciences in 1971.[2]

This chapter provides an overview of the recent developments in the policy analysis field around the world as well as the impact of globalization on
the practice and education within the field in the United States. It discusses
the shifts that have occurred both in the definition of clients and in how
clients and analysts interact with one another. It also comments on the re-

lationship between analysis and politics. As noted in the introduction to this book, policy analysis today exists in a highly volatile environment, and the field itself has been defined and evaluated in terms of these pressures. Finally, the chapter provides a picture of the staff members who are now recruited and hired for positions as policy analysts.

Policy Analysis beyond the United States

Until about 2000, the literature on policy analysis was focused almost entirely on experiences within the United States. The exception to this pattern is found in a 1984 book by Brian Hogwood and Lewis Gunn, *Policy Analysis for the Real World*, whose preface presciently signals a set of concerns that developed in later years. They noted:

> The problem of generating suitable and readily available teaching material for British courses has not yet been overcome. Although our primary interest was in producing policy analysis materials for British students, our experience has made us aware of the limitations of much American literature for *American* students, particularly those who have previously thought of policy analysis as merely American politics rehashed, or as arcane mathematical techniques. . . . Much of the literature about particular techniques concentrates on technical points and assumes that the "optimal" decision will automatically be taken and enforced by a single, authoritative decision maker. This literature fails to discuss the use and limits of policy analysis techniques in real-world political settings.[3]

By the first decade of the twenty-first century, the concerns expressed by Hogwood and Gunn were being addressed by a range of scholars around the world. The introduction of these issues produced a literature that indicated that the field was rich and varied and, in particular, was attentive to the context of the systems in which policy analysis took place. The creation of a journal, *The Journal of Comparative Policy Analysis: Research and Practice*, is evidence of this interest. It defines its mission as follows:

> The *Journal* aims to stimulate the further intellectual development of comparative policy studies and the growth of an international community of scholars in the field. It gives priority to comparative studies adhering to the following criteria:

1. Contribute to comparative theory development.

2. Present theory-based empirical research.

3. Offer comparative evaluations of research methods.

4. Derive the practice implications of theory-based research.

5. Use conceptual heuristics to interpret practice.

6. Draw lessons based on circumstances in which compared policy-related issues have in common certain manipulable policy, program, or institutional variables.[4]

Evidence of a global perspective on policy analysis was found in the programs of a variety of professional meetings (e.g., the International Political Science Association created a new Comparative Policy Analysis section) and in the publication of a number of textbooks and edited volumes from around the world. The following are examples of publications dealing with policy analysis in a number of countries:

- H. K. Colebatch, ed., *The Work of Policy: An International Survey* (New York: Lexington Books, 2006), with contributions from the Netherlands, Japan, Croatia, South Korea, New Zealand, and Finland;
- Claudia Scott and Karen Baehler, *Adding Value to Policy Analysis and Advice* (Sydney: University of New South Wales Press, 2010), a book written with the support of the Australia and New Zealand School of Government;
- Iris Geva-May, ed., *Thinking Like a Policy Analyst: Policy Analysis as a Clinical Profession* (New York: Palgrave Macmillan, 2005); and
- Michael Howlett, *Designing Public Policies: Principles and Instruments* (London: Routledge, 2011), which highlights Canada.

These and other approaches suggest that there are many ways to sort out developments in the field. One can easily list the range of these developments. They include types of policy issues, the diverse relationships between analysts and clients, the types of analysis required, its time frame, the stage of the policy process where it occurs, where in the system it occurs (e.g., whether it takes place inside or outside government), the impact of the structure of the government involved, the placement of analysis in central agencies versus program agencies, whether analysts and clients are career or political actors, the appropriate skill set found in analysts, and the boundaries between policy analysis and management.

It is difficult to characterize the patterns that have emerged as a result of the globalization of the policy analysis field. Some countries have actually

renamed existing data and planning offices and cast them as policy analysis-
organizations. In other countries, career staff (usually generalists) who traditionally acted as advisers to the party in power have become the core of
the policy analysis enterprise. The demise of the Soviet Union provided the
impetus in some nations for an organizational unit that could provide advice
on alternatives to previous approaches. In still other settings, policy analysis
units have been established within autocratic governments to provide at least
a facade of openness and a move toward democracy.

The expansion of the field across both the Atlantic and Pacific oceans provided American policy analysis scholars with a modified view of the field.
David Weimer characterized the results of this experience:

> First, the relative importance of different goals, if not the goals themselves,
> will differ across regimes and societies. Most obviously, different countries
> are likely to have different constitutional constraints that must be satisfied
> in routine policymaking. . . . Second, the sets of plausible policy alterna-
> tives are likely to differ across countries as well. The differences may result
> from anticipation of goals or tradeoffs among them. It may also be a conse-
> quence of certain types of generic policy alternatives not being commonly
> used in a particular country.[5]

Policy Analysis in Parliamentary versus Shared-Power Systems

Variation in policy analysis approaches can be attributed to the structure of
government (e.g., whether it is a centralized or federal system) or to the historic demands of eliminating colonialism, achieving democracy, or responding to the end of the Soviet Union. But if anyone was pushed to come up with
these comparisons, they would have been likely to emphasize the differences
in the political structure between a parliamentary system, where the executive branch is viewed as a part of the legislative branch, and the shared-power
institutional design found in the United States between the legislative, executive, and judicial branches. It appears that a number of important attributes
found in the early days of policy analysis in the United States have parallels
to the practice of policy advising in a parliamentary system.[6] This discussion
first examines the similarities between these two systems and then analyzes
differences that were found between them from the field's earliest days.

Similarities

Policy advising/analysis only takes place inside government. The classic view of policy advising in a Westminster system is based on working relationships between departmental policy advisers, ministers, and members of Parliament. These relationships are defined by government guidelines and are viewed as a part of decision making involving ministers and cabinet officials. The parliamentary system intertwines the legislative and executive branches to make it clear that this combination produces "government" policy.

Although the US system involves a more complex decision-making process emerging from the shared powers between the legislative, executive, and judicial branches, the early days of policy analysis in the United States focused only on decision making within the executive branch at the federal-government level. There was little indication that the original policy analysts were concerned about competing views that would emerge from Congress or from organizations outside government.[7] The development of networks (a set of actors—e.g., individuals or organizations—who are involved in a policy area) as a decision-making form has further complicated this situation.

Policy advising/analysis is produced for a top client inside government. The policy adviser in a Westminster system is expected to provide full and accurate information to an elected official who is a part of government. These elected officials are accountable to the electorate through the Parliament and the ballot box. Advisers are career public servants who will provide full and accurate information to the Parliament about the factual and technical background to policies and their administration. It was assumed that policy advisers were providing information to individuals at the top reaches of government (the ministers or central government officials, e.g., those in the cabinet). The concept of "ministerial responsibility" defines this relationship.

The early US policy analysts were also expected to provide full and accurate information to a political appointee involved in the decision-making process. Crucial to the original design of the profession was the relationship between an analyst and a client inside government. Clients were usually cabinet officials or other high-level political figures (e.g., those in the White House). As discussed in chapter 2, this model was modified in the United States with the proliferation of policy analysis units both inside and outside government.

Policy advising/analysis is a closed process with minimal if any expectations about transparency. The relationship between individual policy advisers and their clients is viewed as confidential in a parliamentary system and the advice that is given during the advising process is not open to public scrutiny.

Advisers are expected to remain personally anonymous, and particular views should not be ascribed to individual analysts. Given this set of expectations, the presence of competing advice is not acknowledged.

The original policy analysts in the US federal system were expected to emphasize the confidential relationship between themselves and the decision makers. Even if they produced policy alternative memos with recommendations, those documents were not to be accessible to the public.[8] In addition, these analysts were usually the only individuals in the agency or department who were thought to possess analytical capacity, and thus there was not competing advice from other parts of the institution.

Policy advising/analysis focuses on the formulation of new policies. Because the policy adviser in a parliamentary system usually is dealing with issues from the perspective of top officials, the major objective of the role is to influence specific actions related to the political, economic, and social agenda of the government of the day. Thus the adviser highlights the outcomes of policy change and the strategies and resources required to achieve these outcomes. Details about putting the policy into operation or changing the details of implementing existing policies would not be a part of the agenda of the top officials.

The early policy analysts in the United States also did not focus on the details of policy implementation. Indeed, Dror specifically defined the role as avoiding administrative reforms, implementation management, and other organizational matters. He wrote: "To move into such items cannot but ruin the essence of policy analysis as focusing on policymaking,"[9] Rather, the activity was related to the crafting of new policies and programs. In some cases, the policy analyst provided a way for a cabinet official to conceptualize the department as a whole and provide a sense of how various pieces in the department fit together.

Differences

Staff members have different backgrounds and career structures. Policy advisers in a parliamentary system are usually experienced officials within the career public service. They are expected to be politically neutral and to be able to serve any government, regardless of its political complexion, with an equal degree of loyalty and efficiency. For the most part these advisers are valued for their ability to meet standards of rigor, honesty, relevance, and timeliness. And in most cases they are trained as administrative generalists rather than program or policy specialists.

The US policy analysts who worked in the federal government in the early years of the profession were expected to be individuals who would come from academia or think tanks with sophisticated training in analytical skills (often with PhDs in economics or operations research). They were not expected to be career public servants but individuals who would stay in government for relatively short periods and then move out. Staff changes might be related to changes in the political structure. Although these individuals were highly qualified professionals in terms of their analytical abilities, they were generalists in terms of program or policy. And though some of the analysts had political links to political officials, this was rarely emphasized. This pattern changed in the second generation of developments in the field.

Organization of the policy advising/analysis activity differs. Because it is so clearly integrated into the career public service system, much of the emphasis of policy advising in parliamentary systems involves individual advisers dealing with individual clients. With a few exceptions, the advising process has not focused on separate organizational structures that collectively offer advice. At the same time, policy advisers seek information from others within and outside government. And when advisers are dealing with central agencies, they need to develop relationships with others in program areas.

From the earliest days, policy analysts in the United States were assigned to organizational units that had significant autonomy in their operations. Often called "policy shops," these units began as relatively small units ranging between ten or fifteen and twenty-five or thirty people. With the exception of the individual who ran the office (who was usually a political appointee), the focus of the activity was on the office itself rather than the individual analysts within it. These offices were expected to reach out to others in the policy research infrastructure (e.g., think tanks, consultants, brain trusts, ad hoc study groups, university institutes, and institutions for advanced study) by assisting with data collection and problem analysis but focusing on decisions to be made inside the department.

Differences in the skill set expected for policy analysts. The parliamentary system adviser is expected to operate to provide policy advice in the context of the specific issue being discussed. Policy advising thus is not formalized as a specialized activity but is believed to include people with a detailed knowledge of the technical, legal, and administrative aspects of policy issues. At the same time, staff in parliamentary systems were drawn from individuals with generalist training and background. In addition, advisers are expected to have a clear understanding of the constraints on the effective implementation of policies. The early policy analysts in the United States emphasized the use of formal analytic techniques. These techniques began with the PPBS process (relying on operations research and some economic analytic approaches) and soon moved to formalized processes related to cost-benefit analysis. As Arnold Meltsner described the first generation of analysts, they employed both technical and political skills; the selection of approach centered on the preferences of the analyst's client.[10]

The level of formalization of the analytical process differs. The policy adviser in the parliamentary system is expected to move through several steps in the process. They include

- taking a difficult and sometimes poorly understood problem or issue and structuring it so that it can be thought about in a systematic way;
- gathering the minimum necessary information and applying the appropriate analytical methods;
- formulating effective options addressing, where necessary, mechanisms for implementation, monitoring, and evaluation; and
- communicating the results of the work to the government in a timely and understandable way.[11]

Advisers are not always expected to make a recommendation for the decision maker. However, they are expected to reach a professional judgment about the underlying situation and appropriate possible courses for policy.

By the end of the first decade of policy analysis in the United States, the policy analysis process had been explicated and formalized. Some of this systemization occurred as a result of the appearance of policy analysis graduate education programs in the United States and what became the professionalization of the field. A logical model emerged that defined the analytic process; it tended to follow these steps:[12]

- Define the problem.
- Assemble some evidence.
- Construct the alternatives.
- Select the criteria.
- Project the outcomes.
- Confront the trade-offs.
- Decide.
- Tell the story.

The structure of government creates different levels of clients with differing authorities. A parliamentary system allows for the coherence of policy development across the government. As such, the actors who become policy advisers' clients include both cabinet-level officials and officials of central agencies (e.g., prime minister's offices or other government-wide units). Because the executive branch is a part of the legislative branch, the decisions that are made by these actors become the formal policy of the system. With a few exceptions (e.g., when the upper chamber of the legislature is controlled by different parties than the lower chamber), there is no need to negotiate a policy once it has been decided.

The policy analysts operating during the first decade of the profession in the US federal government did not always have clients who had the final authority to determine policy. The policies that were recommended by the executive branch often had a strong influence over the final determinations worked out between the executive and legislative branches. However, unlike the officials in a Westminster system, these clients did not have the authority to create new programs or establish new policies without agreement from Congress (or, in some cases, from the judiciary).

Changes That Have Occurred in the United States: The 1960s Compared with Today

As noted above, policy analysis in the United States has changed quite dramatically since its early days in the 1960s as well as its developments since the 1990s. In some cases the areas of similarity are no longer operative. In a few cases the areas of difference have been minimized, but many stay the same. And new variations between parliamentary systems have made it more difficult to generalize about a single approach associated with Westminster systems that often differ markedly from each other.

The 1960s: The Activity Takes Place inside Government

In the early days of the policy analysis field, there was significant similarity between the US activity and parliamentary advising because both focused on decisions made inside government. Today, however, policy analysis in the United States has moved far beyond government. It is found in all nodes of the policy system; not only does it occur inside government but it is also found in interest groups, nongovernmental organizations, and state and local agencies. These groups often approach the policy role with a specific policy agenda in place. In addition, decision making within network systems further complicates the relationship.

Some of this movement beyond government has occurred as the policy system itself has emphasized the role of third parties through grants and contracts with nonprofit organizations or the private sector. Indeed, the growth of these actors has contributed to a field in which the most visible analysts are not found inside but outside government. For many parliamentary systems, however, this development has either not occurred or, if the outside groups are present, they are not the major actors in the ever-changing policy advising enterprise. In Australia, for example, career public servants no longer enjoy the monopoly on policy advice they once held. There has been an allocation of public funds to think tanks and government-funded advocacy centers. As a result, some of the similarities between the systems in the early years of policy analysis have diminished and moved into the "mixed" category.

The 1960s: The Clients of Advising/Analysis Are Found in the Top Reaches of Agencies

The shifts that have taken place in the United States in the policy analysis field have changed this category of similarities. The clients who are found inside government are no longer limited to top agency officials. The proliferation of policy analysts and analysis offices throughout agencies' nooks and crannies means that the offices found at the agencies' top reaches no longer have a monopoly on the production of analysis. As a result, the analysts attached to these offices now must negotiate with analysts in other parts of the agency. In some cases, ideology—not information—has become the currency of policy debate. In addition, clients have moved from being individual officials to collective bodies or even institutional processes within the agency.

Similar developments have occurred in at least one parliamentary system, Australia's, which has seen the introduction of the concept of "contestability," a belief by governments that policy advice is best when it emerges through a contestable market. In other countries the structures of staffs include a proliferation of policy advisers throughout the system. As such, the similarities between the two systems are mixed.

The 1960s: There Is Limited Transparency and Openness in the System

Concern about transparency and open access has increased in both settings over the years. The passage of the Freedom of Information Act in the United States (and its subsequent amendments) did shift at least part of the burden of proof away from the citizen's need to establish the right of access to an agency's information to the agency's need to show why the information should not be made accessible. The Obama administration in the United States has emphasized transparency issues and made them a major goal. Agencies do have the ability to keep information nonaccessible if they can show that a document in question is still at the draft stage or is a part of an ongoing decision-making process. In some settings, it is believed that this has led to practices whereby analysts avoid putting information and options on paper. At the same time, the availability of the internet has made documents and information easier to access. Although parliamentary systems have increased transparency in the process, they still continue to emphasize the confidential relationship between the policy adviser and the individual official.

The 1960s: Work Focuses on the Development of New Policies

During the early stages of the US policy analysis profession, analysts saw their role as primarily focused on the formulation stage of the policy process. During that period they were operating in a context where new policies and programs were being developed. The analysts were important actors in an environment characterized by a strong belief in progress, abundance, and the possibilities of public-sector change. The mood of society also was supported by a reliance on expertise and analytical experts. As the field developed and the mood of the Vietnam-era society took shape, the analyst's agenda focused less on new programs and policies and—instead—on changes that might be made in existing efforts. In addition, both policymakers and analysts became more aware of the implementation problems that were experienced in the new programs and sought to understand the reasons that these problems emerged. The fiscal realities faced by both types of systems have led to an emphasis on the budgetary consequences of implementation decisions.

These developments have spawned an acknowledgment that analysis could take place at all the stages of the policy process. Analysis plays a role in bringing policy issues to the policy agenda, and it is involved in the formulation of policy details, in ascertaining the details of implementation, and in the evaluation process. In some instances analysts associated with particular policies or programs have personally moved from an analytic role to an implementation role (i.e., to being actually involved in managing a program). This increasing focus on implementation has led to a blurring of boundaries between management and policy development; this has also been supported by the contemporary interest in performance management, which sometimes links evaluation activities to performance assessment.

Performance management activities have also been emphasized in some Westminster systems. In addition, the role of central government agencies has provided the setting for what are called "whole of government" responses, which emphasize coordination across policy, program, and service delivery lines.[13] In Australia, for example, policy advisers often have dual responsibilities for policy advice and for program implementation. Implementation includes the oversight task of dealing with contractors that compete for the rights to deliver services.

The 1960s: Policy Analysts Are Found inside Government

By the late 1970s it had become clear that policy analysts in the US system had moved from short-term or in-and-out career paths to become careerists. With the exception of the top staff members, who were political appointees, most of the analytic staff members were now permanent career civil servants. However, there was some movement from government positions to congressional staff positions to interest groups or think tanks; but the bulk of the staff members were civil servants. (See the examples of policy analysis organizations and staffs in chapter 4.)

Although Westminster systems have made attempts to bring in individuals from the outside to serve as policy advisers, the classic civil service career path continues to be the predominant pattern in some settings. In Australia, however, large numbers of ministerial advisers have been brought in who are not public servants as such but public employees employed without pretense to traditional standards of impartiality and merit. As such, they are similar to the political appointees in the US system.

The 1960s: A Focus on Methodology, Not Policy Substance

The early US policy analysts were recruited for their expertise in analytical methods, not for their knowledge about specific matters of policy substance. As staff members assumed career status, they tended to focus on specific policy and program areas. Increasingly, they were recruited for their knowledge of those areas. The career movement that took place usually involved different positions (sometimes outside the executive branch) in that policy field.

Most Westminster systems are based on career staff members who are viewed as administrative generalists, not as policy specialists. There are some indications that this may be changing in some countries.

Today: The Level of Formalization of the Analytical Process

The image of the policy analyst as a quasi-academic staff member whose product is a set of written documents no longer describes many practicing US policy analysts. However, there are still those who fit the profession's original model. An increasing number of analysts make their contribution to the process through meetings and other forms of more informal interaction. In some settings the stylized approach to analysis that ends with formal recommendations has been replaced by interactions where the analyst is only one of a number of participants in policy discussions. In addition, there is a sense of urgency about the need for decisions, and thus there has been a blurring of lines both between managers and analysts and between analysts and more traditional academic researchers. The universal availability of information on the internet allows broader access to information than was possible in the past, when information was largely controlled by the analysts.

Today: The Approach to Information and Data

The proliferation of policy analysis both inside and outside government has supported an approach to information and data that moves far beyond a positivist orientation. As Carol Weiss has described it, it is difficult to think about information without also acknowledging interests and ideology.[14] (See chapter 7 for a further discussion of this issue.) Majone's view about information as evidence for policy positions also seems to describe the current situation.[15] Policy advisers in a Westminster system rarely wrap themselves in a positivist framework but always frame their approach around their clients. For example, a report by the Australian Auditor General's Office describes information gathering in a way that emphasizes flexibility, high quality, and transparency.[16] In addition, the information available on the internet often crosses national boundaries.

These and other changes have contributed to the existence of a policy analysis profession in the United States that has a number of attributes. In many ways, the academic approach to the field has not responded to the changes in the world of practice. The boundaries between policy analysis and management have become increasingly blurred. And at the same time, policies are actually being implemented by state and local governments and private organizations that may not be willing to share information about their experiences. Perhaps most important, they have contributed to a significant modification in the skills that are viewed as essential for individuals hiring in the field.

Changes have also taken place in parliamentary systems that have modified the practice of policy advising. Several patterns are worth emphasizing. First, some Westminster systems have now experienced coalition governments that make it more difficult to establish firm control by one party over government policy (e.g., this occurred in New Zealand). Second, some of the New Public Management approaches have led to changes in the role of central agencies as well as a focus on outcomes and performance assessment. These are emphasized in the growth of third-party contracts. Third, there has been some movement in the development of analytic groups that are outside government. Fourth, the basic parliamentary structure allows these systems to work toward the "whole of government" approach and coordination that is extremely difficult to achieve within the US system. And fifth, the academic field of policy analysis seems to be further developing in a number of countries.

Today: Dealing with Globalization

Perhaps the most dramatic changes dealing with globalization in the policy analysis field in the United States have taken place in the classroom. US programs offering a master's degree in public policy increasingly include students from a range of other countries. It has been a challenge for faculties to develop curricula that meet the diversity of interests and needs of this group of students and, at the same time, provide the core courses for American students. Some US programs offer separate experiences for international students, whereas others have tried to deal with both sets of students together. And still other programs simply place international students in the structures and curricula that have been developed for the US academic market. The combined approach not only provides training in policy analysis for international students but also gives American students some exposure to different political, economic, and social settings—if the international students are encouraged to contrast their experiences with those of their American colleagues. Given the globalization of a number of policy issues (e.g., the environment and health care) that were traditionally treated as domestic problems, some advocates of the combined approach believe that this is an effective way to expose American students to the worldwide dimensions of issues.

Today: Clients

As has been described in chapters 1 and 2, the original concept of the client of the policy analyst was an individual who has authority and is usually located on the top rungs of a public organization. This was modified in the second generation of the profession. Meltsner's depiction of four types of policy analysts with both political and technical skills (see chapter 1) did acknowledge the different roles played by clients as well as the different expectations about the relationship between analyst and client. But even Meltsner's description seemed to assume that the policy analyst would have a monopoly role in this advising process. By the end of the twentieth century, the image of the policy analyst as the adviser to the prince (as in Machiavelli) had been replaced by an image of an individual operating (usually in a public organization) along with other policy analysts in both public and nonpublic organizations. The proliferation of policy analysis units within federal agencies meant that there was now a range of clients as well as a range of types of analysts performing different tasks and roles. As described in chapter 2, clients could be decision makers, institutional processes, organizational maintenance, and even the analyst himself or herself.

Yet another development has occurred in the twenty-first century that has had a major impact on the world of policy analysts and how they think about clients. Views about decision-making processes have moved to quite a different approach. The individual client was often framed in the hierarchical decision-making model, where decisions followed the traditional hierarchical structure and thus assumed that the client would have the authority and power to make a decision. By the end of the twentieth century, however, many policy analysts saw decision making as the result of a bargaining process. Thus the proliferation of analysts and analytic organizations fit nicely into the bargaining relationships between multiple players, most of whom were located somewhere within the governmental structure and could be identified.

By the first decade of the twenty-first century, another approach was added to the decision-making repertoire: the use of networks. Although networks have captured the interest of scholars in a variety of fields in both the United States and abroad, it has not always been clear how they operate as a formal decision-making approach. Networks are conceptualized as structures that reach across a range of organizational boundaries and, according to Rhodes, operate as "a cluster or complex of organizations connected to each other by resources dependencies and distinguished from other clusters or complexes by breaks in the structure of resources dependencies."[17] The participants in the networks were not always easy to define, and networks often were fluid and constantly moving.

McGuire and Agranoff describe a network as a structure that "includes governmental and nongovernmental agencies that are connected through involvement in a public policymaking and/or administrative structure through which information and/or public goods and services may be planned, designed, produced, and delivered."[18] Their analysis focuses on the operational limitations of networks caused by power imbalances, overprocessing, and policy barriers. They note that networks represent both formal and informal approaches, and many of them do not possess the formal authority to act. Others, however, merely exchange information and identify areas of problem-solving approaches. When networks contain a mixture of actors with different resources, it is not always clear how those without formal authority can operate within those relationships.

These are issues that are embedded in situations where the client for the work of a policy analyst is the network itself. Because the network is not an entity with clear or simple goals, how does the analyst determine the interests of the body when—by design—it contains players drawn from multiple interests and settings? And many of those interests represent very different perspectives and thus confront substantive policy conflicts. These conflicts can emerge from the combination of public-sector and private-sector players, representatives of interest groups, multiple public agencies, and players from the various nodes of the intergovernmental system. In addition, studies of various networks indicate that the interaction within the network itself is crucial and thus it is difficult to focus on substantive policy outcomes when the process of interaction is so important to its success.

McGuire and Agranoff note that it is difficult to conclude that networks are replacing governmental agencies or that networks are controlling government. It is not always clear where the boundaries lie between a government agency and a network. But these scholars and others suggest that it is important for researchers to look at the reality of who actually makes decisions in and through networks.[19]

Although there is fairly widespread acknowledgment that decisions are often made by networks (rather than individuals or only government officials), it is not clear how these developments affect the policy analysis process. When a policy analyst confronts a complex array of individuals, interests, and organizations as his or her client, it is difficult for this analyst to figure out which interests will or should prevail.

Today: The Economic Environment

Policy analysts have always been concerned about questions related to the cost of a proposed action. The early interest in cost-benefit analysis (see the discussion in chapter 6) not only pushed analysts to think about the overall cost of an action but also gave them a framework within which to think about who pays for and who benefits from decisions. In this sense cost-benefit analysis required analysts to think about the consequences of their recommendations for real people and to acknowledge that there might be differential costs and benefits to different categories of individuals.

During the early years of the profession, analysts rarely based their decisions only on cost calculations. Recommendations were not expected to be based only on the lowest-cost alternative; instead, analysts tried to trade off multiple values and to determine the ratio between costs and benefits. It certainly helped that the environment of the early 1960s was largely one of growth and possibilities. By the end of the 1960s, analysts were operating in a Vietnam War environment where there was an acknowledgment that it was hard to have both guns and butter. But it was still possible to ask questions that involved determinations of the abstraction "the public interest." During the second phase of the profession, beginning in the mid-1970s, the proliferation of policy analysis offices made it obvious that there were multiple interests at play in most policy decisions. Analysts worried about both costs and benefits but calculated them in terms of their clients. It was the political process that eventually made the trade-offs between the interests of multiple actors in terms of bargaining and negotiation.

As the twenty-first century began, the September 11, 2001, terrorist attacks on the United States and two subsequent wars in Iraq and Afghanistan interacted with more conservative views that advocated a limited role for government and drove to enact lower tax rates. These and other factors led to a fiscal condition that entailed a high debt level, resistance to increasing taxes, and skepticism about the effectiveness of government action.

This financial and economic crisis created a climate in which cost was discussed without thinking about benefits. It pushed analysts to think in short-term rather than long-term frameworks. Debate was often posed in ideological terms, and issues were captured by highly politicized interests. Debates became increasingly based on budget numbers, not on real assessments of program effectiveness. The green-eyeshade technocrats were much less interested in the details of a program than in its cost. Advocates for new programs were pushed to make assessments of future costs, even though they knew that these programs contained significant uncertainties about how they would be adopted and implemented and thus what their real budget costs would be. The availability of data via the internet reinforced the illusion that budget allocations were complete or even accurate. And fiscal issues mixed with increased politicization to push decision makers to further emphasize short-term policy changes.

Today: Changing Skills and Staff

As described in chapter 1, the original depiction of policy analysts was conceptualized by Arnold Meltsner in the 1970s based on his interviews with the first generation of policy analysts in the federal government; he differentiated between two types of skills—technical skills and political skills—and he created four types of policy analysts.[20]

The original edition of this book contained a modification of Meltsner's typology to reflect the changes that had occurred in the field (see chapter 2). This modification added a number of skill categories to the technical and political skills; these were organizational skills, evaluation skills and—most significantly—issue-specific skills around program and policy areas. This framework differentiated between types of clients, emphasizing the dynamics that occurred as a result of the proliferation of policy analysis inside government agencies. However, this typology did not reflect the growth of the policy analysis profession outside government.

Today, a large percentage of the policy analyst jobs are found outside government. They rarely include any executive-level jobs. It appears that few of the policy analysis shops in the federal government are searching for candidates. Those who enter these offices tend to come via the Presidential Management Fellowship Program, which is a two-year paid government fellowship sponsored by the Office of Personnel Management for recent graduate students who seek a two-year assignment in a US government agency.

A review of existing job searches indicates that many organizations are looking for people who have substantive knowledge of specific policy areas when selecting new staff members. Individuals such as Veronica Lopez (see her profile at the beginning of this chapter) come into policy analyst positions because of their specialized knowledge of a policy sector. In addition, organizations seem to be seeking written communication skills, an ability to do collaborative teamwork, and computer skills. They also focus on candidates' oral communication skills as well as evidence of their organizational abilities. A number of organizations are looking for individuals who have the ability to pose issues in a way that is understood and useful to policymakers. Interestingly enough, groups vary in terms of the academic background desired. Some groups look for people with BAs, others focus on master's-level graduates, and a few, more technical, groups seek those with PhDs. If the organization is involved in international work, it often seeks evidence of international experience as well as language skills. If a policy analysis organization is identified with particular ideologies or policy positions, it might require potential staff members to show their commitment to their positions.

The specialization in a policy sector that seems to be the norm for recruitment and career development of policy analysts outside government seems to be quite different than the pattern inside government, particularly the federal government. Individuals who become career federal public servants are likely to have a career structure that involves moving around from policy area to policy area.

The Policy Analysis Field in the Twenty-First Century

This chapter has briefly described the modifications that have taken place in the policy analysis field as the twenty-first century has begun. These changes have occurred both in the world of practice as well as in the academy. The modifications seem to be more pronounced in the academic world as the field reaches its midlife. Although the policy analyst practitioners represent diverse and varied roles and skills, the academic face of the field seems to have swung back to more traditional academic perspectives. As a result, there does appear to be a disconnect between the world of practice and the academy.

David Weimer has written about the differences between the expectations embedded in policy research and those of policy analysis:

> Whereas policy research tends to focus on only a few of the values inherent in an issue, such as efficiency or equity, good policy analysis takes a comprehensive view of values, considering them explicitly. Whereas our policy research often focuses on a single policy alternative, often one that has been tried, good policy analysis considers a range of alternatives, including at times, truly novel approaches. Whereas our fellows in the research community care very much about our methodological innovations

and cleverness, the primary clients of policy analysts are decision makers who care about the good judgment supporting predictions. . . . Whereas we tend to choose policy problems that allow us to apply tools commonly used in our own disciplines, good policy analysis is eclectic in its methods, using whatever methods help make better predictions. Whereas we tend to focus our policy research on a single impact, such as the one most consistent with the purported purpose of a program, good policy analysis considers all the likely impacts of policy alternatives and confronts the tradeoffs among them.[21]

There are several patterns that seem to be evidence of a retreat to traditional academic perspectives within the academy. First, the differentiation between policy research and policy analysis has become much less clear.[22] Policy research approaches draw on broad social science research and do not focus on the relationship between the policy analyst and the client he or she is advising. In this sense the work is less sensitive to the advising role of policy analysts. Second, faculty members are increasingly recruited from traditional academic fields and have been evaluated through the performance criteria of those fields. Third, fewer faculty members than in earlier years either come to the academy with experience as practitioners or are encouraged to spend time in a practitioner role during sabbaticals or other forms of leave. Fourth, the academic work of the faculty tends to retreat into technocratic postures, is atheoretical, and avoids policy issues (often those that are termed "wicked problems") that require attention to framing questions and problems related to defining appropriate strategies. Much of the work that is accomplished may be important methodologically but does not confront the types of policy problems where there are limited formal data sets. Given these patterns, long-term perspectives are much harder to accomplish.

Although the Association for Public Policy Analysis and Management (APPAM) continues to reach out to both academics and practitioners, both the annual Research Conference and its *Journal of Policy Analysis and Management* tend to emphasize more traditional academic approaches. Also, the practitioners who are most active in APPAM come from more academically oriented think tanks. In its call for papers for its 2012 fall conference, APPAM did signal a somewhat different approach: "As part of APPAM's new strategic plan, we are seeking to expand integration across perspectives, disciplines, methods and policy areas. . . . We encourage submissions that reflect diversity of perspectives, and the program committee will look specifically for such submissions."[23]

Conclusion

At least three different generations can be identified in this depiction of the development of the policy analysis field. And it is likely that another generation will come to pass in the future. It is not surprising that this field is constantly developing and moving because it operates within a highly turbulent environment. At this writing in the second decade of the twenty-first century, it is clear that the effects of globalization have had a significant influence on the field. And shifts in the type of decision making also have created challenges for policy analysts because analysts are now clearly in so many nooks and crannies in the decision-making world. Thus it is relevant to look at the work they do and at the skills and background experience they need.

Notes

1. The term was originally described by Horst Rittel and Melvin Weber, "Dilemmas in a General Theory of Planning," *Policy Sciences* 4 (1973): 155–69.

2. See Edith Stokey and Richard Zeckhauser, *A Primer for Policy Analysis* (New York: W. W. Norton, 1978); Arnold Meltsner, *Policy Analysts in the Bureaucracy* (Berkeley: University of California Press, 1976); David L. Weimer and Aidan R. Vining, *Policy Analysis: Concepts and Practice*, 5th ed. (Upper Saddle River, NJ: Prentice Hall, 2011); and Harold Laswell, *A Pre-View of Policy Sciences* (New York: American Elsevier, 1971).

3. Brian W. Hogwood and Lewis A. Gunn, *Policy Analysis for the Real World* (Oxford: Oxford University Press, 1984), v–vi.

4. See the website of the *Journal of Comparative Policy Analysis: Research and Practice*, www.jcpa.ca.

5. David L. Weimer, "The Universal and the Particular in Policy Analysis and Training," *Journal of Comparative Policy Analysis* 14, no. 1 (2012): 4.

6. I have used a draft report of a working group in the Australian government, titled "Performance Assessment of Policy Work," December 1991, as a classic expression of the world of policy advising in a parliamentary system. Although this document provides a picture of activities in just one parliamentary government at one point in time, it is a useful example of the practice of policy advising in a Westminster system. However, because there are important variations in parliamentary systems, some of these observations may be less accurate for some systems. See also John Uhr and Keith Mackay, eds., *Evaluating Policy Advice: Learning from Commonwealth Experience* (Canberra: Federalism Research Centre, Australian National University, and Commonwealth Department of Finance, 1966).

7. Although analysts might come from outside of government, competing views from those outside organizations (e.g., think tanks) were not emphasized.

8. The original Freedom of Information Act was not passed by Congress until 1966. Even with increased coverage, draft memos were not to be accessible to the public.

9. Yehezkel Dror, "Policy Analysis for Advising Rules," in *Rethinking the Process of Operational Research and Systems Analysis*, edited by Rolfe Tomlinson and Istvan Kiss (Oxford: Pergamon Press, 1984), 107.

10. Meltsner, *Policy Analysts*.

11. These are spelled out in the 1991 Australian document "Performance Assessment of Policy Work."

12. See Eugene Bardach, *A Practical Guide for Policy Analysis: The Eightfold Path of More Effective Problem Solving*, 4th ed. (Washington, DC: CQ Press, 2011).

13. Management Advisory Committee, "Connecting Government: Whole of Government Responses to Australia's Priority Challenges," April 20, 2004, appendix 3.

14. Carol H. Weiss, "Ideology, Interests and Information: The Basis of Policy Positions," in *Ethics, the Social Sciences, and Policy Analysis*, edited by D. Callahan and B. Jennings (New York: Plenum Press, 1983).

15. Giandomenico Majone, *Evidence, Argument, and Persuasion in the Policy Process* (New Haven, CT: Yale University Press, 1989).

16. Australian Auditor-General, "Developing Policy Advice Better Practice Principles," November 2001.

17. See R. A. W. Rhodes, "New Directions in the Study of Policy Networks," *European Journal of Political Research* 21, no. 2 (1992).

18. Michael McGuire and Robert Agranoff, "The Limitations of Public Management Networks," *Public Administration* 89, no. 2 (2011): 266.

19. E.g., see Kathleen Hale, *How Information Matters: Networks and Public Policy Innovation* (Washington, DC: Georgetown University Press, 2011).

20. Meltsner, *Policy Analysts*.

21. Weimer, "Universal and the Particular," 2–3.

22. See Aidan R. Vining and David L. Weimer, "Foundations of Public Administration: Policy Analysis," in *Public Administration Review, Foundations of Public Administration*, 2010.

23. Announcement of changes to the APPAM fall conference proposal process.

Chapter 4

Profiles of Practice

This chapter presents relatively short profiles of nine organizations that illustrate a number of ways in which the policy analysis profession is practiced. Though these groups do offer examples of the variegated landscape of policy analysis practice, they are not meant to encompass all possible variations. These organizations were selected because they emphasize several attributes: diverse origins, the role of analysis for legislatures, state as well as national focus, and political agendas. Only one of the organizations is an example of a traditional federal government policy analysis office (although several other offices are discussed in chapter 1). All but one of the examples involve organizations within the United States. The last example—the Danish SFI organization—provides a picture of an organization in Europe that shares some attributes with groups in the United States but places its activities within a parliamentary system and a political culture that are quite different from American activities.

The profiles include information on the organization's staffing patterns, patterns of growth and development, definitions of clients and audiences, methodologies and analytic techniques, sources of information, and challenges and dilemmas. The data used to develop the profiles were drawn from various information sources, including interviews with staff, extant analyses of the organization, and scrutiny of reports and other products issued by the organization. The profiles attempt to present the organizations as they define themselves and are not meant to offer a critique of their roles or effectiveness.

To one degree or another, all the organizations have had to deal with problems balancing the values of analytic neutrality with advocacy. As is shown below, each organization has confronted this dilemma in its own somewhat different way. The groups also differ in other respects. Some of the organizations focus on national-level decision making, whereas others emphasize issues in state-level institutions. They vary in age; several of the organizations began their operations before the 1960s, whereas others are more recent.

The Public Policy Institute of AARP (formerly the American Association of Retired People) began in 1985 as an organization that sought to link research to both lobbying and its large and active membership. It continues to do this today.

The Office of the Assistant Secretary for Planning and Evaluation (ASPE) in the US Department of Health and Human Services is the oldest domestic department-level policy analysis office in the federal government. Over the years, the changes in ASPE have been quite dramatic.

The California Legislative Analyst's Office (LAO) is the oldest and perhaps premier state-level policy analysis office. The LAO, which was created to provide the California legislature with an analytic voice that was not dependent on the governor, has also undergone many changes in its environment that have required modifications in its work.

The Center on Budget and Policy Priorities is a Washington-based organization that was created in the early 1980s to provide an alternative source of information to the policy positions then being taken by the Reagan administration. Although the center is embedded in a defined set of values, it has sought to produce rigorous analytic work that is useful to policymakers in Washington as well as in the states and localities, and also to the public, the press, and other groups that share its values.

The State Fiscal Analysis Initiative network, founded in 1993, describes itself as "a network of state-level nonprofit policy organizations working for equitable, responsible and sustainable budget and tax policies." It began with member groups in twelve states and currently functions as a network of approximately forty groups.

The Century Foundation (formerly the Twentieth Century Fund) was created after World War I by a philanthropist who believed that social problems could be addressed when information became available. Over the years, the fund has responded to shifts in society, supporting publications and research in a wide range of domestic and international issue areas.

The Congressional Research Service (CRS) of the Library of Congress is the major source of information and analysis for the US Congress. As such, it must deal with the multiple and conflicting client perspectives found among the membership and committees of the House of Representatives and the Senate. It operates within all dimensions of the legislative process and seeks to anticipate issues that will come before Congress.

The Danish National Centre for Social Research (known as SFI) was founded in l958 as a part of the Ministry of Social Affairs and was designed to conduct research that focuses on welfare state policies.

The Heritage Foundation was created in the 1970s by a group of conservatives who believed that Washington-based think tanks were being monopolized by liberal researchers and analysts. It has excelled in providing information that is easily digested and accessible to busy policymakers.

The AARP Public Policy Institute: Policy Analysis Linked to Lobbying and Membership

The Public Policy Institute (PPI) of AARP was founded in 1985 soon after John Rother joined AARP as its principal policy and strategy leader. Rother came to the organization in 1984 from the Senate Aging Committee, where he saw the potential for the use of research in advocacy. To that point, he saw how lobbying for older Americans was not based on research but emerged as a result of information already available to both lobbyists and congressional staff.[1]

During the first years of its existence, PPI drew on some people already on the AARP staff but mainly recruited new individuals hired specifically because of their expertise on retirement and health issues. Marilyn Moon was recruited as the first head of the office; she was a highly visible individual who was known for her work on health issues. The initial mission for the organization was threefold. First, it sought to add credibility to advocacy work by grounding it in evidence, particularly during the process of considering new policies. Second, it would develop options for the leadership groups in the organization to consider. And third, it would link to other, already-established policy research organizations that dealt with issues affecting older Americans.

During most of its life, PPI has reported to Rother, who was a vice president of AARP responsible for both research and lobbying. Trained as a lawyer, Rother tried to blend a staff that used diverse approaches. One group (largely the lobbyists) saw the effort as helping the organization come to decisions that would be the basis for lobbying activities. Another group was from the research community and saw its mission as furthering knowledge in the areas of interest to AARP. The two groups both had legitimate concerns, but it was not always easy to find ways to combine their perspectives. For some, PPI's major mission was translating research into policy, not doing original research of its own.

The policy analysts in PPI respond to several different clients. One client is their "boss," the head of the policy organization. Another is the other national office staff and volunteer-based bodies within AARP. And Congress (and state decision makers) are the ultimate target audience for its efforts.

Unlike many other public interest groups operating in Washington, AARP has a large membership of approximately 37 million individuals that can be mobilized as a valuable resource in lobbying. This membership supports both a large national office as well as offices in all fifty states and three territories. A board of directors directs the affairs and resources of the organization and is made up of both working and retired individuals who represent a broad range of experience useful to the organization. The board sets guidelines for the organization and hires the top executives to run its day-to-day operations. Many board members have been active in AARP at the state level or have had careers in public service in areas of concern to the organization.

The AARP National Policy Council (NPC), an advisory committee to AARP's board of directors, is composed of volunteers who represent a diverse cross section of AARP members and have a proven record of public policy experience and interest. The NPC helps the board to perform its governance responsibilities in setting AARP's policies and strategic direction. The presence on the NPC of seven regional representatives, three board members, and AARP's president-elect facilitates integration among AARP's state offices, national staff, volunteers, and the board.

Members of the NPC develop and make public policy recommendations to the board of directors regarding AARP's federal, state, and local legislative and regulatory issues. In making public policy recommendations for the board's consideration and approval, the NPC studies public policy options and considers the opinions of members, guidance from the staff, and analysis from nationally renowned policy experts. Official policies are approved by AARP's independent, all-volunteer board of directors.

An annual policy meeting followed by a board policy conference is held for both national and state members to examine and discuss the organization's policy positions. This session focuses on a range of policies that should be modified, accepted, or eliminated. Observers at and participants in these sessions note that the volunteers who are engaged in these discussions were thoughtful and often able to think about long-range views (focused on policies for their children and grandchildren).

The result of the policy discussion is a publication titled *The Policy Book* that integrates views from members and others through communications, policy forums, surveys, and polls and serves as a guide for volunteers and staff in advocating for change.[2] It also issues *The Priorities Book*, which "offers a brief overview of AARP policy positions, reflecting our mission to enhance quality of life for all as we age. We lead positive social change and deliver value to members through advocacy, service and information to make things better for society and play a positive role in communities of all kinds."[3]

At the federal level AARP supports legislation that reflects these policies by lobbying the administration, Congress, and regulatory agencies. In addition, these policies serve as the guide for advocacy efforts in the states and territories. Because the states and territories differ from one another, state AARP leaders work with the national office staff to interpret the goals for local leaders and help them select policy issues and strategies.

The PPI staff works within this complex organizational structure. In some cases it is involved in the agenda-setting process and provides background information that is useful in early stages of the process of establishing a policy agenda. This provides an opportunity to think about longer-term strategies and identify emerging issues. In other cases PPI staff provide analysis that supports positions that have already been defined and established. In these cases PPI and the lobbying staff are required to work closely together and usually to think in short-term frameworks. One observer noted that the difference between the lobbying agenda and the policy analysis agenda gives protection to people thinking about big ideas. Sometimes it is useful not to be at the table where immediate issues determine the approach.

The PPI staff itself is organized in four teams, each of which deals with a cluster of issues that have been important to AARP since its beginnings:

- *The Consumer Team* conducts research and policy analysis, and brings together thought leaders to develop and advance AARP's public policy agenda on consumer protection. The team focuses on critical marketplace practices and regulatory developments that affect financial services and literacy, credit practices, fraud and deceptive practices, energy and telecommunications, and advance planning issues such as guardianship and powers of attorney.
- *The Economic Team* analyzes and develops policies related to the economy and its impact on financial security, particularly security in retirement. Key research topics include the solvency of the Social Security program and the adequacy of benefits for low-income retirees; the adequacy and coverage of workplace pensions; individual retirement saving, managing assets in retirement, and the income of older Americans; Supplemental Security Income and other programs to protect low-income families and retirees; workplace flexibility, training, age discrimination, and other issues related to the older workforce; and the equity and efficiency of tax policies and the adequacy of tax revenues.

- *The Health Team* conducts research and policy analysis, and brings to-gether thought leaders to develop and advance AARP's public policy agenda on health care. The team examines critical public policy issues that affect access to health care services, their quality and safety, the cost of care, and public health. Its goal is to foster sound and creative solutions that meet the health care challenges of an aging society and to inform state and national policymakers, opinion leaders, research-ers, program planners, and administrators.
- *The Livable Communities/Long-Term Care Team* focuses on expanding consumer access and choice to an array of affordable long-term care options, with an emphasis on improving home and community-based services, supporting family caregivers, and making communities more livable.

In addition, staff in the PPI work on strategic initiatives with external part-ners and foundations on a range of projects designed to improve the care and services available to older Americans.

During the early years of its operation, PPI's products emphasized reports and publications. These included policy research reports, monthly reports on unemployment, fact sheets on a range of policy issues, in-depth reports, and briefs on topical issues. More recently, however, the organization has empha-sized the dissemination of existing work and reaching out to experts outside the organization for policy ideas. It has organized forums on topical issues and what it calls innovation roundtables on policy developments. In 2011 seven forums were held in collaboration with other national organizations. These drew more than 1,000 policymakers and analysts, congressional staff, academic experts, government officials, and stakeholder leaders. Nine inno-vation roundtables were organized in 2011 to bring together national experts for confidential discussions to help AARP develop policy options on key is-sues. These meetings sought to bridge ideological gaps in order to reach new solutions. In addition, PPI sponsored six internal AARP dialogues to bring to-gether national office staff and state offices to discuss research and options for policy development related to health care, economic security, and caregiving.

In 2011 PPI staff members gave approximately 150 presentations at confer-ences and stakeholder meetings around the country. The organization's re-ports (which are available on its website) attracted nearly 50,000 downloads. Media coverage of reports and citations of PPI experts appeared in more than 400 articles in 2011, an increase of almost 25 percent from 2010.

PPI worked with almost all the state offices in 2011, and it largely provided expertise on a range of legislative issues. These included health care reform, Medicaid, the legal protection of seniors, utilities and telecommunications, transportation, and housing. It provided analysis and guidance to the various units of AARP's national staff—including the lobbying office, the NPC, communications, membership, and the AARP Foundation.

A significant percentage of the nearly sixty PPI staff members had academic and professional backgrounds in specific policy issues on AARP's agenda as well as training in the field of gerontology. Job searches within PPI clearly emphasize the need for individuals who are knowledgeable about the specific issues on AARP's policy agenda.

The Office of the Assistant Secretary for Planning and Evaluation in the Department of Health and Human Services: A Classic Policy Analysis Shop That Changed over Time

The Office of the Assistant Secretary for Planning and Evaluation (ASPE) in the US Department of Health and Human Services (HHS; formerly the Department of Health, Education, and Welfare), is the oldest of the department-level federal agency domestic policy analysis units. When ASPE was created in 1965 as the Office of Program Coordination to perform the Planning, Program, and Budgeting System (PPBS) functions, the unit reported to an assistant secretary, who in turn reported to the undersecretary of the department.[4] ASPE's mission statement reads: "The Assistant Secretary for Planning and Evaluation is the principal adviser to the Secretary of the Department of Health and Human Services on policy development issues, and is responsible for major activities in the areas of policy coordination, legislation development, strategic planning, policy research and evaluation, and economic analyses."[5]

During ASPE's first days, a small staff of eight people was given specific areas of program responsibility and collected and analyzed data to inform the multiyear PPBS planning process. Over the years the office varied in size; its largest growth occurred during the Carter administration, when more than 300 individuals worked in the centralized policy office. At its lowest, there were 85 staff members. At this writing there are approximately 140 individuals. The office's growth was triggered by at least two factors in the 1970s—the transfer of staff from the policy analysis unit of the Office of Economic Opportunity, and the interest of the department's secretary in policy analysis activities.

The impact of the office not only was affected by the size of the staff but often was determined by the makeup and type of the staff's professional training. Perhaps most important was the personal relationship between the department secretary and the assistant secretary for planning and evaluation. During some periods ASPE was a close adviser to the secretary; in others the office was an arm's-length think tank that did not play an important role in the decision-making process.

Many of the original ASPE staff members were PhD-holding economists; some, in fact, had come to the department from the Department of Defense, where they had been involved in the PPBS process. As the years went on, staff members were drawn from many different fields, and more staff had master's degrees (particularly in public policy) than doctoral degrees. Increasingly, staff came to the office with either academic or work experience in one of the issue areas with which the office was concerned.

ASPE's office structure was mainly drawn along specific issue lines. When the office was devised, its structure actually mirrored the program categories used in the PPBS process. This approach, at the time, was viewed as a radical organizational structure. Before the Social Security Administration was removed from HHS in 1995, an income security unit included welfare and Social Security. Units also were organized to specialize in health, social services, and education (before education became the responsibility of a separate cabinet department in 1979). Functional rather than issue-specific units included a group called program systems, which coordinated the planning and legislative functions, and at one point, an evaluation unit, which tried to improve the department's overall evaluation activities. The program systems unit could be viewed as a residual of the original PPBS responsibilities, given that it was assigned the job of providing crosscutting policy and policy support for the department's planning activities and data policy systems, and of providing statistical, scientific programming, modeling, computer systems, and other technical services for staff.

Many staff members made ASPE the longtime location for their careers. Information that was gleaned from a survey of current and former staff members indicated that they had a high level of job satisfaction, believing that their time in ASPE provided them with mentors and an environment that supported constant learning about new approaches and strategies.[6]

As discussed above, ASPE's role in HHS has been modified over the years. Although the office still appears on the organization chart within the Office of the Secretary, the staff's role now involves interaction with other parts of the department as much as advice giving to either the secretary or the deputy secretary. These changes have been caused by several developments: the movement from an emphasis on the development of new policies to a mixed portfolio that includes attention to existing programs, the demands of research and evaluation management, shifts that are attributable to fairly dramatic transitions from one president to another, and the imperatives of working with many more analysts both inside and outside the department.

Although ASPE's clients have remained the secretary and deputy secretary, its role has changed, depending on the nature and number of the HHS secretary's other advisers. When ASPE had more competition, its clients also became more numerous and less clear-cut. Yet in many instances, the top officials actually relied on others to provide advice; these included a range of special assistants, individuals who staffed the executive secretariat (the traffic cop function), the budget office, or the program units themselves. When new staff members entered the department through the Presidential Management Intern (later the Presidential Management Fellowship) Program, ASPE found that other units—particularly the Office of the Assistant Secretary for Management and Budget—were hiring individuals whose training was similar to that of persons hired by ASPE.

ASPE was usually asked to comment on proposals submitted by others at HHS, but often it was just one of a number of voices that were heard rather than the secretary's ultimate source of advice. The early ASPE operations were often associated with the efforts of a secretary to exert more centralized control over the program units. The commitment to centralization varied, depending on the secretary; during the Clinton administration, HHS was managed internally on a highly decentralized basis.[7]

During the Clinton administration ASPE staff members became increasingly involved in policy initiatives that emerged from the White House. Particularly in the areas of welfare reform and health reform, ASPE staff members were directly involved in crafting alternatives that would surface as presidential initiatives. In the case of the Clinton health reform effort of 1993, they were assigned to work on the health policy task force on a full-time basis. Similarly, they often took major responsibility for organizing and staffing intradepartmental task forces on particular issues. Similar assignments were also given to ASPE staff involved in welfare reform proposals.

The focus on policy specializations within ASPE tended to support a fairly diffuse ASPE management strategy. In many cases both the assistant secretary and the deputy assistant secretaries were chosen because of their specialized knowledge of a policy area—particularly welfare or health. As a result, the role of ASPE as a generalist voice within the department was diminished, often at the same time that the overall staff role of units within the Office of the Secretary also diminished. In some instances, analysts who had been around for many years were associated with particular policy positions, and their perspective on the issue was very predictable. Specialization also led to the development of strong relationships between ASPE staff and others both inside and outside the department with an interest in a particular policy area.

ASPE staff in the health policy area, for example, often include individuals who have had past experience in think tanks, academic settings, legislative areas, and interest groups.

The methodologies and analytic techniques that were employed during the early years tended to rest on economic models and variants of the PPBS approach. However, as the years progressed, the ASPE staff was likely to emphasize skills as *policy* experts rather than *policy analysis* experts. When asked what skills were the most important for ASPE staff, they picked specific program knowledge as the most important. This was true for individuals drawn from different disciplines; even the individuals trained as economists ranked specific program knowledge highest, followed by statistics, microeconomics, and cost-benefit analysis.

Performing research and evaluation functions within ASPE led to an interest in other skills, including research design and evaluation techniques. The large-scale evaluations and demonstrations that moved from the Office of Economic Opportunity to ASPE also supported hiring people who had simulation skills. With budget cuts, however, these kinds of efforts are very rare. The institutionalization of the office also was responsible for an emphasis on a range of other skills: an ability to write clearly, an ability to speak and make presentations, and skills in group interaction. When former staff members were asked what term best described their role in ASPE, they listed *expert* as the major role, followed by *advice giver, coordinator, researcher*, and *technician*.

Although there is a high level of job satisfaction within ASPE, its past and present staff members are fairly clear that they did not perceive many of their work assignments as successes. Failure was attributable to a number of factors, most of which involved political problems: a lack of support in the administration or department, not enough political will, a lack of interest from top decision makers, rough politics, a closed window of opportunity, congressional resistance, or collision with political ideologies.[8]

Though some ASPE staff members enjoyed their involvement in administration initiatives and interaction with White House staff, sometimes this participation also bred situations in which they felt a lack of control over their assignments. They were more likely to feel negative about an assignment in an unfamiliar area. Conversely, they were more likely to feel positive about assignments that allowed them to have a high degree of interaction with others inside ASPE, inside the department, and outside the department (e.g., with other agencies, researchers in academic settings, think tanks, interest groups, and state and local officials).

In the past, the final product that emerged from ASPE's assignments was likely to include the elements of a classic policy analysis: alternatives, recommendations, strategies for adoption, implementation issues, and cost estimates. Products of successful projects were more likely to include recommendations than anything else, whereas the examples viewed as unsuccessful were likely to end with the specification of alternatives. Although not all products included detailed attention to implementation issues, there was increased concern about these questions over time. In the successful examples memoranda were the most frequent products of the analytic work. Other products were proposed legislation, briefings, reports, meetings, and policy papers. In recent years there has been a tendency to minimize the writing of formal issue papers, which have been replaced with interactive discussions during the budget and legislative development processes. Major decisions were also made outside the department, for example, the crafting of the Patient Protection and Affordable Care Act, which was done in Congress and in the White House.

Although today's ASPE continues to exhibit some of the attributes of the policy shop of the 1960s, in many ways it is very different. Though the office has always had a high level of fragmentation, in the past it was also able to operate as a coherent whole. Because other offices within HHS play an important role in determining policy initiatives (particularly the budget office and the operating divisions), it is not at all clear whether ASPE will be able to provide an overall perspective on developments or proposals that reflects a centralized perch in the department, which is currently managed and structured as a highly decentralized organization. If there is a centralized perspective on issues, it is more likely to come from the department's executive secretariat or from its public affairs office. Because staff members have been encouraged to become specialists, their ability to operate as generalists has been diminished. In addition, many of the decisions that had been made inside the department have been eclipsed by the increasing role of the Office of Management and Budget.

The California Legislative Analyst's Office: Analysis in a Changing Political Environment

The California Legislative Analyst's Office (LAO) was established in 1941 to provide the state legislature with fiscal analytical capacity. Before that time, the legislature did not have the ability to independently review the governor's budget or to assess the administration of policies enacted by the legislature. Earlier attempts to establish such an office had not been successful. In 1941 the legislature did pass a bill to establish a similar office, but it was vetoed by the governor. To circumvent this opposition the legislature changed its own joint rules to allow the office to be created. In 1951, however, the sitting governor did sign legislation codifying the joint rule that created the LAO and the Joint Legislative Budget Committee, which oversees the LAO.[9]

When the LAO was established, it was the only analytical staff available to the legislature. As such it was a very important tool for the body and was involved with committee hearings. Over the years, however, staffs were built up within the committees and the LAO focused its responsibilities on fiscal issues, primarily through analysis of the state budget and proposed legislation. Eventually the staffs of the fiscal committees in both the Assembly and the Senate became more partisan.

The LAO is charged by statute to make recommendations to the legislature, not simply provide options to the members.[10] Because the legislature was in session for only part of the year, the office was able to use the nonsession time to develop budget issues, learn about the operations of programs, and perform special projects for committees.

Up to the mid-1990s the growth of the LAO staff mirrored the population explosion in California and the growth of the state budget. The staff size, which was approximately forty people in 1960, grew to more than one hundred in 1990. The early staff was composed of individuals with a variety of experiences: auditing backgrounds, prior experience in government, or experience as agents of the Federal Bureau of Investigation. In the late 1970s focused recruiting efforts were made to bring in students who were graduates of the public policy schools. A master's degree became the minimal qualification, and the recruitment effort resulted in an infusion of new talent. Given the relative youth of the staff, it was not surprising that many of its members left the LAO and moved to other parts of state government; this movement created a network of alumni that facilitated information exchange within the state apparatus.

In the early 1990s, however, things changed. The office staff size was more than cut in half because of a voter-approved measure reducing the legislature's budget. Although the LAO was valued, the legislature was faced with a choice between cutting back on personal staffs of the members or decreasing the size of the LAO. Especially at its reduced size, the office itself continues to operate as a flat organization with strong collegial relationships among staff members. The LAO is known as a highly productive work situation within state government, and though not as large as it once was, it has regained some of its staff capacity and currently has more than fifty-five staff members.

According to Elizabeth Hill, the former head of the LAO, "one of the most important values that the office has adopted is that of service, which we have defined as 'contributions that make a difference.'"[11] Contributions include high-quality, objective products that can be used to frame and influence policy discussions. The LAO defines eight functions in its mission: (1) analyzing issues and making recommendations to solve fiscal and policy problems; (2) providing nonpartisan advice and policy alternatives; (3) responding to inquiries for facts and for programmatic and technical information; (4) raising important fiscal and policy issues for the legislature; (5) critiquing proposals for state spending and revenue raising; (6) forecasting state revenues and expenditures; (7) serving as the fiscal and programmatic watchdog by overseeing the executive branch; and (8) estimating the fiscal effect on state and local governments of statewide ballot measures.[12]

Although the LAO's functions remain fairly constant, its role has changed as a result of the term limits imposed on members of the legislature. The much higher turnover of members has meant that the office plays a very important institutional memory role. This has emphasized its ability not only to critique proposals but also to provide information and offer solutions to members who do not have a legislative track record on issues.[13] Given the shorter length of service of members, it is also important for the LAO to build trust with members over a shortened period of time.

The changed environment and the reduction in staff size have modified the work of the office. In addition, the decrease in staff size doubled the assignments and portfolios of the staff, necessitating a focus on higher-level issues.

The main work of the LAO is done for the legislature's fiscal committees, but the organization defines all 120 members of the California legislature as its "bosses."[14] Individual members may ask for analyses or cost estimates for particular proposals. When individual members make such a request, the LAO treats that relationship between the member and the LAO as akin to an attorney–client relationship.

The operating oversight of the LAO is done through the Joint Legislative Budget Committee—a fourteen-member committee made up of eight senators and eight Assembly members. This body has been strictly bipartisan, with representation given to minority party members. The rules of the committee require approval by five Senate and five Assembly members. The LAO's budget comes directly from the legislature's budget, not from the regular state budget—thus avoiding a potential veto from a governor.

The LAO's products reflect the multiple audiences with which it is concerned. In fact, the downsizing forced on the office pushed a change in its analytical agenda, which now emphasizes a range of products that will be available to the legislature on a short-turnaround, timely basis. The LAO no longer prepares a single, large book containing all the analyses of the governor's budget proposals. Instead, it publishes shorter, more digestible pieces by program area (for example, K–12 education). Many of its key reports involve fiscal forecasting—economic, revenue, and expenditure trends. This function has become a particularly important and visible one in recent years as the state has dealt with chronic budget deficits. In addition, the office also releases reports of various lengths on specific issues that highlight policy rather than fiscal issues. Whereas the budget was the flagship document for the office, these other reports have become more important to members. Reports now contain more graphics and are shorter and easier to consume (e.g., with concise executive summaries). All LAO reports are now available on its website.

The LAO employs a wide variety of methods in its work. The taxation and fiscal forecasting projects involve modeling and very sophisticated techniques. Others are much less sophisticated. But whether the analysis is quantitative or qualitative, analysts are encouraged to translate that work into understandable language. As one manager put it, "We tell the staff that they should write their reports so their family members can understand them." Although the office used cost-benefit analyses extensively in earlier years, it has not relied on that technique more recently. The staff found that it was difficult to quantify benefits and thus is more likely to present cost estimates alone. The work that has been performed recently has emphasized solutions and options.

The advent of new technology has made it possible for the staff to create its own independent databases. The staff members who do the fiscal forecasts and expenditure analyses work with program people in the agencies but are not as dependent as they had been in the past on data produced by the executive branch. At the same time, staff members rely on various sources of data from state departments and other official documents as well as on analyses produced by federal agencies and information from local officials, lobbyists, and academics. The office accentuates the importance of understanding the details of program implementation, and staff members frequently visit implementation sites.

The LAO emphasizes its role as a neutral, nonpartisan, and third-party source of advice to the legislature. It operates in an environment that has become increasingly partisan, both within the legislature and in relationships between the governor (of one party) and the legislature (of another). Its role is constrained by a number of attributes: a "crowded advice world," where information is available from many sources; a legislature that is tied to specific demands from constituencies; a conflict between qualitative and quantitative orientations (with legislators often relying on personal communities and immediate fix-it approaches); the limits of policy analysis; and the office's reputation as a "nay-sayer."[15]

The term-limited environment within California has created new realities for the LAO that are likely to impact its future operations. It is increasingly important for the office to address the needs of the legislature—to highlight solution paths and long-range issues. The changes in federal–state relationships as well as state–local relationships require a different form of analysis than was used in the past. In addition, the LAO has been increasingly concerned about marketing its products, and thus it had attempted to be more methodical about the dissemination of its reports, developing briefings, providing webcasts, and making presentations to groups with which it had not met earlier.

The Center on Budget and Policy Priorities: Analysis That Combines Rigor with a Point of View

The Center on Budget and Policy Priorities (CBPP) was founded in 1981 as a Washington-based organization that would provide an alternative source of information about the social policy program initiatives of the Reagan administration. As the founder, Robert Greenstein, described it:

Because the Reagan administration was the main source of information for the several months in which the proposals were debated and then made into law, the presentation that poor families were being protected was largely accepted by the media and by many policymakers. There was no alternative source of analysis and information on the impacts of these proposals other than some more academic analysis that wouldn't come out until one or two years later, *after* the decisions had already been made. . . . [Also] President Reagan was able to change the budget process by which these decisions were made. [Groups] that were concerned about programs for the poor were used to the "old" budget process and had difficulty adapting to and understanding how the "new" budget process worked, and they were less effective as a result.[16]

The CBPP started its operations in December 1981 with three people on its staff. Greenstein had been a political appointee in the Carter administration, during which he headed the Food and Nutrition Service in the Department of Agriculture. By 1998 the staff had grown to 55 people, actually doubling in the previous six years. This growth occurred as the organization increased the range of its activities, expanding into new areas. The current staff totals approximately 120 people and includes the staff of the International Budget Partnership as well as the staff of the State Fiscal Analysis Initiative, which coordinates a network of state policy organizations. The CBPP is now located in an office building near Union Station, on the fringes of Capitol Hill. The organization is funded primarily through grants from a large number of foundations and individuals.

Very few of the policy staff members have doctoral degrees, but most have master's degrees in public policy, public administration, or business administration. In addition, the staff includes several lawyers and a few economists (people who are interested in applied work). Staff members are hired for their understanding of strategy as well as analysis.

A number of members of the staff come to the CBPP with experience in the federal government—in the Office of Management and Budget, the Congressional Budget Office, congressional committees, and analytic shops in federal or state departments. Some staff members are hired directly out of school, often after serving an internship in the organization. Approximately five people on the CBPP's staff have been there for two decades, and many staff members have been there more than ten years. Several of the longer-term staff members have changed roles; others have left and subsequently returned. Staff members work collegially; senior managers compose teams for specific issues.

As it describes itself, the CBPP combines a number of roles as it works on its agenda. These include:

- in-depth expertise in both federal budget and tax policy and programs and policies to reduce poverty and inequality;
- strategic expertise in crafting policy strategies and designing alternative proposals, not just in broad terms but also in the specific policy details that have large consequences for millions of people;
- credibility and stature in working effectively with White House officials, members of Congress and their staffs, the media, and large numbers of other national and state nonprofit organizations and other stakeholders; and
- an ability to coordinate a network of highly regarded state policy organizations that have a track record of conducting effective policy work in their states.

The strategies that the CBPP employs combine analytic work that dissects proposals and places attention on their effects with a communication strategy as well as efforts to advise policymakers and advocates about the potential effects of proposals. Over the years the CBPP's agenda has reflected a range of policy issues that have been part of the national debate. Expansion of the low-income tax credit program was one of its original agenda items, as was its work helping states reduce taxes on low-income working families and improving federal nutrition programs. Work on all three issues continues today. The devolution of responsibilities from the national government to the states stimulated a shift in the CBPP's work in the 1990s (see the description of the State Fiscal Initiative that follows). In 1995 the CBPP launched work on health insurance; over the years it focused particularly the Medicaid program and the State Children's Health Insurance Program. In 1997 work began on low-income housing, and at the same time the CBPP established the International Budget Partnership. Work on Social Security was an important issue in 2005. And current attention is also placed on budget process reform and protecting its impact on low-income citizens.

The CBPP focuses on several types of clients (or what it calls its *audiences*). These clients include actors at the federal level: policymakers across the political spectrum (in Congress and the administration), the media (the organization reaches the general population largely through both print and electronic media), and other nonprofit organizations. At the state level the audiences include state nonprofit organizations (helping them develop) and, to a lesser extent, state-level policymakers and media.

The CBPP's work at the state level also created momentum for outreach campaigns across the country on issues such as the Earned-Income Tax Credit. More than six thousand organizations and agencies across the country have participated in this effort, which the CBPP describes as "the nation's largest sustained private sector campaign to promote a public benefit." Other campaigns have been waged on child care and children's health coverage under Medicaid. As one staff member noted, these campaigns not only provide information and give technical assistance across the country but also elicit information on the state of implementation (which is useful to the organization for its federal policy work). In addition, state-level audiences help the CBPP develop its work agenda, responding to the concerns that are raised outside Washington.

The CBPP employs a wide range of methodologies and analytic techniques in its work. Much of its focus is on the budget, and staff have in-depth knowledge of the budget and the tax system. The organization does not have its own microsimulation model and relies on data from the Congressional Budget Office, the Census Bureau, and other sources. It also conducts its own miscrosimulation analyses, particularly of the antipoverty effects of various policies. It frequently distills complex data, making them more accessible to decision makers. The CBPP does not do cost-benefit analyses. In many cases the CBPP's reports are based on a careful reading of legislative language or statistics and explicating the impact in ways that will be clear to a broad audience. Thus, its reports and graphic presentations seek to broaden the terms of the debate and communicate to a nontechnical audience. It is expanding its audience through the internet, where it is not unusual to have 10,000 hits on its home page on a day when a report or statement is released. Major reports or statements can reach 25,000 hits a day.

Although closely tied to a value orientation, the CBPP is constantly aware of the advocacy-neutrality issue. Because it wants people who do not agree with its positions to rely on its work, it imposes stringent internal quality-control checks before reports or statements are released. Greenstein has described the organization's approach:

> Some people have said, "Well, you can't be seen as doing credible, trusted analyses and have a point of view—and have a policy agenda at the same time." We have been able to do it, but the reason is because we only work in areas we really know, and we make sure that in those areas that our work is very solid and credible. We don't simply put forward pieces of information or analysis that would support where we would like to see the policy go. We try to cover all of the relevant pieces of information in our analyses. So we have learned from this not to jump into areas we don't know, to make the foundation of all our work the credibility of our work and the accuracy of the work. And we have found that the more we have built recognition and trust for the quality of our work the more effective we actually are in making recommendations and advancing specific policy changes.[17]

One Washington journalist commented that "while this crew is renowned for its dogged advocacy, the dirty little secret about them is that they're very effective in working with people they don't agree with. . . . Their weapons in these battles are reliable data, sound analysis, and an ability to deliver it when needed."[18]

The CBPP tends to respond to what is already occurring and stays fairly close to the adoption stage of the policy process. It is usually close to policies and issues that are getting attention or that are likely to get attention in the foreseeable future. Demographic changes in society and growing income disparities will likely continue to concern the organization.

There has been significant interest in the work of the CBPP from nongovernmental organizations around the world. The organization has had a direct influence on the development of similar institutions in several countries. The CBPP has the advantage of American transparency of processes and availability of information, but other organizations in quite different environments have also found its experience useful.

The State Fiscal Analysis Initiative Network: Balancing Advocacy and Analysis in a Federal System

The State Fiscal Analysis Initiative Network (SFAI), which was founded in 1993 and is coordinated by the CBPP, describes itself as "a network of state-level nonprofit policy organizations working for equitable, responsible and sustainable budget and tax policies." It began with member groups in twelve states and is currently a network of approximately forty groups. Its goals are to improve state tax and budgeting systems, strengthen policies for low- and moderate-income families, and expand public debates over budget issues. Its analytic work highlights reliability, timeliness, and accessibility.

In 1992 the CBPP confronted two realities. First, the implementation of a range of federal programs had been handed to state governments, with limitations that varied from program to program; and second, the states' fiscal conditions were having a dramatic effect on their ability to carry out the federal goal of providing a safety net for lower-income and vulnerable populations. According to one observer, "As state-level cuts in social programs became more widespread, the growing outcry from nonprofits and other poverty advocates helped focus attention on the severity of the budget problems and the inadequacy of states' tax systems and fiscal policymaking structures."[19]

Conversations began between the CBPP and the Ford Foundation as both organizations shared their concerns.[20] The potential complexity of the effort that would be needed to address the two pressing realities and the resources that would be required for it seemed too large for a single funder. As a result the initial effort included support from the Charles Stewart Mott Foundation and the Annie E. Casey Foundation alongside that from Ford. The combination of multiple funders (each of whom had its own perspective and existing portfolio) and the diversity of US states led to a program design for the effort that acknowledged variations in how specific state analysis programs were structured and developed.

Three key assumptions undergirded the effort: (1) The shifts in funding responsibility from the federal to the state level had disproportionately harmful effects on lower-income and vulnerable populations; (2) relevant information and fiscal analysis were not in place at the state level; and (3) the analysis needed should be undertaken on a state-by-state level.[21] In addition, the funders agreed that the best location for the effort would be a policy research activity within a locally based nonprofit organization. At the same time, there was a need for the groups to learn from each other, and the network that was envisioned would also include the CBPP as a provider of technical support.

In many ways the structure of the SFAI mirrored a collaborative approach to federalism. It provided a general framework for the effort but allowed each of the players to structure its own focus and specific approach. Each state program was quite distinct, and yet, at the same time, the central actor (the CBPP) would serve as a facilitator, convener, and provider of technical assistance for all the states' activities. The state groups were encouraged to learn from one another, and meetings twice a year provided them with a venue for networking and disseminating the results of their work. SFAI governs itself through a steering committee whose members are selected by their colleagues. Observers have noted that the network owes much of its success to the deliberate lack of centralization.

The strategy that was devised at the beginning of the effort was quite unusual and continues today. Each of the three foundations made grants on their own to both individual state-level organizations as well as the CBPP. The Ford Foundation continued its focus on transparency and improving democratic decision making. Casey built on its work on children and families and sought to strengthen the quality of data used in decision-making processes on children's issues. Mott emphasized access to the economic mainstream for working families and those living in poverty.[22] Other foundations later joined the original funders but largely continued their approach; these newcomers included the Kellogg Foundation, the Open Society Institute, and the Stoneman Family Foundation. In 2009 the Council on Foundations presented its Award for Distinguished Grantmaking through Collaboration to SFAI's funders. It noted that the network of funders had helped to "broaden the debate around budget and tax policy through public education and the encouragement of civic engagement."

The twelve original state organizations reflected a variety of structures and hosts. Projects were launched within children's advocacy and legal services organizations, a faith-based advocacy coalition, a university policy shop, and an association of nonprofits. Two of the founding groups were union-supported organizations that were already focusing on tax and budget policy. As new groups have been added to the network, the picture today shows that approximately two-thirds of the groups are "embedded" in larger nonprofits and the rest are stand-alone budget and tax policy organizations.

As the SFAI effort grew and matured, both funders and member groups recognized the need to develop formal criteria for admitting new members that would also serve as standards for evaluating existing members. Formal criteria were developed by the CBPP and the SFAI Steering Committee in consultation with other members. These criteria are used in multiple ways: to be considered for a planning grant, to join the network as a full member, and as an accountability mechanism to evaluate the state program.

Eleven criteria have been established by the SFAI:[23]

1. breadth of state tax and budget issues analyzed;
2. focus on policy outcomes;
3. credibility (accurate, transparent, and bias-free analysis);
4. timeliness (availability to policymakers, advocacy groups, and others);
5. accessibility (understandable to a varied audience);
6. long-term focus;
7. accountability and diversity (reflecting the broad array of constituencies);
8. strong, sustainable, diverse organization;
9. part of the network;
10. outreach; and
11. media/communication (dissemination).

However, despite this set of network-wide expectations, each member organization is self-governing and thus has its own board and priorities. Even those "embedded" organizations have distinct advisory committees in addition to the parent group's board.

Oversight of the SFAI's activities is quite complex though largely informal. The CBPP acts as a leader in the field, a research partner, a convener, and a provider of technical assistance and training. The CBPP's own analyses of state fiscal issues often clarify priorities and options for the state partners. Model state reports are distributed through the network and provide the state groups with key data and policy analysis on a state-by-state basis. Two training conferences are held each year—an introductory session for new SFAI staff members to the network and its activities; and a major policy conference for 350 people, including SFAI staff and the staff of other state and national organizations with interests in fiscal policy. The network's funders rely on the CBPP for its assessment of the productivity of the state programs as well as its efforts to help the group improve.

The relationship between the state programs and the CBPP has been described as one of creative tension. Unless it is not meeting the minimum SFAI standards, no group is required to accept the CBPP's recommendations.

One observer noted that the groups "are comfortable with the structure as a loose confederation, and would chafe at any effort by the CBPP to direct more of their work. One group told us the real strength of SFAI is allowing states to act on their own and make strategic decisions independently of the network."

SFAI groups are usually a part of broad coalitions within the state and have often led those collaborative activities. Their collaborators include antihunger advocates, churches, community organizers, environmental advocates, labor unions, local governments, social service providers, and service clubs.

Despite their differences and the great variety of contexts in which they work, all the state programs struggle with the need to balance analysis and advocacy. The staff of the SFAI groups is drawn from very different backgrounds. Some have come from advocacy organizations and have emphasized short-term fixes to budget and fiscal problems. In an era of stringent budget cutbacks, these proposals focus on the survival of programs and services, but at the same time, they attempt to find longer-term solutions that seek new sources of revenue. Other staff members come to the network from experience either in governors' offices or legislative bodies. Still others have emphasized their technical training in budget analysis and see their role as specialized analysts. Some SFAI staff members have a background in specific policies and programs (e.g., programs for children) and may have had experience actually delivering services. Most of the state programs have staff members who have had training in policy and fiscal analysis, often through master's in public policy programs. A typical SFAI program has a strong director, at least two strong policy analysts, and a mix of two to four staff members with capability in communications, outreach, fund-raising, and administrative activities.

As the SFAI network has expanded and developed, its individual state programs have increasingly emphasized the way that they have organized their communications efforts. In the early years communication strategies were largely an afterthought; reports were disseminated to policymakers and statehouse reporters and, as the Web developed, they were posted online. Failure to develop relationships with journalists or to use various channels to reach multiple audiences limited the impact of SFAI's work. SFAI groups vary widely in the competence and effectiveness of their communications efforts. Some websites are neither user-friendly nor comprehensive. Efforts have been made to find resources to hire communications staff and to provide training on media strategy, skills, and relationship building. The staff of the CBPP has assisted state programs in this effort.

The network's goals and activities are described as follows on its website:

- *Improve state tax and budgeting systems:* States need to raise adequate revenue in a fair, responsible, and sustainable manner in order to meet critical responsibilities such as education, public safety, and health care. SFAI organizations analyze major tax proposals and develop and promote options to make tax systems better. They also assess how proposed changes in federal policies would affect state finances. SFAI groups make sure policymakers and the public understand the implications of arbitrary spending limits and other budget gimmicks. And they identify long-term strategies for sound state budgets and strong state economies.

- *Strengthen policies for lower- and moderate-income families:* SFAI groups work at the state level to improve economic security and opportunity. They do so by analyzing the barriers that can prevent low-income families from improving their lives and by identifying sound policy solutions, like fairer tax systems, better health care, affordable child care, work supports, and income assistance.

- *Expand public debates over budget issues:* The budget is a state's single most powerful decision-making tool. But too often budgets are written and debated in terms that most citizens (and even many policymakers) cannot understand. SFAI groups provide the translation. They analyze budget trends and options to make clear the crucial choices that states face. By widely disseminating their work and interacting with the news media, SFAI groups shape the debate and make it accessible to advocates and the public.[24]

The Century Foundation: Research Committed to Solutions and Action

In 1919 Edward Filene, who was known for his retailing innovations in the Boston area, turned his attention to broader civic issues and established a nonprofit foundation through which he could funnel contributions to the causes he supported.[25] The organization was originally called the Cooperative League, and Filene's goal was "to enlist the greatest minds he could find to disburse his funds in a way that could change the world."[26] He is quoted as saying: "In the formation of a program . . . it is my earnest hope that we shall avoid the pitfalls of purely academic research. . . . There is plenty of money to be had in this country for research merely for the sake of research, but far too little of it for intelligent and effective application."[27] During its early years the organization (which was renamed the Twentieth Century Fund in 1922, and the Century Foundation in 2000) acted in a more traditional philanthropic manner by providing funds to organizations that shared its goals (including the League of Women Voters and various municipal reform efforts). With the advent of the New Deal, however, the foundation began to shift more of its resources to its own activities rather than to outside groups. Many of these activities involved the writing and publication of books and reports on relevant issues.

During the first months of the Roosevelt administration, the Twentieth Century Fund's recommendations on the regulation of securities markets became the nucleus for White House policy. Other reports on labor relations and pension reform also had a direct impact on New Deal initiatives. In 1936 the fund distributed 20,000 copies of a short pamphlet that was critical of the Townsend Plan (an old-age pension proposal). The organization not only reacted to issues that were on the policy agenda and worked closely with officials in the administration and in Congress but also sought to raise questions that had not yet been considered. From the 1930s on, the fund focused on problems associated with providing access to quality health care.

Many of the Twentieth Century Fund's board members served in the Roosevelt administration during World War II, but the organization continued to operate. During this period it attempted to anticipate the issues that would be before the country when the war was over, particularly questions related to the economic demands that would be unleashed internally as well as issues related to economic recovery abroad.

During the postwar period the Twentieth Century Fund's portfolio included significant projects that entailed paying attention to both domestic and international development. A series of influential reports focused on the interrelationship between economic stabilization and full employment at home and issues related to international concerns, particularly the Cold War. The fund's publications in the 1960s were a combination of reference works and books dealing with a wide range of issues. This era has been described as a time when the fund almost became a data collection agency, surveying and analyzing basic information. Beginning in the late 1960s, the organization stimulated a series of task forces on specific issues, assessing alternatives and collecting information to support its positions.

At the present time what is now known as the Century Foundation operates out of an elegant brownstone in New York City, with a staff of approximately twenty-five people. It also has a small staff of five people in its reopened Washington office (which had closed in the early 1970s). Staff members have a variety of skills and experience; some have economics backgrounds, and others have backgrounds in specific policy areas. Over the years the changes in the composition of the staff have been subtle. In addition to researchers, the staff has usually included individuals with experience in communications and the press. The staff also is supplemented by a number of fellows, consultants, and part-time people working on specific projects and providing new ideas to the permanent staff. At the present time the foundation supports between seventy and one hundred projects.

Emphasis on the media—particularly through op-ed pieces or short editorials—has characterized the foundation's dissemination strategy. The past president of the foundation, Richard Leone, described the approach:

> For good or ill, modern government must live with a political culture that emphasizes the sensational, communicates in sound bites, and is experienced in "real time." Leaders struggle to re-create trust among a citizenry convinced of the venality of the experienced and of the virtues of amateurs, awash in flickering images of sex, violence, and corruption, and entranced with the notion of a talk show version of direct democracy. Perhaps it is not surprising that many Americans feel that things are out of control. They yearn for a renewed sense of confidence that we are headed in the right direction and that we have the right leadership to take us there. Yet they seem angered by any argument that contends that the complexity of their problems requires solutions involving both patience and sacrifice.[28]

August Heckscher, an individual intimately involved with the Century Foundation, commented on its uniqueness: "The Foundation has been in many ways a model of what a small foundation should be. Its projects were defined amid protracted and often highly philosophical discussions among men of strong convictions. Its project directors were chosen not merely on the grounds of acknowledged expertise, but because they seemed to have unfulfilled capacities and a fresh way of looking at things."[29]

Unlike those of many other foundations or research enterprises, the Century Foundation's board members play an important role in defining new areas and are directly involved in shaping its program. Suggestions may actually be made for modifications in proposals for projects. In some cases the board has resisted proposals by the staff to move into specific policy areas, believing that the time was not opportune to support work in one area or another. Also, to scope out issues, the board has created task forces drawn from a range of individuals with expertise in a particular area.

The location of the Century Foundation in New York City is somewhat unusual for an organization that focuses on national policy. To some at the foundation, operating in New York City is a way of avoiding partisan labels. Though the organization has always had strong connections to Washington, it has emphasized a somewhat different audience than Washington-based groups. The foundation defines its mandate as affecting people who vote, and it seeks to stimulate public debate. Consequently, it wants its publications to be readable and accessible. Most of its books include a clear analysis of data and recommendations based on that analysis. Its projects focus on issues and approaches that are realistic and that will stimulate the development of the political will to act on their recommendations.

The Century Foundation's products are distributed in a number of different forms. Over the last several years it has produced a series of relatively short pamphlets called "The Basics," a series that focuses on issues in which there are conflicting claims and disagreements. These include topics such as welfare reform, Medicare reform, poverty, tax reform, Social Security, and block grants. These publications seek to clarify issues by collecting the best available information. Interestingly, these publications are similar to pamphlets issued by the foundation during the New Deal, particularly one titled *Will the Townsend Plan Work?* That early publication, circa 1936, announced that it sought to contain much factual information essential to a general public understanding of the issue at hand.

The books that have been released by the Century Foundation are of several types. The volumes that were published in the 1960s tended to be resource books for scholars. Publications include works on Megalopolis (the dense urban settlement running from Boston to Washington) by Jean Gottman; a variety of domestic and international economic issues; and *Asian Drama*, a work by Gunnar Myrdal. The books published in the 1970s and 1980s focused on a wide range of domestic issues (e.g., urban issues, campaign finance, governance, nursing homes, regulation, blacks in the military, and civic service) as well as many international questions. Some of these volumes were published by the foundation itself, but others were issued by other publishing houses.

During this later period the Century Foundation released a number of reports that drew attention to a variety of economic, social, political, and cultural institutions. These reports were developed by task forces and included studies of the arts, communications issues, community development corporations, employment, veterans, and energy issues. In 1979 the foundation cosponsored the first of two task forces on the US presidential debates.

Beginning in 1989 the Century Foundation initiated a series of books intended to explore the new underpinnings of American foreign policy. And in the 1990s it sponsored projects that attempted to respond to what were defined as "assaults on representative government."[30] Among these was a series of case studies analyzing the impact of a federal balanced budget amendment on specific states. A publication titled *New Federalist Papers* provides essays that examine the current status of the American governmental structure. In recent years the foundation has published books on health policy issues, election reform, and regulation.

Over the years, the Century Foundation has engaged in some projects in collaboration with other organizations that share similar views. Sometimes projects are jointly sponsored; in other cases, publications are issued in collaboration with other publishers or organizations. The foundation has also emphasized the availability of information via the internet. Its website is affiliated with the Electronic Policy Network, which provides exposure for progressive ideas.

The Century Foundation has defined itself as a nonpartisan but not neutral organization that is deeply rooted in the bipartisan progressive movement in America of which the organization was a part. As it focuses on the future, it emphasizes the relationship between the past and the future, noting that "the Foundation's plans for the future are solidly grounded in a progressive tradition that would be quite familiar to its founders."[31]

Upon the advent of the twenty-first century, as noted above, the Twentieth Century Fund changed its name to the Century Foundation. However, this name change does not represent a change in its value orientation. Brewster Denny, the former chairman of its board, described the agenda for the future:

> As we move on to the end of the century, we must work on those ever present health of the polity issues. We must attend to the search for economic justice after an era when national policy was aimed at making the rich richer and the poor poorer, hardly a new concern for the Fund. For the third time in this century, we must focus on finding a system to keep the peace in a very different world from the one before it. . . . But perhaps the most difficult challenge we face is that the twenty-first century is the century of Malthus—the world's very physical environment is in grave peril.[32]

The Congressional Research Service of the Library of Congress: Analysis Linked to the Intricacies of the Legislative Process

The Congressional Research Service (CRS) of the Library of Congress is one of several analytical institutions designed to provide information and policy analysis to Congress. The origins of CRS date back to the creation of the Library of Congress in 1800. In 1914, however, Congress appropriated money to the Library of Congress to provide a Legislative Reference Service (LRS) to assist Congress by providing data related to the development of legislation.[33] The Legislative Reorganization Act of 1946 established the LRS as a permanent body, enlarged the service, gave it the ability to hire senior specialists, and called on it to assist committees in the "analysis, appraisal, and evaluation of legislative proposals."[34]

The creation of CRS and its identification with the policy analysis movement came in 1970 with the amendments to the Legislative Reorganization Act. Its name change from the LRS pointed to its new research and analysis emphasis, highlighted a close relationship between the organization and the Congress, and provided for a degree of independence from the Library of Congress. The 1970s amendments allowed CRS to almost triple the staff of the LRS over the next decade to a high of almost 900 in 1980 and to become a major adviser in congressional deliberations. At this writing the CRS staff includes 640 people, of whom about 350 are analysts and attorneys and about 100 are information professionals.

In fiscal year 2011 CRS prepared nearly 4,000 new written products, maintained more than 7,000 CRS Reports, and conducted more than 6,000 personal briefings, consultations, and seminars. It also maintains a website that is accessible only to Congress that contains all its written products and other resources relevant to the issues on the legislative agenda; the site recorded nearly 2 million hits in fiscal year 2011.

The CRS analytical staff is drawn from a range of sources, including graduates of public policy and law schools. The newer staff members are teamed up with the more experienced ones; the collegial atmosphere of the organization reinforces a commitment to promote from within. Once in a position, CRS analysts are eligible for promotions without competition to the high level of a GS-15 on the federal civil service pay scale. Given this, it is not surprising that the average tenure of staff members is nearly fifteen years.

The CRS office is organized according to a combination of subject areas and disciplines. Divisions include American law, domestic social policy, foreign affairs, defense and trade, government and finance, and resources, science, and industry policy. A Knowledge Services Group houses the information professionals, many of whom serve in consultancies in the subject divisions. Staff members are often combined into interdisciplinary teams, which are drawn from different subject areas as well as diverse disciplines.

The analysis performed by CRS attempts to respond to the question "What is the legislative hook?" The staff interacts constantly with players in the legislative process, a relationship that resembles a confidential consultant–client relationship. The role of policy consultant is reinforced by the longevity of the staff (in terms of both knowledge of issues and personal relationships). Robinson describes this as a situation where staff members know "firsthand what ideas had been tried by the committee before, the reactions of interested parties, procedural tactics tried, committee jurisdictions threatened, legislative outcomes and their impacts, and some notions about what options might be pursued usefully at the present stage of debate."[35]

In its early years CRS was characterized by high volume and quick turnaround, a pattern that caused one staff member to describe the organization as "a reference factory."[36] However, since the early 1970s, Congress has expected, and the organization has placed, increased emphasis on legislative consultation, interdisciplinary work, and analytical work.

CRS has devoted considerable attention to processes that allow it to forecast issues likely to be of interest to Congress. Beginning in 1987 it instituted a planning system whereby senior managers meet twice a year to identify the top twenty or so major issues that are likely to reach the legislative stage.[37] This list is reviewed with the congressional leadership and is used to organize interdisciplinary teams that become expert in the issues and are able to respond to future congressional requests.[38] More recently, however, the agenda for CRS has been focused on specific legislative interests, and therefore the CRS website and the research agenda of its analysts are organized around 160 to 170 specific issues before Congress.

Many legislative initiatives have a fairly long time frame; the legislative process may include making initial inquiries, holding hearings, crafting draft legislation, and moving to decisions. The CRS role is designed to respond to the demands of all these legislative stages. Robinson has described this process:

- provision of background papers to the committee to increase understanding of the issue,
- assistance in the design of congressional hearings to gather more information,
- suggestions for witnesses at the hearings,
- provision of possible questions for members of Congress to ask witnesses to draw out needed information,
- presence at the hearings to supplement questioning,
- development of options for dealing with the problems discussed,
- possible legislative specifications for implementing policy directions selected by the committee (CRS does not draft legislation),
- presence and expert consultant at committee mark-ups of bills,
- periodic appearances as witnesses to testify,

- occasional availability on the floor of the House or Senate as expert resources during floor consideration,
- help in preparation of conference agendas and decision documents, and
- attendance and assistance at conferences to resolve differences between the two houses.[39]

Much modern-day legislation often does not follow this regular process, and CRS has had to adjust in order to support a legislative environment that sees much more omnibus legislation, a greater emphasis on appropriations, and legislative agendas set by the leadership rather than committees.

For a senior analyst, however, the highest priority is to be brought to the table, trusted by the members of Congress and their staffs, and invited to participate in the creation of new legislation. In some cases CRS may be most successful when it convinces members of Congress not to enact legislation.

The work produced by CRS is not available to the general public, unless members of Congress release it in some form. Analysts and attorneys prepare tailored, confidential memoranda for members and committee offices as well as CRS Reports for Congress available to the general congressional audience. Other forms of content are available on the CRS website.

Unlike some other organizations CRS lists the names of the analysts as authors of publications, indicating a point of contact for further questions about an issue. In addition to creating written products, CRS emphasizes its ability to interact directly with congressional staffs and members of Congress. CRS has increasingly emphasized its role of providing direct legislative support, in which staff members participate in legislative development and provide impact estimates of policy options. This role often rests on the analytic studies that have been completed within the organization. CRS staff regularly brief members of Congress in their offices. Timeliness is one of the most important attributes of CRS's work.

Although the congressional infrastructure makes up the basic client pool for CRS, over the years the relationships between CRS staff members and congressional committees and subcommittees have shifted. They have been affected by several realities: the size and capacity of committee and subcommittee staffs, turnover among members of Congress, changes in leadership in the House and Senate, and the level of partisanship or conflict on an issue. Committee staff size has declined, and recent Congresses have been composed of a large number of new members. In this climate CRS has been able to move into what may be viewed as a void.

CRS does have an in-house capability to do modeling, create microsimulation models, and perform fiscal analyses. However, it operates in a culture that tends toward qualitative methods and an oral tradition. Thus it emphasizes the importance of writing skills and ease in personal interactions for its staff.

CRS places its commitment to objectivity and nonpartisanship at the center of its values. Robinson notes that the "role of the service is to inform the decision-making process, not to make the choice or to press for one set of values over another. This premise also underlies our policy of not making recommendations."[40] It accepts the goals of members of Congress and tries to help them avoid mistakes and to understand both the intended and unintended consequences of proposals. It is careful about the use of language as it presents its findings (e.g., it would use the term "global climate change" instead of "global warming"). It is clear that it works only for Congress, not for the executive branch or the general public.

CRS has several challenges as it faces the future: pressures on resources, obstacles to collaborative work, a need to keep up with the technology that is available to today's congressional staff members, and how to more effectively publicize CRS services to a Congress whose members and their staffs rapidly turn over. At the same time CRS leadership emphasizes the importance of multidisciplinary approaches and a clearer focus on the legislative agenda. The ability to anticipate what will be on the agenda will become even more important. In addition, CRS will be faced with an aging staff; more than 50 percent of its analysts and attorneys are currently eligible for retirement. The CRS recently revamped its first-line management structure to place a greater emphasis on research management and to also serve to establish successors to current managers as they reach retirement age.

The Danish National Centre for Social Research: Balancing Research and Advising

The Danish National Centre for Social Research (known as SFI) was founded in 1958 as a part of the Ministry of Social Affairs of the Government of Denmark and was designed to conduct research that focuses on welfare state policies. Although it was located within the ministry, it was created as an autonomous unit and was not a part of any larger organizational shift.[41] Today, SFI has a broader scope than at the beginning of its life, when it was designed to carry out analysis more strictly dealing with the ministry's portfolio. Unlike many other policy research organizations, it combines a more traditional research agenda that deals with issues (e.g., employment, integration and labor market conditions, economic and family-related issues, and other national and international social conditions) with work that reflects the agenda of the central government unit in the Ministry of Social Affairs. It is an example of a policy analysis organization outside the United States that shares some attributes with American counterparts, but the organization itself reflects the distinct political culture of a Northern European and Scandinavian country that has a parliamentary system and is a classic welfare state.

SFI describes itself as an organization that conducts research and carries out commissioned projects in the area of welfare state politics and disseminates the results. It provides international research, independent evaluations, professional data collection, consultancy, and dissemination, and it produces internationally qualified research studies on the effects of social programs. It disseminates its findings to the public via its website and by publishing reports, working papers, a quarterly magazine, press releases, and presentations. It frequently invites people to attend after-work meetings, at which its own researchers give presentations. Dissemination of its work is designed to reach as broad an audience as possible. Peer-reviewed articles in international journals are viewed as extremely important, but also the organization seeks to make its work accessible to a range of possible users.

The evolution of SFI as an organization mirrors a number of influences during the twenty-first century emerging from globalization, national developments (affecting economic shifts as well as modifications in the research and education fields), and shifts that have occurred within the policy analysis field itself. Historically, the Danish research system was tied to autonomous units governed by what was called "collegial democratic self-management." The governance of both research units and universities was controlled by collegially elected bodies that made decisions that affected the research agenda as well as other issues affecting faculties, departments, employees, and students. Given the social democratic political culture of Denmark, it was not surprising that self-government emphasized that political orientation. At the same time, the Danish focus on corporatism emphasized governance-oriented management processes and skepticism about hierarchical solutions.[42] That led to a tradition where policy formulation involved unions, social democrats, interest organizations, and groups tied to workers, farmers, and academics.

Changes adopted in 1993 modified the autonomy of the units somewhat, but it was not until 2003 that more fundamental changes were made that included governing boards with a majority of external members. Although these changes did require that top managers be qualified academically, they were based on a perspective that constrained the historical autonomy of research and university enterprises. As one observer commented, "the university not only has to communicate knowledge to the surrounding society, but also to transfer knowledge."[43]

An evaluation of SFI was commissioned in 2006 in connection with the changes in the Danish university and research institute system. The panel charged with this assessment was asked to determine how well the organization met its primary mission "to provide research-based evaluation and knowledge to enable legislation and administration."[44] This panel focused on seven dimensions of the organization's activities: (1) the formulation of relevant objectives, (2) productivity, (3) the quality of research, (4) the quality of reviews and evaluations, (5) synergy between (3) and (4), (6) dissemination of SFI's work, and (7) international cooperation and SFI's PhD training.

The issues that were highlighted in the 2006 report emphasized the difficulties of defining what "research-based evaluation" meant and noted that some organizational features within SFI seemed to cultivate dualism rather than synergy between research and policy evaluations. Three issues received special priority. First, SFI needed to find ways to stimulate more synergy between the two boxes of research versus policy evaluation. Second, "methodological dualisms pervade much of SFI's research, with the gulf between qualitative and quantitative work too wide, and the distribution of quantitative skills too uneven."[45] And third, the report called for the preservation of SFI's status as an independent institution: "SFI's principal asset lies in the broad legitimacy of its policy-applied research, and its independence from political institutions as well as from any particular academic milieu is an optimal arrangement considering the goals that define its activities."[46]

An additional evaluation of the organization in 2009 conceptualized SFI as a national research institute and emphasized the dual nature of the sources of the group's substantive agenda. SFI gets approximately 30 percent of its budget through basic funding, and the remainder relies on funding project by project. Research constitutes approximately half of its activities, and the other half is commissioned by the government (mainly the Ministry of Social Affairs and the Ministry of Employment) through competitive grants.[47]

The government work is financed by a core grant from the government, whereas the second source is project-related financing received either from research councils or from authorities for evaluations of different social policy programs.

The government-supported agenda emerges from regular meetings between the SFI staff and government officials. Staff members present research findings to the officials and collaborate with them on the development of future research agendas. Over the years, personal contacts have been established between the government staff and SFI staff. Information on research themes is shared with the appropriate ministries. The result of this process is an agenda that is both negotiated with the government and, as well, self-generated. However, most major projects are supported by competitive grants.

SFI competes with departments within universities for much of the research project–related funding, but, according to the participants in the 2009 review, "SFI has a much broader research competence on the functioning of the welfare state" and serves as a resource for all the universities in Denmark, particularly as a result of its long-term commitment to empirical research as well as the development of high-quality databases.[48] The corporatist tradition in the country means that university departments often carry out policy analyses in collaboration with ministries, municipalities, and decision makers in general.

According to the 2009 review, "SFI should not be a part of one university but an institute independent of a specific university and that SFI instead should collaborate with all universities in Denmark on research regarding the functioning of the welfare state."[49] It also observed that the balance between core financing and other sources of financial support is crucial. It noted that "core financing is necessary for the infrastructure of the institute, for developing databases, for theory and method development, for following up on research projects and also policy evaluations with scientific articles and monographs, for cooperation with the universities, for the training of PhD students, and also for financing the time necessary for formulating applications for research projects and policy evaluations."[50] However, databases are rarely supported by core funding.

In 2010 another review group was commissioned to generate recommendations concerning SFI's Impact Evaluation Research. Unlike the earlier teams, this group was composed of four individuals from countries other than Denmark, which reflected the increased concern within SFI about global challenges that led it to seek out the experiences of individuals from both Europe and North America. The 2010 group emphasized strategies for improving the quality of current research and recommended that SFI "strengthen collaborations with external researchers by establishing relationships with foreign research institutes, academic departments, and researchers. SFI could encourage an exchange of graduate students, have international researchers be listed as SFI affiliates, develop a more regular seminar series involving international researchers, and develop a newsletter to increase the organization's visibility."[51] In its *2010 Annual Report*, Ole Gregersen, SFI's executive director of research, observed that "social policy issues often repeat themselves internationally. Some of the issues facing us here in Denmark have already cropped up in the Netherlands or the UK or in Sweden, or perhaps one of these will see such issues in the future. We want to be better at exploiting this knowledge."[52]

SFI has a staff of approximately 140 people; 60 of them are researchers from a number of different academic disciplines. Sociologists and economists are the largest group within the staff, but it also includes political scientists, anthropologists, and psychologists. Most of the staff members have at least a master's degree, and many of them began their careers at SFI. As one staff member put it, "we grow our own." Approximately 20 PhD students from other universities are a part of the staff at this writing. In the past PhD program graduates stayed on and moved to senior research positions. Few if any of the staff members had experience inside government.

The work products of SFI tend to focus on the creation of policy agendas but also include work that is relevant to both adoption and implementation issues. The group's research component gives it the ability to explore a range of issues and employ multiple research methods, and yet be in the center of policy discussions within the country. For some observers, SFI has to deal with conflict between internationally funded research agendas and the expectations of those who seek policy advice. The staff members of SFI are increasingly involved in collaborative activity with researchers from other countries and often present their work at professional meetings.[53]

The Heritage Foundation: Linking Research, Marketing, and Ideology

The Heritage Foundation, which was founded in 1973, is a Washington-based organization that seeks to "formulate and promote conservative public policies based on the principles of free enterprise, limited government, individual freedom, traditional American values, and strong national defense."[54] According to its then-president, the organization was "started to counter the overwhelming liberal intellectual climate of Washington in the 1970s. . . . Sure, there were other think tanks, but the most influential of them—such as the Brookings Institution and Urban Institute—were part of the problem, not part of the solution, in our opinion."[55] During its early period Heritage sought to differentiate itself from other conservative groups, particularly the American Enterprise Institute, by focusing on influencing the discussion of issues before decisions were made.

When the organization opened its doors, it had a staff of nine people; by its twenty-fifth anniversary in 1997, 180 individuals worked for it.[56] The current staff totals approximately 250 individuals. During its first five years, the

Heritage staff operated in a crowded building with one copying machine, several electric typewriters, and—like many other groups at the time—no computers. However, it did have a compulsory prayer meeting every week.[57] By early 1980, a research team was assembled made up mostly of men and women in their thirties who were working toward their PhDs. They were drawn from a number of fields, but many of them were economists. However, Heritage did not rely solely on its in-house capacities. Support was obtained for a number of chairs (the holders of which were sometimes former cabinet officials) and visiting fellows. Some of its programs support young scholars who are interested in furthering the conservative agenda. Other programs provide support for academics to spend a year at Heritage. In addition, the organization pulls together groups of outside experts in specific areas to help it develop reports and studies.

The Heritage Foundation has amassed a significant endowment and receives funding from various sources. It currently has an endowment of approximately $140 million and an annual budget of more than $75 million. In addition, it has received support from a number of foundations that support its agenda. It does not take government funds. In 1983 it moved into its own building, located in the shadow of the Capitol. Before that occurred, according to the Heritage historian Lee Edwards, the president of the foundation "could not put out of his mind that Heritage was headquartered in a string of town houses while the Brookings Institution had its own eight-story building, a visible symbol of its power and prestige."[58] In addition, the organization has an office in Moscow.

According to its supporters, Heritage has defined itself as the "institutional center of the conservative movement," which thus is committed "to furthering and strengthening the American conservative movement."[59] Heritage seeks to bring together what it views as three generations in the modern conservative movement—the first generation made up of intellectuals of the 1940s and 1950s, the second generation made up of the organizers and activists of the 1960s and 1970s, and the third generation made up of contemporary writers, activists, and others who, according to the *New York Times,* are "formidable ideologues and scathingly articulate."[60] In addition, Heritage has tried to redefine the concept of a Washington think tank by pushing more aggressively than other tax-exempt policy research organizations on advocacy of issues and policy. While arguing that it does not lobby, it clearly disseminates its views to those who are believed to be interested in these positions.

The Heritage Foundation emphasizes activities that further the conservative agenda. Its president, Edward Feulner, is quoted as saying that the question is not "Where are we going?" but "What can we do to ensure that we get where we want to go?"[61] In a number of areas (e.g., welfare), Heritage played a major role in framing the debate. In 1994, when the Republicans took control of Congress, the John F. Kennedy School of Government at Harvard University was not asked to hold its regular orientation conference for new members of Congress. Instead, Heritage and another conservative group organized an orientation meeting as a conservative school for freshman congressmen.

Heritage has defined its audiences to include members of Congress, key congressional staff members, policymakers in the executive branch, the nation's news media, and the academic and policy communities. During the Reagan years, much of its attention was focused on the executive branch; when the Republicans assumed control of Congress, increased emphasis was on influencing the legislative branch. There is movement in and out of government; thus, a significant number of individuals affiliated with Heritage assumed positions in the Reagan administration, and others worked on Capitol Hill either before coming to Heritage or afterward.

The Heritage Foundation's products are fine-tuned to meet the needs of its defined audience. In 1979, anticipating Ronald Reagan's election, Heritage attempted to answer the question "What is the conservative agenda, particularly for the First Hundred Days?" An outline of a publication titled *Mandate for Leadership* was developed through a team process that included every key department and agency in the government. According to Edwards, more than 250 experts served on twenty teams; none of the team members were compensated for their involvement. The final report—which was ready for the new Reagan team— became the action plan for the new administration.[62] It was followed by additional similar reports in 1984, 1989, and 1996.

Although many Heritage people moved into positions in the Reagan administration, there was sometimes tension between Heritage's positions and those of the administration. There were several instances of conflict between the think tank and the State Department during the Reagan administration, and also subsequently during the Bush years. During the 1990s Heritage concentrated on Congress and found strong supporters among the Republican leadership.

Heritage has developed a fairly eclectic approach in the way it distributes its message. It supports the writing and publication of a range of books and extensive monographs on a wide variety of subjects; and it issues short reports and background publications aimed at the busy decision maker. It publishes a journal. It emphasizes the production of what is called "the minibook"—a condensed version of a popular study or book that is given free to supporters and friends. What Edwards called a "cultural jackpot" took place in 1993, when former education secretary William Bennett discussed his study of cultural indicators on Rush Limbaugh's radio program.[63] Within forty-eight hours, 73,000 people called Heritage to request copies of the study.

In 1995 Heritage began publishing the *Index of Economic Freedom*—a report that developed a set of criteria whereby members of Congress could judge the performance of countries around the world in attaining what was defined as "economic freedom." Briefing books on specific issues are also distributed. According to Edwards, when Ronald Reagan met with Mikhail Gorbachev in 1985, Gorbachev brought up a Heritage report during the first ten minutes of the meeting.[64] The organization's international emphasis was indicated by the attention given to former British prime minister Margaret Thatcher during the organization's twenty-fifth anniversary.

From its founding, Heritage developed what was called the Resource Bank, which has been described as a master Rolodex including the names of two thousand scholars and more than four hundred think tanks, public interest law institutes, educational organizations, and other policy groups across the country. Part of this effort involves the encouragement of state-level think tanks that share the Heritage agenda.

Throughout its existence, Heritage has focused on marketing its work to the media. This includes the broadcast media as well as the print media. In 1984 Heritage won an award from the Public Relations Society of America for its marketing campaign. The imperative for marketing the work is that it can be read quickly and argued simply and that it is timely. During the past few years, the group has expanded its use of the internet, thereby expanding its distribution capabilities.

Although the organization has its own supercomputer that allows it to devise its own economic and budgetary projections, much of its work relies on secondary analysis. It attempts to be on top of analyses done by others on relevant policy areas.

President Feulner has emphasized the Heritage Foundation's commitment to its basic principles and expects that these principles will continue to characterize its work. During the past decade, it has attempted to single out a handful of issues for special emphasis, somewhat narrowing its earlier broad focus. Its financial base allows it to expect to function as the best-endowed think tank that is most frequently quoted in Washington.

Conclusion

As these short profiles indicate, policy analysis organizations come in many shapes and sizes. Not only are they different from the original concept defined by Dror in terms of their location, staff characteristics, and role, but in some respects they are also different from one another. These differences can be analyzed in terms of many different attributes; however, for the purposes of this discussion, it is useful to highlight several characteristics, some of which illustrate similarities as well as differences. These include the stage of the policy process the organization emphasizes, the clients of the organization, staff hiring patterns, the form in which work and products are packaged, the use of technology, and accountability relationships. Table 4.1 summarizes the profiles of the organizations discussed above, and it emphasizes the diverse goals of the groups, their policy orientation, analytic approach, and major products.

The Stage of the Policy Process

Most of the nine organizations have an agenda that responds to events in the political and policy world. Issues that are analyzed appear on the agenda of a new president, a new cabinet official, or a member of Congress. In this sense, the analysis is reactive to an external agenda. Several of the organizations do, however, have their own issue agenda and see their role as placing issues on the formal policy agenda. This is particularly the case for the Heritage Foundation. AARP works at several stages, depending on the issue at hand. ASPE is typical of the classic policy analysis offices in its emphasis on the formulation stage of the policy process. Both of the groups involved in the legislative process—the LAO and CRS—emphasize the adoption stage of the process, as does the CBPP.

Clients of the Organization

As has been discussed, policy analysis was originally envisioned as an activity that responded to the top officials in the government agency and that had a monopoly on analysis. All the organizations that have been described have moved far away from that model. All of them—to one degree or another—participate in the give-and-take of decision making in a pluralistic setting. Though the values or orientation of each organization may emphasize a particular set of clients or audiences, all acknowledge that many other actors are also involved in policymaking.

ASPE analysts experience multiple and competitive relationships both inside and outside HHS (including other executive branch players, Congress, and interest groups). Both the LAO and CRS deal with legislative settings that have entrenched and even stylized partisan differences. The CBPP interacts with a wide array of audiences, including other advocacy organizations with similar policy agendas as well as those with the formal authority to make decisions. Heritage has a similar set of relationships. Because of its relationship to the research community, SFI sometimes sees other academics as its client. Perhaps of all the organizations, the Century Foundation has a less defined set of clients or audiences, given that it directs its activities toward the general public as well as decision makers.

Staff Hiring Patterns

As Arnold Meltsner noted, even the early days of the policy analysis profession were characterized by some variation in the kinds of people who were hired as policy analysts. But if there was a predominant type of staff member in the 1960s, it was likely to be an individual with a doctorate, usually in economics or operations research. All the organizations profiled here have departed from this model. The individuals who make up the staffs of these groups are much less likely to be technician analysts (in Meltsner's terms). Few of them would have considered working in a job environment that was similar to that of an academic institution. Many of the individuals hired have actually been graduates of master's-level programs in public policy or related fields. Increasingly, the staff hired come to policy analysis organizations with expertise in a particular policy or program area. In addition, several of the organizations (e.g., CRS, LAO, and the CBPP) have sought to hire staff members who have had hands-on experience with program implementation.

The Packaging of Work and Products

If there was an accepted model for policy analysis in the early days of the profession, it was likely to have been a memorandum that included problem definition, background information, options, some formal analytic approach (e.g., cost-benefit analysis), and a recommendation. None of the organizations that have been profiled seem to emphasize this form (although some of them do continue to develop options papers).

Some of the organizations discussed (CRS and LAO) stay away from recommendations, although they may actually present options to their clients. Others have gravitated toward the production of position papers (the Heritage Foundation and the CBPP). Still others (ASPE) have tended to move

Table 4.1 A Range of Policy Analysis Institutions

Organization	Year Founded	Goals	Policy Orientation	Analytic Approach	Major Products	Stage of the Policy Process Emphasized
AARP Public Policy Institute	1985	Provides analysis to membership organization in lobbying federal and state levels	Focuses on policies of interest to members	Eclectic in methods, highlights dissemination	Materials for membership, presentations to policy players	Adoption, some agenda setting
Office of Assistant Secretary for Planning and Evaluation, US Department of Health and Human Services	1965	Provides analysis to decision makers in the department	Focuses on specific program and policy areas	Eclectic, increasingly noneconomic	Memos, evaluations, briefings	Formulation
California Legislative Analyst's Office	1941	Provides California legislature with analytical capacity	Deals with diverse membership of legislature	Fiscal analysis, increasingly focusing on nonfiscal issues	Reports to members, some public documents	Adoption
Center on Budget and Policy Priorities	1981	Provides analysis on impact of national and state policy proposals on the poor	Works closely with advocacy groups	Eclectic, budget orientation	Reports, materials for state and national groups	Adoption

Center on Budget and Policy Priorities, State Fiscal Analysis Initiative	1993	Improves state tax and budgeting systems; policies for lower and moderate income citizens; expands policy debate	Responds to diverse state realities	Eclectic, budget orientation	Depends on state; reports; dissemination strategy emphasized	Depends on state agenda; agenda setting and adoption
Century Foundation	1919	Uses research to address national and international problems	Directs efforts toward general public, decision makers	Research, packaging of existing information	Books, reports, op-ed pieces	Agenda setting
Congressional Research Service	1970	Provides information and policy analysis to Congress	Responds to congressional needs, anticipates future needs	Eclectic, both substantive and process expertise	Advice to members, nonpublic briefing materials	Adoption
Danish National Centre for Social Research	1958	Conducts research and evaluation of welfare policies, works with government agencies	Social policies; links to global academic players	Largely traditional research and evaluation	Reports, dissemination strategies	Agenda setting
Heritage Foundation	1973	Promotes conservative public policies	Works closely with media	Research and marketing	Reports, magazine, media information	Agenda setting

away from written documents and instead engage in the interactive process of decision making, using their analyses as the basis for bargaining. The absence of written documents may also be a way for government agencies to avoid requirements of the Freedom of Information Act, and thus protect analysts from negative reactions to alternatives that are speculative and produced to educate decision makers.

In the 1960s many of the documents that were produced by policy analysis units were relatively technical. Although they may have included an executive summary for busy decision makers, the documents included fairly sophisticated analyses and—wherever possible—relied on a quantitative presentation of data. In recent years, by contrast, a number of the policy analysis organizations discussed above have sought to package their work in a way that emphasizes the importance of communicating clearly to nontechnical audiences. The Heritage Foundation has excelled in this area, producing short documents that are understandable to generalist audiences. In the early years of the policy analysis profession, the dissemination and communication of work was only a second thought for some organizations. Today, however, dissemination strategies are defined early in the process.

The Availability of Technology

Computer technology and the availability of the internet have dramatically changed the way policy analysis organizations operate. In the 1960s policy analysts either were dependent on data systems produced by others or were required to invest in very expensive simulations for their own work. Computers and data availability have made all the organizations profiled much less dependent on others for data. This is true for the LAO, CRS, the Heritage Foundation, and the CBPP. The technology has also provided a way for individuals around the globe to share work and sources. At the same time, government policy analysis organizations such as ASPE do not have the resources to invest in the types of simulations and demonstration projects that they were able to mount in earlier years to develop data.

Accountability Relationships

In the early years of the profession, policy analysts were viewed as accountable to their clients (often defined through the hierarchy of a government organization) and to professional norms (borrowed from the norms of research and the academy, emphasizing objectivity and neutrality). Although the two sets of expectations could conflict with each other, the clash between them was rarely viewed as a major problem, as table 4.1 shows by comparing the nine examples.

The organizations that have been described in this chapter have a much more complex set of accountability expectations than did the early analysts. All the groups have struggled to find a way to present their work as fair and evenhanded, even when the organization itself has a point of view or an agenda (e.g., the CBPP). Some of the groups (LAO, CRS, the Century Foundation, and AARP) have characterized their work as nonpartisan. Experience over the years has given many policy analysts the ability to differentiate between advocacy positions and partisanship. Both of the legislative organizations have tried to avoid work that appears to assume an advocacy posture. When it moves into a concern about implementation or follows its own recommendations to the operation stage, ASPE can assume an advocacy posture (advocating its own position).

The organizations discussed in this chapter provide a sense of the richness of the policy analysis profession in practice. Individuals who are entering the profession have a variety of settings from which to choose and an array of issues with which they can deal.

Notes

1. Rother left AARP in 2011. Except for a few years during the early 2000s, both the PPI and the lobbying shop reported directly to him.

2. See AARP, *Policy Book 2011–2012: Setting Public Policies* (Washington, DC: AARP, 2011).

3. See AARP, *The Priorities Book: Building a Better Future* (Washington, DC: AARP, 2011).

4. This discussion is drawn from Beryl A. Radin, "Policy Analysis in the Office of the Assistant Secretary for Planning and Evaluation in HEW/HHS: Institutionalization and the Second Generation," in *Organizations for Policy Analysis: Helping Government Think*, edited by Carol H. Weiss (Newbury Park, CA: Sage, 1992), 144–60. This chapter reports on data collected in 1988 on seventy professional staff members who had been in the office between 1965 and 1988. Additional respondents were added to the study in 1998 to update the findings.

5. Office of the Assistant Secretary for Planning and Evaluation, *All About ASPE: A Guide for ASPE Staff* (Washington, DC: Office of the Assistant Secretary for Planning and Evaluation, n.d., c. 1999), A-1.

6. Ibid.

7. See Donna E. Shalala, "Are Large Public Organizations Manageable?" *Public Administration Review* 58, no. 4 (July–August 1998): 284–89.

8. Radin, "Policy Analysis," 150.

9. This discussion is drawn from Elizabeth Hill, "The California Legislative Analyst's Office," in *Organizations for Policy Analysis*, ed. Weiss, 256–73.

10. Ibid., 257.

11. Ibid., 264.

12. Elizabeth G. Hill, "LAO Annual Report Fiscal Year 1996–97," December 17, 1997.

13. This is particularly true for the Assembly because many of the newer members of the Senate had already served in the Assembly.

14. Hill, "LAO Annual Report," 260.

15. Ibid., 269–70.

16. Robert Greenstein, "Evolution of the Center's Work," speech to the International Public Finance Conference, Washington, DC, December 3, 1997.

17. Ibid.

18. Steven Pearlstein, "A Powerhouse for the Poor," *Washington Post*, May 4, 2007.

19. OMG Center for Collaborative Learning, "Assessment of the State Fiscal Analysis Initiative," Report prepared for Ford Foundation, March 2005, 2.

20. The main actors in this effort were Michael Lipsky, a well-known academic who had joined the Ford Foundation and was the main champion for the idea at Ford, and Iris Lav, who had just joined the center after working on these issues with public-sector labor unions and helped create an organization in New York that was a model for the network.

21. Drawn from OMG Center, "Assessment," 3.

22. Ibid.

23. Interview between SFAI and the author.

24. "State Fiscal Analysis Initiative," www.statefiscal.org/SFAI-brochure.pdf.

25. Twentieth Century Fund, "The Fund's First 75 Years," in *Twentieth Century Fund 1919–1994: 75th Anniversary Celebration* (New York: Twentieth Century Fund, 1994), 21.

26. "Dedication to Edward A. Filene: His Enduring Imprint," in ibid., 13.

27. Ibid., 13–14.

28. Richard C. Leone, "Message from the President," in *Twentieth Century Fund*, 19.

29. August Heckscher, "Reflections: The Twentieth Century Fund—Yesterday and To-morrow," in *Twentieth Century Fund*, 40.

30. "Fund's First 75 Years," 37.

31. Ibid.

32. Brewster C. Denny, "Message from the Chairman," in *Twentieth Century Fund*, 17.

33. This discussion relies on William H. Robinson, "The Congressional Research Service: Policy Consultant, Think Tank, and Information Factory," in *Organizations for Policy Analysis*, ed. Weiss, 181–200.

34. Quoted by Robinson, "Congressional Research Service," 183.

35. Ibid., 194.

36. Ibid., 182.

37. Ibid., 196.

38. Ibid., 187.

39. Ibid., 188.

40. Ibid., 189.

41. The Danish Parliament passed legislation in 1958 that authorized SFI to carry out research on welfare state policies with a specific aim of dealing with the rapidly growing area of social policies. The idea for the legislation developed soon after World War II.

42. The agrarian party within the country worked for collaborative arrangements and self-governance. There were links between the strong cooperative movement in Danish farming that advocated social networks through unions, clubs, and associations.

43. Jens Oddershede, "Danish Universities: A Sector in Change," February 2, 2009, www.dkuni.dk/English/~/media/845710866496440B9D9FB5B754112DA5.ashx.

44. Reported in "Evaluation of SFI: The Danish National Centre for Social Research 2009," August 11, 2009, 4.

45. Ibid., 7.

46. Ibid., 7–8.

47. Following the 2011 elections, the Ministry of Social Affairs and Integration was formed.

48. Ibid., 8.

49. Ibid.

50. Ibid., 9.

51. "Recommendations Concerning SFI's Impact Evaluation Research," 2010, 1.

52. SFI, *SFI Annual Report, 2010*, 16.

53. During the period between 2001 and 2010, the number of international conference papers grew significantly.

54. Heritage Foundation, *Leadership for America, 1997 Annual Report* (Washington, DC: Heritage Foundation, 1997), 1.

55. Ibid., 7.

56. This discussion relies on Lee Edwards, *The Power of Ideas: The Heritage Foundation at 25 Years* (Ottawa, IL: Jameson Books, 1998). This is a commissioned history of the organization.

57. Ibid., 19.

58. Ibid., 68.

59. William E. Simon, "Foreword," in *Power of Ideas*, by Edwards, xiii.

60. Edwards, *Power of Ideas*, 88, quoting the *New York Times*.

61. Ibid., 118.

62. Ibid., 45–47.

63. Ibid., 121.

64. Ibid., 76.

Chapter 5

Dealing with Two Cultures
Politics and Analysis

When John Nelson arrived at the Department of Defense in 1961, he really didn't pay much attention to any form of politics, neither the form that came from outside the government nor the internal variety. He reported directly to the top reaches of the department and was insulated from any internal political machinations. In addition, the procurement issues in which he was involved were rarely defined as political battles. He knew that there were many defense contractors who followed the procurement decisions within the Department of Defense carefully, but it seemed as if they exerted their influence on the process during congressional deliberations. In fact, his marching orders from the secretary made it clear that he was expected to develop recommendations that were the best possible approach to issues and to ignore the political landscape. His analysis was meant to provide an alternative to the line-item budget process used by Congress that was extremely responsive to political pressure. Because his office had control of the Planning, Programming, and Budgeting System process, he believed his work would be taken seriously.

He expected a similar arrangement when he moved to the Department of Health, Education, and Welfare during Lyndon Johnson's presidency. A strong president who knew how to get his way with Congress provided a setting that was very responsive to the work that he did. Indeed, there were fewer skirmishes with members of Congress than with the staff of the Bureau of the Budget in the White House.

Nelson had very little to do with the myriad interest groups that were involved in the issues before him. In large part, his clients—the top officials in *the department—were able to convince these groups to support the proposals that came out of the policy office. That really wasn't difficult to do, because the growth in programs meant that every group got more. He did find that the career staff in the department's budget office was not particularly convinced by the analyses he had completed. It was committed to the incremental allocation patterns of the past and didn't want to be viewed as rocking the boat.*

Rita Stone knew that the child care issue was a very divisive one. When she was working at the Children's Defense Fund (CDF), she learned that President Richard Nixon had vetoed an earlier piece of legislation that had received fairly strong support from Congress. Expansion of the child care block grant evoked strong views from many different groups. Some groups believed that women should stay home, which would make the need for child care irrelevant. Other groups pointed to the work pattern in the United States—that women were in the workforce and needed child care support.

Recent polls and focus groups had indicated that the child care issue could be an important one in the upcoming congressional elections; this did set out the possibility of support from Republicans who had not been advocates in the past. However, divided government—a Republican-controlled Congress and a Democratic president—made this issue very volatile. In addition, it was important to frame the proposed program in a way that would bring in a broader coalition of support than simply people who worked in the child care community. Otherwise, there was the possibility of a divide-and-conquer situation in which interest groups that ought to have been supporters would be pitted against one another. She was particularly concerned about the CDF's response to various proposals, both because of her own past experience and because she knew that both the president and the first lady were supporters of the CDF's agenda.

Ironically, Stone found that it was more difficult to get agreement within the executive branch than to gain support from the outside. There were at least ten other analysts working on this issue inside the department. In addition, there were strong differences between the department, the White House, and the Office of Management and Budget.

Veronica Lopez often felt that she operated in a world that was very like the Tower of Babel. Her movement from a role as a clinician treating ill children to global health policy issues put her in touch with a wide range of individuals and organizations. Although they all professed to be concerned about health issues for children, they all spoke different policy and program languages and had real difficulty communicating with one another. Yet her own experiences gave her the facility to speak all those languages and to understand the reasons why each of these actors emphasized different aspects of pediatric health questions. She felt she had a room full of hats. Each hat fit her just fine, but it was a challenge to figure out which one was appropriate for her current job.

As she had moved from position to position, she understood the complexity of the issues that she had made her life's work. She had experienced the realities of pediatric health policies at both the state and federal levels in the United States. Her experience at Centers for Disease Control and Prevention had brought her in contact with the many interest groups involved in health policy in the United States as well as the multiple agencies involved in the work. She had learned about the differences in health systems in the Latin American countries and the difficulty in figuring out the criteria that could be used to evaluate their success or failure. And her most recent job at the Bill & Melinda Gates Foundation had required her to work with a wide range of nongovernmental organizations around the globe as well as other foundations that shared her agenda.

All these experiences introduced her to a world characterized by a very untraditional set of political relationships—one where the actors shared some general approaches but emphasized very different policy issues within the shared goals. All these actors were faced with scarce resources and thus had to make determinations based on differences in emphasis. Even at the Gates Foundation, she learned, different program areas competed with one another for resources. She had expected this competition within the formal political structure (like Congress) but not in the loose and ever-changing health policy network.

This chapter deals with the classic conflict between the culture of analysis and the culture of politics. It describes the imperatives of the two cultures, the variety of political demands, the analyst's response to politics, the politician's response to the analyst, and issues dealing with analysis, democracy, and accountability.

Two Cultures

The writer C. P. Snow has provided us with a framework to describe the conflict between two very different cultures. Although Snow wrote about the conflict between literary intellectuals and physical scientists, his description of the gulf between these two worlds is applicable to the conflict between the world of analysis and the world of politics: "Between the two a gulf of mutual comprehension—sometimes (particularly among the young) hostility and dislike, but most of all lack of understanding. They have a curious distorted image of each other. Their attitudes are so different that, even on the level of emotion, they can't find much common ground."[1]

But whereas Snow's two cultures had limited requirements for interchange, the cultures of analysis and politics are inextricably connected in the field of policy analysis. The cultures are distinct and not equal. The political culture puts pressure on the norms of analysis (e.g., systematic thought and freedom from deliberate bias). In a sense the two cultures exist as master and servant.

A panel at a spring meeting of the Association for Public Policy Analysis and Management during the Reagan administration that sought to review the developments in the policy analysis field illustrates the problem. The panel included Richard Darman, who, at the time had left the administration and was teaching at the John F. Kennedy School of Government at Harvard University. Darman recited the various analytic methods that had been used over the years, beginning with the Planning, Programming, and Budgeting System, and moving to management by objectives and zero-based budgeting. Now, he said, "we have a new form—I D E O L O G Y."[2]

The literature in the policy analysis field is replete with illustrations of conflict between the two cultures. Most frequently, the dichotomy is established as a conflict between analysts and politicians. It is also defined as a conflict between intelligence and power, and between studying and action. Whatever the mode of framing the dichotomy, it is clear that there are differences between the two cultures in values, time, uncertainty, evidence, and meanings. There are instances in which the two sets of actors sit across from one another without ever engaging in what could be viewed as an exchange.[3] They do not even speak the same language because, as Alice Rivlin noted, there is a "tendency of particular groups of policy professionals to talk to each other in code."[4]

If we think about Machiavelli as a policy adviser, it is hard to read his advice to the prince without thinking about politics. Indeed, Yehezkel Dror's description of the new profession of policy analyst highlighted the failure to be attentive to political issues as one of the weaknesses of systems analysis. He chastised the systems analysts for their "neglect of the problems of political feasibility and of the special characteristics of political resources."[5] He further criticized the economic approach to systems analysis for its lack of attention to the political dimension of problems and failure to engage in political feasibility testing. Yet he did not really address these deficiencies in any detail in his early work.

Arnold Meltsner was one of the few early writers to give sustained attention to questions involving political feasibility and skills in political analysis.

Meltsner sought to move the field to a methodology that allowed for analysis of political feasibility, including the identification of actors, their beliefs and motivations, resources, and the sites of their interactions.[6] His emphasis, however, was on the development of micro-level political skills, and thus he did not pay significant attention to partisan and societal value conflicts or to appropriate political strategies that might be attached to the policy analyst's recommendations.

During the early years of the policy analysis field, there seemed to be an implicit acceptance that analysts would be governed by the norms of neutrality and objectivity that were embedded in their culture. Dror himself recognized these limitations, and in a later work he noted that many of the responses by contemporary policy analysis to the needs of handling politics were inadequate. He wrote that some analysts view politics as an enemy and actually regard politics as "ripe for reform by policy analysis."[7] He posed the conflict between the two cultures in a 1984 work that contrasted the two approaches in a number of ways; see table 5.1.[8]

Table 5.1   Interfaces between Analysis and Politics

Policy Analysis	Politics
Clinical and semidetached, with concern	Fighting and deep personal involvement
Uncertainty and complexity explicating	Situation-simplifying and ignoring
Searching for more options	Rapidly overloaded and option-rejecting
Posing need for decision criteria and value choice	Avoiding clear-cut choices in order to maintain essential consensus
Long-term perspective	Pressing troubles are enough
Emphasizing interrelations between various problems and decisions	Piecemeal approach
Constraints and costs constantly considered	Hopeful thinking and optimistic assumptions preferred; sometimes visionary
Doubtful and reevaluation-oriented	Dissonance-repressing, biased to see "successes" everywhere, and tending to escalate commitment to doubtful decisions

Source: Yehezkel Dror, "Policy Analysis for Advising Rulers," in *Rethinking the Process of Operational Research and Systems Analysis*, edited by Rolfe Tomlinson and Istvan Kiss (Oxford: Pergamon Press, 1984), 115.

The Imperatives of the Two Cultures

The attributes associated with the task of policy analysis include problem definition, definition of goals, information collection, choosing and applying analytical techniques, devising options or alternatives, and making recommendations. It is assumed that these tasks will be accomplished when analysis is clearly separated from the decision-making process. Historically, the policy analysis function was situated squarely in the formulation stage of the policy process—a stage that was viewed as separate from the adoption or implementation phase. As in the tradition dating from Machiavelli, the policy analyst was the adviser, not the decision maker.

By contrast, what we call *politics* is a much less precise set of activities. Politics takes many different forms. At the most basic level, it is important to remember, as Deborah Stone reminds us, that policy analysis is political argument and that policy conflicts are produced by political conflicts. Yet she writes: "Inspired by a vague sense that reason is clean and politics is dirty, Americans yearn to replace politics with rational decision making. . . . Policy is potentially a sphere of rational analysis, objectivity, allegiance to truth, and pursuit of the well-being of society as a whole. Politics is the sphere of emotion and passion, irrationality, self-interest, shortsightedness, and raw power."[9] She argues that though most social scientists and proponents of policy analysis try to develop a middle ground between these two spheres, that approach is not appropriate. *"Reasoned analysis is necessarily political.* It always involves choices to include some things and exclude others and to view the world in a particular way when other visions are possible" (emphasis in the original).[10]

Benveniste has noted that most issues involve a range of political actors (including implementers and beneficiaries), not simply the political figure who may be analogous to Machiavelli's prince.[11] And as the familiar maxim puts it, politics is the art of the possible—a reality that usually pushes a decision away from the search for the best solution (or what economists call maximizing) to a feasible solution (or what economists call satisficing).

The fragmentation of the American political system also provides different opportunities for those who advocate particular positions to raise their concerns. The agenda-setting and adoption stages of the policy process provide the setting for political argument.[12] In contrast to the policy formulation stage, both the agenda-setting and adoption stages are essentially political processes, and thus political reasoning and argument predominate. Therefore, analysis has a more difficult time finding a way to insinuate itself into the dynamics of these two stages. Analysts cannot insulate themselves from the dynamics of politics, interest groups, and deadlines. Information takes on particular meaning when it is attached to specific positions and is articulated by participants in the decision-making process who have arguments to make.

A Variety of Political Demands

One can see the impact of political issues both on the organizations for which policy analysts work and at the level of the individual analyst. In both instances analysis is affected by macropolitical issues as well as by micro-level political pressures. The following discussion is a relatively broad-brush presentation of the range of political demands that policy analysts must face.

Macro-Level Politics

Policy analysts and the institutions where they work are affected by a variety of macro issues. These include pressures that emanate from the actual structure of government and from elections, partisanship, interest group politics, coalition building, and ideological battles.

The structure of government. The structure of the American system of government itself creates a series of political pressures on the policy analyst. At the most basic level, the American system of shared powers (in which authority is dispersed among the executive, legislative, and judicial branches) effectively means that there are very few cases in which any one institution—let alone any one person—has the power to make a clear-cut decision. In this sense, unlike policy analysts in countries with parliamentary systems, analysts in the United States must deal with multiple policymakers.

Actors within the executive branch of the federal government are hardly homogeneous. On many issues there are strong differences among departments and agencies, the Office of Management and Budget, and the policy staff at the White House. Other kinds of differences are found between presidential and cabinet styles of management.

Unlike the decisions made by Machiavelli's prince, decisions in the US political system almost always involve bargaining and negotiation between levels of government. The US system of federalism also creates a set of difficult pressures on the analyst. Very few domestic policy decisions are made unilaterally at the national level; even if the decision is made by the national actors, state and local agencies have been given increasing responsibility for the actual implementation of programs. It is difficult to determine general patterns of responses to policy changes, given the disparities between the states and localities in resources and political culture.[13] For instance, policy analysts who attempted to predict implementation patterns in the welfare reform debate produced very different scenarios, depending on the assumptions that were made about the response of one state or another to the proposals. Even when organizations such as the State Fiscal Analysis Initiative Network (SFAI) try to emphasize specific areas and approaches, they realize that federalism in the United States means that it is inevitable that states will have different responses to shared problems.

The fragmentation implicit in the structure of government creates situations in which various institutions are able to impede decisions even if they cannot make a decision on their own. As a result, the power to kill a policy is much greater than the power to create one. And whereas the diverse institutional perspectives are predictable, the substance of the conflict between them is not always obvious.

The conflict between the executive branch and Congress over sampling processes in the 2000 census was an example of the dynamics that result from the interests of the various institutional actors. Though almost all the analysts involved in the issue believed that sampling was appropriate, the Republicans who controlled Congress did not want to allow the Census Bureau to embark on this path. Their arguments were both explicit and implicit. The opponents argued that sampling violated the constitutional requirements for the actual counting of individuals. At the same time, it was expected that sampling could have changed the data that would determine the apportionment of congressional seats. Those who advocated the sampling procedure argued from a position of technical expertise, whereas the Republicans in Congress perceived the issue to be a clear-cut political problem.

The electoral process. The regular schedule of elections in the United States also establishes a set of political pressures on the practice of policy analysis. Some issues rise to the surface because they have salience as campaign issues. Elections (in both two-year and four-year cycles) especially have an impact on the policy organizations that operate inside the government in both the executive and legislative branches. Presidential elections are usually followed by significant changes in executive branch personnel (unless the incumbent president is reelected), both at the decision-making level and in the individuals who might be appointed to head policy shops. Elections frequently produce divided government, where legislative powers may be in the hands of one political party while the executive branch is in the hands of the other. Shifts in power in the legislative branch can also provoke changes in leadership, particularly among those who chair legislative committees and the staffs who serve them. Perhaps few changes were as dramatic as the imposition of term limits on the legislature in California, but elections often produce changes at both the state and federal levels.

During its more than thirty years of operation, the Office of the Assistant Secretary for Planning and Evaluation in what is now called the Department of Health and Human Services has experienced dramatic shifts in its environment as a result of elections. Career staff members who have been in this office for many years have found that changes in personnel can shift the focus from one set of issues to another or from one analytic approach to another. During the Reagan administration, the entrance of a set of officials who wanted to eliminate many of the department's programs provoked a defensive stance on the part of the office's staff. Some staff members found they were spending much of their time creating arguments for the maintenance of programs that were being attacked, rather than focusing on the new officials' agenda. Some of them left, but others remained and played an important role in crafting block grant proposals and other aspects of the Reagan agenda. In addition, during the early period of the Reagan administration, the assistant secretary for planning and evaluation was an influential adviser to the department's secretary.

Partisanship. Although the American political system is usually described as a set of institutions that operate on highly personal rather than party disciplinary lines, partisanship is a reality for many of the issues that confront the policy analyst. This is particularly important today—an era characterized by divided government in both national and state settings. It is increasingly common for the executive branch to be controlled by one political party and the legislature by the other one, or for one house of the legislature to be controlled by one party and the other house by the other party. In addition, most legislative committees are highly conscious of the separation between the majority and minority members, and separate staffs respond to the agendas of the two separate sides of the aisle.

Both the California Legislative Analyst's Office and the Congressional Research Service operate in a partisan environment. The presence of majority and minority members of committees makes it clear that there are different perspectives on issues that must be somehow satisfied. This is very different from the experience of either government policy analysis units or advocacy groups, where there are clear positions and relatively consistent agendas. Both of the legislative units work hard to find ways to produce work that is useful to any party and to establish reputations as nonpartisan institutions. These two organizations do not attempt to ignore the partisan overlay under which they work but rather accept it as a point of departure and find ways to work within it. They may complete analyses that reflect opposing perspectives by presenting clearly different options for an issue.

Interest group politics. The vast array of organizations that make up what Heclo called issue networks provides another set of realities for the practice of policy analysis.[14] Heclo notes that issue networks "comprise a large number of participants with quite variable degrees of mutual commitment or of independence on others in their environment; in fact it is almost impossible to say where a network leaves off and its environment begins."[15] In some cases, ongoing relationships have been cultivated among interest groups, congressional committees, and career officials, which together provide an informal infrastructure for the exchange of information. In other cases interest groups are highly fragmented and polarized, and the policy debate over issues is increasingly adversarial. The multiple perspectives that are articulated provide an opportunity for the production of analysis attached to specific positions. This supports a view that it is difficult to disentangle these perspectives from the information that is produced by interest groups.[16]

The Center on Budget and Policy Priorities and its SFAI program operate in a highly charged interest group environment because they are focusing on issues affecting low-income citizens. When they work on issues involving the provision of services to these citizens, they know that their positions may not reflect the perspective of other interest groups or the administration, even when the White House is controlled by the Democrats. Similarly, the AARP Public Policy Institute experiences a volatile issue environment with many different players. There are very strong differences among the players engaged in these issues, both in policy goals and in the interpretation of the data that describe the problems to be attacked. Although the center's value perspective is clear and it seeks to serve the cluster of interest groups whose members share values with it, it is committed to the production of policy analysis work that does not appear to be a narrow brief for policy positions. It seeks to do work that is viewed as credible, even by those who do not agree with its policy positions.

Coalition building. The fragmentation of the American political system—largely as a result of its multiple institutions—has made it extremely difficult to make decisions. Most decisions require coalitions of support from actors with diverse interests and perspectives. Coalitions are usually temporal and are characterized by policy positions that are broad enough to enable the various players to see a win–win situation. The analysis that is effective in this situation is often strategic rather than substantive.[17] Analysts are required to find new ways to frame an issue and to respond to the vagaries of the decision-making processes.

The Century Foundation has attempted to play a role in this process by defining issues in a way that broadens, rather than narrows, the policy space considered. It focuses on producing information that could be used by the general public, often through the media, to understand basic issues and move toward more effective government. The state-level SFAI groups emphasize the importance of developing coalitions.

The emergence of ideology and single-issue politics. Many students of the American political system have argued that the United States—unlike many parliamentary systems—operates in a nonideological and pragmatic fashion. Though the fragmentation of institutions and the imperatives of coalition building do minimize the strength of ideologically based positions, ideology and single-issue politics have played an increasing role in American politics. In some cases this occurs because an issue divides society (e.g., the Vietnam War or abortion). In other cases it is related to an attempt to find ways to think about policy positions in a comprehensive and rationalized way.

The Heritage Foundation's concern about serving as a voice for the conservative movement in the United States has led it to emphasize the role of ideology in politics. It has sought to define a set of policy positions that can frame the details of political discourse, and thus to establish what it views as a coherent blueprint for conservatives because it proceeds from a clearly defined set of principles. The Center on Budget and Policy Priorities, by contrast, proceeds from a general set of values rather than a clear policy blueprint.

Micro-Level Politics

Political pressures on the policy analyst not only emerge from the macro-level political system but also from the micro-level relationships found in organizations and in choices implicit in the analytical process. It is useful to briefly examine the dimensions of this micro-level situation.

Organizational politics. When policy analysis offices enjoyed a monopoly position, located at the top reaches of the organization and accessible to the top decision makers, they were less likely to be concerned about internal organizational politics. For some offices—such as the Policy Planning Staff of the State Department—the decentralized nature of the organization did make it more difficult for the analytical staff to feel as if it were affecting policy.[18] As the policy analysis function proliferated and was diffused within organizations, it became clear that a new form of court politics was emerging. Just as internal political battles were commonplace (often among individuals responsible for various aspects of program implementation), so, too, disputes arose between policy analysts located in different places within the bureaucracy (e.g., between a department's policy analysis unit and the analysts in the Office of Management and Budget). Some of these battles stemmed from long-standing arguments about responsibilities or approaches to policy issues.[19] Others reflected the pecking order in the organization, based either on personal relationships or on budget levels. In some cases the decision chain within an organization is likely to be most important; the analyst who is the last one to speak to the decision maker may have the last word on the issue.

Intraorganizational politics are usually less complex in highly centralized organizations, but there may still be conflicts between those holding various perspectives who seek to exert control. Policy analysts in these centralized roles may find themselves debating with budget analysts or lawyers over the appropriate decision path.

The politics of analysis. The choices that must be made by the policy analyst in the process of organizing and accomplishing analytical work do represent another variety of politics. The determination whether to make political feasibility calculations in the analytical process is perhaps the clearest of this type of pressure. Despite the suggestions made by Meltsner on approaches to accomplishing political feasibility analysis, many analysts choose to avoid this type of approach.[20] Assessment of supporters, opponents, and indifference requires quite detailed information about the decision environment. The analyst's knowledge of the details of the policy substance is not adequate to make these determinations; Meltsner's policy analyst as technician is not likely to have been trained to frame issues in this manner. The analyst needs to be able to understand the players and their motives. In some cases, however, the client may want the analyst to stay away from these political assessments, holding on to these calculations himself or herself. Volatile political environments are especially difficult for analysts who emphasize class research methodologies.

Whether or not the analyst makes detailed political feasibility calculations, it is important for the individual working on an issue to have some sense of the underlying reasons why the work is being done. Analytic work can serve a variety of hidden or not-so-hidden agendas. Studies may be commissioned as a way to delay or avoid a decision or, conversely, to speed up its consideration. The appointment of blue-ribbon commissions with responsibility for writing a report is sometimes a way to slow down a decision process while giving the impression of action.

There are implications of political choices in most of the analytic stages. The choice of topic for analysis provides a clue about the level of importance of a particular issue. The analyst's specification of the preferred state or goals of the effort involves value choices. In most instances policies have multiple and often conflicting goals; the emphasis on one or another of these goals represents an important choice.

Several considerations flow from the analyst's relationship with a client. Each client transmits implicit information about power relationships, both within the organization and in society at large.[21] Though this is clearest in the case of elected officials who come to their positions with relatively well-articulated agendas, it also occurs at other levels. Clients communicate preferences about policy approaches as well as the legitimacy of target populations to be served by the policy under consideration.

Analysts often find themselves in a situation where they have multiple clients. The original conception of the policy analyst's role was that of an individual who advised an individual decision maker (ruler), but policy analysts now find themselves attempting to satisfy multiple clients who may have very different perspectives and motivations about the issue. The increased interest in networks may mean that the multiple clients are known to exist but do not operate together in a formal setting. In a hierarchical bureaucracy, the analyst may find himself or herself in a situation where the work is first given to a superior with one perspective on the issue and then transmitted up the chain of command to other decision makers with views that are different from those of the first-level client. Analysts who work within legislative settings, such as those in the Congressional Research Service, usually try to avoid making recommendations and simply produce analyses that lay out multiple options.

The interpersonal relationship between a client and an analyst has also become more difficult and complex. One can expect the relationship between the two to be characterized by highly personal responses that are not often predictable. It is not always clear why trust relationships are built up between client and analyst. But as the policy analysis function has become more bureaucratized, analysts may never have a face-to-face relationship with their clients and find it difficult to receive feedback on their analytical approaches. In those cases where the client's views are well known, the analyst must determine how open the client is to reexamining those views. This determination can be a tricky business; there is always a risk that an analyst will be sent to an organizational Siberia (i.e., never given an important assignment in the future) when he or she questions the beliefs of a client.[22]

During the early years of the field, there was a tendency to assume that the goals articulated by the decision makers were appropriate and provided sufficient guidance for the analyst. Soon, however, analysts confronted problems with this assumption and recognized that goals and objectives in public policy are usually multiple, ambiguous, and conflicting. For example, when analysts examined the compensatory education programs supported by the then–Office of Education, they found that improvement in test scores was not the only goal of the programs. Rather, the programs were also devised to provide financial support to school districts. Clients who ignore this intergovernmental and policy complexity are likely to find their positions overruled, and analysts do not serve their clients well if they fail to deal with this complexity.

Other aspects of the analytical process reflect important judgments. The criteria that are established and the weights (if any) that are given to them are expressions of values and beliefs. The balance among criteria of efficiency, effectiveness, and equity is crucial. Sometimes an analyst may be so concerned about efficiency values that these drive out other concerns. This is especially problematic when analysts limit themselves to the rationale and techniques derived from the economic model, because the economic model puts a premium on efficiency and often assumes away other criteria. The selection of an analytic technique may also reflect implicit choices about constituencies and issues. If a methodology does not allow—or indeed drives out—the possibility for the calculation of political feasibility, then many factors that will eventually determine the decision are ignored.

The Analyst's Response to Politics

Some years ago, Alice Rivlin wrote that despite all their expertise and sophistication, policymakers still make big policy mistakes: "Policy analysts often seem paralyzed, recognizing the futility of chasing easy solutions, but confounded by their own sense of the complexity of issues. They lose the floor—indeed often hand over the microphone willingly—to the intellectual patent medicine salesmen."[23] Though she did not use the label "politician" to describe those intellectual patent medicine salesmen, the association was fairly obvious.

Others are somewhat less pessimistic. Yehezkel Dror suggests that policy analysts can handle politics in several ways: by mapping the political fields in which the decision makers operate, by generating options more favorable to political realities, by paying attention to the relationship between the decision maker's own political power and the recommendations that would be made, and by accepting the decision maker's ideological position as a frame of reference.[24] However, Dror did acknowledge that the inclusion of politics in policy analysis will likely require what he called "paradigmatic innovations in policy analysis."[25]

David Weimer and Aidan Vining have emphasized the importance of thinking about political issues in terms of strategies. They suggest four strategies that can be used to achieve policy outcomes and to counsel policy analysts to think about strategies as well as substance in their work: co-optation, which means getting others to believe that the idea you suggested is theirs; compromise, which means making modifications in proposals that evoke more political support; heresthetics, which entail manipulating the agenda or the rules of decision making; and rhetoric, which means using language that either clarifies or obfuscates a policy position.[26]

There have been various responses to the conflict between analysis and politics. Some analysts are not able to acknowledge that their own values and beliefs might shape their approach to issues. Although not thinking of themselves as apolitical, other analysts inside government agencies try to protect themselves from external overt political pressure or agendas, often moving away from high-profile assignments to less-visible activities.[27] Sometimes these projects are technical in nature, but more often they involve the satisfaction of working on interesting topics with good colleagues inside the department and with others outside the agency who are interested in the work. At any rate, the analysts seek to distance themselves from highly volatile issues. This behavior was not uncommon during the Reagan administration in the Office of the Assistant Secretary for Planning and Evaluation of what was then the Department of Health, Education, and Welfare, where some analysts strongly disagreed with the positions taken by the administration. Conversely, some analysts (even those who did not agree with the issues on the Republican agenda) engaged the issues and provided policy analyses to their political bosses.

In other instances policy analysts realize that their impact will be only at the margins of decisions. They acknowledge that the essence of the decision will be a political choice that reflects decision makers' values. The analysis that is available may be useful in the details of the policy design but will not determine the large contours of the policy.[28] This is a particularly difficult reality for some analysts to accept, particularly those whose analytic methodologies or personal values lead them to make very different sorts of recommendations. The recent debate on welfare reform is an example of this type of discomfort.

Another response has been for analysts to become identified with particular political or value commitments. Though they may not have begun their careers with that intent, this move has occurred as analysts who specialize in particular policy areas become convinced of the truth of their recommendations and, as a result, move into an advocacy posture. They may continue to work inside the government, but their policy preferences are well known and others may view them as the close colleagues of analysts attached to advocacy groups that highlight particular client groups, policy issues, or political stances. The change in administration from Carter to Reagan provoked a move by analysts from government to advocacy groups. Some analysts who had been working inside government moved to the advocacy groups with which they had dealt or, in the case of the Center on Budget and Policy Priorities, actually started a new organization.

Others have responded to the changes in the political environment by deciding to stay within the system and to attach themselves directly to the political actors or move directly into a decision-making role. The shelf life of such a strategy may be short, particularly in an era characterized by frequent shifts in political leadership. It requires an analyst to focus on short-term goals and elevate assessments of relevancy over those of policy effectiveness. Other institutions—such as the Congressional Research Service—have learned to work within the parameters of the political process, acknowledging its constraints and needs.

There is always a danger that analysis that is close to an advocacy role will be viewed simply as rationalization for particular positions. More than twenty-five years ago, Rivlin called this "forensic social science," in which scholars or teams of scholars write briefs for or against particular policy positions: "They state what the position is and bring together all the evidence that supports their side of the argument, leaving to the brief writers of the other side the job of picking apart the case that has been presented and detailing the counter evidence."[29] Analysts who are identified with particular positions or work for interest groups are most susceptible to this danger.

Some writers have been concerned about the failure of the policy analysis field to establish a code of ethics that would guide analysts who find themselves embroiled in sticky political situations. Douglas Amy, for example, argues that policy analysis and ethics are incompatible because a focus on ethics "frequently threatens the professional and political interests of both analysts and policymakers."[30] Weimer and Vining have offered one formulation of the possible dilemma, for which they use Hirschman's discussion of exit, voice, and loyalty and Hirschman's framework to describe alternative responses to value conflicts. They note that "voice" has four dimensions: protest, leak, issue ultimatum, and speak out until silenced. "Exit" also has four: resign, resign and disclose, issue ultimatum, and speak out until silenced. What they term "disloyalty" has sabotage, leak, speak out until silenced, and resign and disclose. There are overlaps between each dimension. All three overlap in terms of "speak out until silenced." Voice and disloyalty overlap in terms of "leak." Exit and voice both indicate a response in terms of 'issue ultimatum." And exit and disloyalty both are likely to use "resign and disclose."[31]

The Politician's Response to the Analyst

Too often, analysts are viewed as the sole actors in the policy analysis process, and too little attention is given to the responsibilities of the client-politician in the relationship. Dror noted that clients/rulers must communicate their interests, values, perspectives, plans, and agenda; and that without this information, analysts cannot be useful in the decision-making process.[32] Laurence Silberman, a former undersecretary of labor, expressed a somewhat cynical view of the relationship between the client and the analyst: "Since most political appointees already have been captured by their constituent bureaucracies, it is hard to see how policy analysis can weaken their effectiveness. On the other hand, if a politician enters into his duties with a sufficiently well-formed notion of what he wants to accomplish, policy analysis can be very helpful."[33]

Politicians who are unhappy with a policy analysis have many ways to respond to it. They can marginalize the analyst or the analytic unit (as discussed above, they can isolate the analyst from a role in decision making). They can trivialize the subsequent assignments that the analyst or the analytic shop receives. Or they can fragment the assignments in such a way that no analyst has the legitimacy to provide a comprehensive perspective on an issue.

Clients can also control the rules for producing or releasing analytic work, which will allow them to control the availability of information in ways that meet their own needs. Policy analysts who see themselves as governed by norms of research find this particularly hard to accept because it violates views about open access to information.[34] The increased interest in transparency in the twenty-first century makes for conflicting views about the availability of information. This may be a greater problem for analysts in consulting firms who are supported by contracts with the government; analysts inside government often expect these types of pressures because they operate in a context that is governed by traditional, hierarchically based rules. In an age of public sector downsizing, consulting firms are increasingly being utilized as extensions of agency operations, and their project managers have imposed the internally generated expectations on them.

Analysis, Democracy, and Accountability

Some writers are concerned that the policy analyst's search for rationality is a way to avoid the demands of democracy.[35] In the mid-1990s, for example, the effort inside the Clinton administration to devise a major health care reform proposal was cloaked in an aura of secrecy, and the individuals who orchestrated the process argued that it was exempt from requirements (e.g., those imposed on federal agencies involving the use of advisory groups). One commentator noted that Americans "have felt an elemental urge to bring social science and technical skills to bear on policy making, and our politics has been changed and reshaped by a yearning to govern ourselves more intelligently—even if doing so means escaping the political process."[36]

The range of institutions and processes associated with American democratic principles does make life very troublesome for a policy analyst; these institutions and processes create a set of pressures and expectations that are much more comfortable for a politician to deal with than for an analyst. Change and uncertainty are constant, which makes it difficult for an analyst to freeze-frame an issue long enough to work on it.

Carol Weiss reports the charge of some critics that "the spread of analysis and analysis organizations has pernicious effects on the democratic process" and the policy experts "hostile to politics and scornful of moral and ideological commitment . . . seek to reduce all issues to matters of practical technical inquiry."[37] However, Guy Benveniste has suggested that the developments in the field have created a different set of pressures. He noted that there has been a shift away from the view that analysts could be apolitical experts. He suggests that during the early period of the field, an analyst "had to appear uncommitted, a mere technician in the world of partisan politics."[38] He found, however, that as the field developed, there has been a shift away from apolitical politics toward partisan advocacy: "One can no longer claim that experts are concerned purely with improving rationality, as the earlier literature was prone to do. They are engaged to deal with means and with underlying value premises. The assumptions that define problems often define underlying value premises. Thus experts have become politically suspect. Many no longer pretend to be apolitical but espouse instead well-known views regarding their values and commitments."[39]

All this makes it very difficult to discern how a policy analyst can be held accountable. Barbara Romzek and Melvin Dubnick's framework for analyzing accountability expectations provides one way to think about these issues. They suggest that there are four types of accountability: bureaucratic, where an analyst is held accountable to superiors inside an organizational structure; professional, where the norms of the profession set the expectations and standards for behavior; political, where the expectations of some key external stakeholder define the expectations; and legal, where external sources that play a role in oversight and monitoring activities define the accountability relationships.[40]

Analysts who operate inside the bureaucracy balance all four sets of demands; most, however, would prefer to be governed by professional norms. Politicians, however, expect the analyst to respond to the accountability expectations that they articulate. And because many policy analysts do not have a defined constituency to look to for support, their relationship with the client (i.e., the bureaucratic relationship) becomes exceedingly powerful.[41] The more an analyst acquires power on his or her own, the more suspect he or she becomes to politicians.[42] This is particularly problematic in policy areas where the boundaries between public- and private-sector actors and issues are murky.

All this suggests that the tensions between the imperatives of the two cultures—the cultures of analysis and politics—are not easy to avoid. They are a part of the day-to-day life of the policy analyst, playing out in different ways in different environments, and the stress that emanates from them is part of the lifeblood of the policy analysis profession and should be expected in a democratic system. Analysts are rarely in the controlling role in this relationship, and most have acknowledged that their legitimacy is derived from elected or appointed political officials. As Aaron Wildavsky wrote, these two approaches of analysis and politics "are twin forms of competitive redundancy that compliment one another by learning from social interaction."[43] For Dror, "policy analysts are one of the bridges between science and politics, but they do not transform the basic characteristics of 'the political' and of organizational behavior."[44]

Notes

1. C. P. Snow, *The Two Cultures and a Second Look* (Cambridge: Cambridge University Press, 1963), 4.

2. The importance of ideology and political labeling is also illustrated by the recent publication of guides to political advocacy organizations. Economics America, a consulting firm specializing in nonprofit organizations, has published two guides—*The Left Guide*, the comprehensive directory of liberal, progressive, and left-of-center organizations; and *The Right Guide*, a comprehensive directory of conservative, free-market, and traditional-values organizations.

3. See the discussion of the two cultures by Beryl A. Radin and Willis D. Hawley, *The Politics of Federal Reorganization: Creating the US Department of Education* (New York: Pergamon Press, 1988), 226–28.

4. Alice M. Rivlin, "Out of the Trenches: A Public Policy Paradox," *Journal of Policy Analysis and Management* 4, no. 1 (1984): 20.

5. Yehezkel Dror, "Policy Analysts: A New Professional Role in Government," in *Ventures in Policy Sciences*, by Yehezkel Dror (New York: Elsevier, 1971), 227.

6. Arnold J. Meltsner, "Political Feasibility and Policy Analysis," *Public Administration Review* (November–December 1972): 859–67.

7. Yehezkel Dror, "Policy Analysis for Advising Rulers," in *Rethinking the Process of Operational Research and Systems Analysis*, edited by Rolfe Tomlinson and Istvan Kiss (Oxford: Pergamon Press, 1984), 115.

8. Ibid., 96–97.

9. Deborah Stone, *Policy Paradox: The Art of Political Decision Making* (New York: W. W. Norton, 1997), 373.

10. Ibid., 375.

11. Guy Benveniste, *The Politics of Expertise*, 2nd ed. (San Francisco: Boyd & Fraser, 1977), 20.

12. For a description of the attributes of the various policy stages, see Robert Nakamura and Frank Smallwood, *The Politics of Policy Implementation* (New York: St. Martin's Press, 1980).

13. For a description of the multiple executive branch actors involved in the decision to create the Department of Education, see, e.g., Radin and Hawley, *Politics of Federal Reorganization*.

14. Hugh Heclo, "Issue Networks and the Executive Establishment," in *The New American Political System*, edited by Anthony King (Washington, DC: American Enterprise Institute for Public Policy Research, 1978), 87–124.

15. Ibid., 102.

16. See Carol H. Weiss, "Ideology, Interests, and Information: The Basis of Policy Positions," in *Ethics, the Social Scientists, and Policy Analysis*, edited by Daniel Callahan and Bruce Jennings (New York: Plenum Press, 1983), 213–45.

17. On this issue, see Meltsner, "Political Feasibility."

18. See Lucien Pugliaresi and Diane T. Berliner, "Policy Analysis at the Department of State: The Policy Planning Staff," *Journal of Policy Analysis and Management* 8, no. 3 (1989): 379–94.

19. See, e.g., Matthew Holden Jr., "'Imperialism' in Bureaucracy," *American Political Science Review* 60 (December 1966): 943–51.

20. See Meltsner, "Political Feasibility."

21. See the discussion of the social construction of policy by Anne Larason Schneider and Helen Ingram, *Policy Design for Democracy* (Lawrence: University Press of Kansas, 1997), esp. chap. 5.

22. See Michael Mintrom, *People Skills for Policy Analysts* (Washington, DC: Georgetown University Press, 2003).

23. Rivlin, "Out of the Trenches," 18.

24. Dror, "Policy Analysis for Advising Rulers," 115.

25. Ibid., 116.

26. David L. Weimer and Aidan R. Vining, *Policy Analysis: Concepts and Practice*, 2nd ed. (Englewood Cliffs, NJ: Prentice Hall, 1992), 319–25.

27. See Austin Sarat and Susan Silbey, "The Pull of the Policy Audience," *Law and Policy* 10, nos. 2 and 3 (April–July 1988): 98.

28. This point was discussed during a panel titled "Do Clients Use Policy Analysis?" Annual Research Conference, Association for Public Policy Analysis and Management, Washington, November 1997.

29. Alice M. Rivlin, "Forensic Social Science," *Harvard Educational Review* 43, no. 1 (February 1973): 61.

30. Douglas J. Amy, "Why Policy Analysis and Ethics Are Incompatible," *Journal of Policy Analysis and Management* 3, no. 4 (1984): 587.

31. David L. Weimer and Aidan R. Vining, *Policy Analysis: Concepts and Practice*, 3rd ed. (Upper Saddle River, NJ: Prentice Hall, 1998), 50.

32. Dror, "Policy Analysis for Advising Rulers," 98.

33. Laurence H. Silberman, "Policy Analysis: Boon or Curse for Politicians?" in *Bureaucrats, Policy Analysts, Statesmen: Who Leads?* edited by Robert A. Goldwin (Washington, DC: American Enterprise Institute for Public Policy Research, 1980), 38.

34. See Charles E. Metcalf, "Presidential Address: Research Ownership, Communication of Results, and Threats to Objectivity in Client-Driven Research," *Journal of Policy Analysis and Management* 17, no. 2 (1998): 153–63. This may be a greater problem for outside analysts who operate through contracts with the government; analysts inside government often expect these types of pressures.

35. See Edward C. Banfield, "Policy Science as Metaphysical Madness," in *Bureaucrats*, ed. Goldwin, 1–19.

36. James Allen Smith, *The Idea Brokers: Think Tanks and the Rise of the New Policy Elite* (New York: Free Press, 1991), 3.

37. Carol H. Weiss, "Helping Government Think: Functions and Consequences of Policy Analysis Organizations," in *Organizations for Policy Analysis: Helping Government Think*, edited by Carol H. Weiss (Newbury Park, CA: Sage, 1992), 15.

38. Benveniste, *Politics*, 115.

39. Ibid.

40. Barbara S. Romzek and Melvin J. Dubnick, "Accountability in the Public Sector: Lessons from the Challenger Tragedy," *Public Administration Review* 47 (May–June 1987): 227–38.

41. Arnold J. Meltsner, *Policy Analysts in the Bureaucracy* (Berkeley: University of California Press, 1976), 157.

42. Benveniste, *Politics*, 27.

43. Aaron Wildavsky, *Speaking Truth to Power: The Art and Craft of Policy Analysis* (Boston: Little, Brown, 1979), 386.

44. Dror, "Policy Analysts," 232.

Chapter 6

The Tools of the Trade

John Nelson was quite amazed at the smooth transition he was able to achieve as he moved from academic work to the RAND Corporation and then to the Department of Defense (DoD). The assignments he was given in DoD fit the market models with which he was familiar. As he examined procurement activities in DoD, he was able to examine various alternatives in terms of their merit, usefulness, price, and cost. Because he was comfortable with quantifying these attributes, he could move toward measurement, assessing alternatives, and estimating the optimal alternative. The structure of the Planning, Programming, and Budgeting System (PPBS) allowed him to fit this framework into a decision-making process.

As the months went by, he found it very satisfying to train other staff members in the application of the analytic techniques and soon was viewed as a senior expert in the PPBS process. When he moved to the Department of Health, Education, and Welfare, however, sometimes he felt like Paladin, the star of an old television western. Paladin "had gun, will travel." Nelson "had analytic technique, will travel." His knowledge of PPBS and cost-benefit analysis did seem to serve him well. Soon, however, he was stymied. He could not figure out how to make comparisons across client groups or to find ways to attribute dollar benefits in policy areas that involved the calculation of the worth of an individual's life.

At first he was so overwhelmed by the amount of work he was assigned that he didn't give this problem much thought. But he became increasingly concerned about the applicability of analytic techniques developed for policy areas in which there was general agreement on goals to areas in which there was significant disagreement in society. Sometimes the program staff in the department pointed out potential problems in implementing his recommendations if they were adopted. Because he was not familiar with the specific program areas, he could not really understand their concerns. Those issues certainly complicated the application of his economic models and contributed to his decision to return to California.

As a result of her master's program in public policy, Rita Stone had become familiar with a range of analytic tools that had been traditionally viewed as a part of the policy analyst's tool kit. Though she thought that this knowledge sharpened her general analytic ability, she found that there was very limited opportunity to use it when she moved into the Department of Health and Human Services. However, her quantitative analysis courses did provide her with the ability to critique work done by contractors and other researchers and to use those findings where relevant. She wished that she had taken some courses in policy and program evaluation because studies of several of the child care demonstration efforts seemed to provide very useful information, but she wasn't always sure that she had the skills to glean the appropriate "meat" from those studies.

Although the department's information about experience with the existing child care block grant was limited, she was intrigued to find out that the Congressional Research Service was developing a microsimulation that provided information on attributes of children served as well as on providers. She had worked closely with the Congressional Research Service staff when she had an assignment on Capitol Hill and knew the individuals who were developing this information. She hoped that this data set was not going to be subject to the range of interpretations that seemed to accompany other child care information sources.

After five years in the department, Stone was somewhat surprised to realize that she had not written anything longer than three pages in length. Though she still viewed her role as a policy analyst, her work was usually presented in briefings, following talking points that organized the main issues and outlined general options for the top officials in the department and the White House. Sometimes she spent the entire workday in meetings, rarely having an opportunity to sit in her office to write, let alone read.

Veronica Lopez sometimes felt that she was operating on a different planet when she dealt with other policy analysts. The analysis that she did herself as well as work of others that she found useful seemed to reverse the analytic process. She began her work by emphasizing the imperative of action and asked herself what she needed to know before she was comfortable making a recommendation for action by those in the organizations in which she worked. In contrast, she often found herself surrounded by analysts who began their work by focusing on the methodology that they would use and let the imperatives of that methodology drive their work. In her view, that approach frequently produced analysis that lost sight of the reality of the policy situations before them.

There were a number of attributes of that type of analysis that she found extremely frustrating. First, most analysts seemed to think that quantitative analysis was the only approach that was appropriate. Thus they began their work by looking for data sets that were already in existence. Second, she found that most of these data sets collected information at the aggregate level and thus didn't provide her with micro-level information disaggregated at the level of specific population groups. This was particularly problematic for her because she was focused on services for Hispanic children both in the United States and in a number of Latin American countries. Third, she rarely found analytic work that provided her with information that focused on issues of quality of services. When she worked in a range of sites, she was not able to figure out why one location was so different from others. It was rare that she was able to find information that gave her the ability to trade off between conflicting—and appropriate—values and goals. And fourth, her action agenda often raised questions about strategy for approaching the issue. She recognized that the alternatives that she would present to her clients/bosses looked to different approaches, not to specific aspects of policy substance.

For many, the field of policy analysis is best understood by attention to the analytic techniques and methodologies that can be applied to the issues that are before decision makers. This chapter discusses the differences between research and analysis. It examines the impact of economic models and techniques in this process, particularly the cost-benefit technique. It also looks to systematic approaches such as criteria analysis and political mapping. In addition, it includes attention to the development of policy evaluation. It outlines the debate over the use of the "classic" policy analysis framework, highlights the skills that a policy analyst should have, and finally includes a discussion of the work environment in which analysts operate.

The tools that are used in policy analysis are often confused with the tools that are found in the research enterprise. Vining and Weimer have commented that they recognize "research on the policy process as distinct from, but nevertheless, potentially informative for political/organizational and policy analysis." They argued "for a narrow definition of policy analysis that requires both a specific client and a substantive focus on advancing social values. We distinguish it from policy research, which shares the substantive focus but not the requirement of a specific client, and from political/organizational, or stakeholder analysis which has a specific client but an instrumental rather than substantive focus."[1]

The dichotomy between policy analysis and policy research is similar to that between applied and pure research. Applied research seeks to apply knowledge and truths, whereas pure or basic research seeks knowledge without concern for its application.[2] Policy analysts, however, seek to compare alternative policies for addressing problems through what David Weimer has termed "neutral competence." This is defined as bringing to bear "appropriate methods for assessing problems and predicting the consequences of policy alternatives as well as neutrality in choosing and arguing for the social values that provide a basis for comparison." Further, he notes that "neutral competence does not mean 'value free.' . . . Rather, it means identifying policy impacts that affect values held by any members of society."[3]

The PPBS Experience

There has always been an uneasy relationship between those who focus on the application of these analytic tools and those who accentuate the substance of the decision before a client. Although Yehezkel Dror's manifesto on the new profession of policy analyst called on these practitioners to reach beyond "a narrow definition of quantitative analysis as a main contribution to treatment of complex issues," there have been instances in the development of the field when policy analysts have operated with a very limited repertoire of analytic tools.[4] As the maxim goes, when you have only a hammer in your toolbox, everything in the world looks like a nail. Over the years, however, the range of techniques has increased, and, at the same time, analysts have become more skeptical about the appropriateness of several of the traditional techniques developed in the early days of the field.

Dror called on the new profession to reach beyond the analytic approach associated with PPBS. Aaron Wildavsky pushed the argument even further and as early as 1968 warned that PPBS was not a helpful enterprise in which to begin the policy analysis activity. Describing the "preconditions" for the use of PPBS in DoD, Wildavsky noted that the system required a small group of talented people who had spent years in the effort and had a common terminology, a collection of analytical approaches, and some inchoate theory to guide them. He also noted that the DoD effort had a top leadership that understood the technique and an organizational commitment to planning.[5]

He warned that "there is grave danger that policy analysis will be rejected along with its particular manifestation in PPBS."[6]

Yet the PPBS experience was so important to the development of the field that it is not surprising that it played a pivotal role in the formative years of the profession. The original conceptualization of the role of the policy analyst was technique-driven. After the demise of PPBS, techniques were drawn from both positivist social science and normative economic models, with the economic models providing the clearest and most powerful basis for an improvement and change orientation.[7] The concept of the "economic man"—the highly rational individual who operates in the broader society as well as inside organizations—was viewed as an important point of departure not only for economists but also for those from other disciplines.[8]

These techniques were nested in the American pragmatic tradition, particularly the one defined by John Dewey, who, though he did not believe in complete objectivity, articulated strong faith in the scientific study of social problems:

> Inquiry must be as nearly contemporaneous as possible; otherwise it is only of antiquarian interest. Knowledge of history is evidently necessary for connectedness of knowledge. But history which is not brought down close to the actual scene of events leaves a gap and exercises influence upon the formation of judgments about the public interest only by guesswork about intervening events. Here, only too conspicuously, is a limitation of the existing social sciences. Their material comes too late, too far after the event, to enter effectively into the formation of public opinion about the immediate public concern and what is to be done about it.[9]

Wildavsky commented, "Policy analysis has its foundations for learning in pragmatism and empiricism. We value what works and we learn what works from experience, particularly experience that magnifies error and failure."[10] Laurence Lynn has suggested that Americans have attempted to apply ideas derived from the social sciences to public problems for some time. He repeats Edwin Shils's comment: "It was the First World War which showed, particularly in the United States, that academic social scientists could be used by governments and by all organizations interested in controlling and modifying human behavior."[11]

In reality, however, economists (particularly microeconomists) appeared to dominate the social science landscape. Few economists were as open as Ralph Turvey in his argument for deference to economists: "My personal feeling is that the value judgments [of economists on discount rates] are, by and large, better than those by non-economists. . . . The point is simply that the people who are experienced at systematic thinking about a problem are usually those who make the best judgment about it."[12]

In his review of the policy analysis field, Peter May summarized some of the arguments against the rational model and its policy analysis applications. The attacks of policy analysts included the following: "reducing complex problems to limited parts by restricting the definition of problems or limiting consequences of interest; . . . focusing on ends while excluding attention to means and historical context; . . . promoting a false sense of value neutrality which masks the inherently normative nature of policy analysis; and . . . embodying an elite model of policymaking for which the desires of analysts can be easily substituted for judgments of elected officials."[13]

Despite the initial goals, optimism, and some skepticism, even the early work on policy analysts in the federal bureaucracy indicated that the concept of policy analysis, once put into place, yielded a more diverse set of roles, functions, and techniques than had been imagined. Arnold Meltsner's study of policy analysts in the bureaucracy, which was based on interviews completed in the years 1970–71, indicated that the policy analysis function took multiple shapes as it interacted with the realities of client idiosyncrasies, organizational cultures and histories, and the special attributes of particular policy issues.[14] Meltsner found that analysts differed in their use of political and technical skills and that they did not have uniform educational backgrounds, policy areas of interest, incentives, or views about the role and impact of the function in the policymaking process. But despite the differentiation in practice, the economists' framework, drawn from the market model, continued to dominate.

Cost-Benefit Analysis: The Economist's Tool of Choice

The choice of analytic approach often depends on the disciplinary background of the individual analyst. Not surprisingly, the predominance of economists during the early days of the field accentuated the use of cost-benefit analysis. This approach was actually borrowed from a project focus (dealing with water projects in the US Army Corps of Engineers) to apply to policy issues. The logic of the analytic approach is appealing—one can quantify the value of both costs and benefits and determine whether a proposed option offers the most efficient path for addressing the problem at hand. As one commentator noted, cost-benefit analysis "is deceptively simple. One adds up the costs of a program, then its benefits. Next, costs are subtracted from benefits. If several options are being considered, the one with the greatest *net* benefit should be selected."[15]

There is a range of technical problems involved in the application of the cost-benefit approach.[16] Identifying and monetizing relevant effects and discounting for time and risk are much easier to accomplish when one is faced with a decision about building or not building a specific dam than when the decision involves a program administered by fifty different states. Even then, as Daniel Mazmanian and Jeanne Nienaber point out, the technique is often less clear-cut than it appears at first blush. The entrance of the environmental movement into the decision environment of the Army Corps of Engineers forced that agency to think about decisions that had value conflicts surrounding them.[17] When environmental advocates began to do their own adversarial cost-benefit analyses, it became very clear that the federal government was facing policy choices involving value disputes, not simply technical determinations.

The Corps of Engineers, according to Mazmanian and Nienaber, began to realize that cost-benefit analysis was not as objective as it had once appeared to be. In practice,

> the accurate estimate of benefits and costs is extremely hard to determine even when the basic concept is not challenged. . . . For example, neither the benefits nor the costs of a flood control project accrue at a single point in time but rather over the life of the project. Benefits and costs must then be apportioned accordingly. But since the actual life of a project is uncertain, how are benefits and costs to be apportioned? The Corps' solution has been to choose either 50 or 100 years as the life of its projects. This serves as a useful basis for computation, but nevertheless it is an arbitrary one.[18]

Lynn notes that there are cases in which sophisticated cost-benefit analysis is relevant but of limited significance. He quotes a study of the influence of analysis in the Department of the Interior to make his point:

> Judicial review of the planning process for [the outer continental shelf] lease sales has given the Department of the Interior an unusual freedom to use cost-benefit analysis as a major factor in balancing competing congressional objectives [in deciding on the number of lease sales to hold in a given planning area]. The results . . . indicate that while there is a statistical relationship between cost-benefit measures and the expected number of sales, the net social value measure must change by an impractically large

number to cause a change in the expected number of sales for a given planning area."[19]

When applied to policy areas such as health, education, and welfare, the problems are even more difficult. In testimony before the Joint Economic Committee of Congress in 1968, William Gorham, the first head of the policy office at the Department of Health, Education, and Welfare, described the dilemma:

> Let me hasten to point out that we have not attempted any grandiose cost-benefit analysis designed to reveal whether the total benefits from an additional million dollars spent on health programs would be higher or lower than that from an additional million spent on education or welfare. If I was ever naive enough to think this sort of analysis possible, I no longer am. The benefits of health, education, and welfare programs are diverse and often intangible. They affect different age groups and different regions of the population over different periods of time. No amount of analysis is going to tell us whether the Nation benefits more from sending a slum child to preschool, providing medical care to an old man or enabling a disabled housewife to resume her normal activities. The "grand decisions"—how much health, how much education, how much welfare and which groups in the population shall benefit—are questions of value judgments and politics. The analyst cannot make much contribution to their resolution.[20]

For some economists, however, efficiency values continue to drive decisions. The concern about efficiency was assumed almost unconsciously and believed to constitute the promotion of the welfare of society.[21] Hank Jenkins-Smith characterized the use of efficiency as a "metavalue" and argued that it "is the pursuit of value maximization—and takes as given the particular values pursued by citizens or public officials."[22]

This mindset was so embedded in the normative economic paradigm that the cost-benefit technique was viewed as a value-free, neutral, and objective analytic approach. Cost-benefit analysis became the analytic technique of choice and found its way into decision processes in government. During the 1970s and 1980s the California Legislative Analyst's Office automatically performed cost-benefit studies of all legislation before the legislature and reported its analyses to the Assembly's Ways and Means Committee. Cost-benefit analyses were required in the federal government in the 1970s and 1980s for all proposed regulations to be issued by agencies. At one point, the World Bank required a cost-benefit analysis of all proposed projects.

To a large extent, the cost-benefit approach presented many of the same problems that had confronted those who used the PPBS technique. It was not possible to find a common denominator for very diverse values and players. Many policies did not have clear ends–means relationships, and a choice of a particular option was not much more "scientific" than choices that came from tossing dice. Policies rarely had simple goals; even a narrow decision about whether to construct a building had a range of objectives attached to it. The building was expected to function efficiently for its explicit purposes, but it was also expected to be built without negative effects on the environment and to be constructed through the creation of jobs for an otherwise underserved segment of the population.

Increasingly, those who used the cost-benefit approach began to recognize its limitations. The calculation of costs and benefits and definition of externalities depended on the values of the client (or—in some cases—of the analyst). The technique could not encompass the vagaries of implementation problems and complexities. Even when an analyst backed away from quantifying costs and benefits and described relationships in qualitative terms, the value conflicts were almost overpowering. Though the technique does have analytic power and provides an analyst with a logical way to think about an issue and establish a framework for value trade-offs, it becomes a risky business to present a recommendation only in the language of the cost-benefit technique. Vining and Weimer have noted that it is particularly difficult to apply the cost-benefit analysis to social policies because the technique raises a number of challenges. They note that uncertainty is problematic and that it is difficult to predict and value behaviors. In addition, social policy areas often involve distributional goals that do not fit easily into the analytic technique.[23]

Lucian Pugliaresi and Diane Berliner point out that cost-benefit and other quantitative and rigorous analytical treatments are often used in agencies such as the Environmental Protection Agency by young analysts with superior and highly technical analytical skills. However, these techniques are very difficult to apply in cases of issues that are broad in scope with extremely difficult trade-offs and large uncertainties.[24]

Experiencing what could be described as an analytic variation of the Rashomon effect (where it is not possible to establish a true sense of an occurrence but only report the various perspectives on that event), groups like the California Legislative Analyst's Office backed away from the use of the cost-benefit technique. Though they continued to do cost estimates, the difficulties found in the valuation of benefits made the technique of limited utility. A series of court decisions involving the federal government questioned the reliance by the White House Office of Management and Budget (OMB) on this analytic approach in several environmental policy areas. According to several legal scholars, OMB's use of the cost-benefit technique raised "serious legal and policy questions":[25] "Under United States administrative law, may OMB play this role [of regulatory traffic cop] and may agencies engage in cost-benefit analysis? Some environmental statutes permit such an analysis, while others explicitly preclude it. In both situations, OMB has reportedly applied cost-benefit analysis. Further, is cost-benefit analysis helpful in formulating complex environmental policy? . . . Cost-benefit analysis in regulatory decision making yields some benefits in rulemaking, in terms of streamlining the process and creating a structure for decision making, but it is not clear that such analysis complies with administrative law principles in all situations."[26]

Other Rational Analysis Techniques

When some analysts used other methodologies besides cost-benefit analysis that had been developed either for the private sector or for the defense establishment, they also confronted problems. Flow charts and decision trees—borrowed from the systems analysis field—could be helpful as long as there was an agreement on the goals of the policy and analysts could figure out what they were trying to maximize. But they were not very useful when policies had multiple and conflicting goals embedded within them and there was no surrogate for maximizing profit.

Impact analysis was one analytic approach that was not borrowed from the private sector; it is a form of analysis that attempts to relate what may be seen as two or more seemingly separate policy tracks. Though impact analysis has been used in several areas, it is best known in the environmental field. Use of the environmental impact statement continues to be fairly widespread and requires analysts to look at the environmental effects of decisions such as building a new prison. Congress mandated the use of environmental impact statements when it passed the National Environmental Policy Act of 1969. This was one of the few times when a legislative body has required the use of a particular analytic approach. The concept of impact analysis has been used in other areas as well—for example, to determine whether policies directed toward one set of goals may have negative effects on specific client groups (e.g., children or the elderly).

Congress also relied on a rational analytic approach when it established a decision process related to military base closings that sought to avoid the politics of such decisions. Because members of Congress were usually unwilling to support base closings in their own districts, the decision process that was adopted in 1989 constrained the ability of members to vote on separate base-closing decisions. Rather, the process established adoption rules that required members to vote on DoD's recommendations as an entire package. The base-closing analytical process involved the establishment of what DoD defined as a "metric or a family of metrics. Each metric is a ratio that expresses an indicator of capacity (maneuver base acres, facility square feet, etc.) with a relevant measure of US-based force structure (maneuver brigades, personnel spaces assigned, etc.) in 1989."[27] Separate metrics were established for each of the three branches of the armed services. For example, the methodology adopted for the US Army included eight categories: administration; depots; industrial; major training areas—US Army Reserves; major training areas—active; maneuvers; schools; and test and evaluation and laboratories. The model that was established for the analysis had much in common with a classic cost-benefit analysis; however, the criteria that were calculated in the analysis were both more detailed and more explicit.[28]

Analytic Techniques for Complex Political Issues

The traditional rational analytic approaches are often difficult to apply to policy problems where there are multiple actors, conflicting views, and limited formal information sources. Several techniques have been used in this type of situation to provide an analyst with systematic but qualitative approaches to think about a policy problem. Two such techniques are described here: policy mapping and criteria analysis.

Policy Mapping

Policy mapping is a process that has been used to define the context, actors, and relationships that allow the analyst to both understand the problem and develop ways to address it. It is a technique that is appropriately used relatively early in the policy analysis process that provides the analyst with a way to define multiple perspectives involved in the issue. It is a way of operationalizing a systems analysis approach of both taking apart a system and putting it back together. One of the earliest expressions of such a map was developed by Donald Schon in 1970.[29] Schon devised a map of what he called the "blindness system"—the interrelated network of people, organizations, rules, and activities that make up a complex of fragmented and disorganized institutions.

During the past several decades, variations on this theme have been devised and the concept of "mapping" is now found both in domestic policy analysis in the United States and in locations in other parts of the world. It is a way to acknowledge that public policy issues rarely involve only government actors; the process includes not only the clients of a program but also various nongovernmental actors. In this sense, it is a way for a policy analyst to try to make sense of the fluid networks that are operative today.

Patrick Dobel and Angela Day developed what they call "A Note on Mapping: Understanding Who Can Influence Your Success," a teaching resource issued by the Electronic Hallway of the Evans School of Public Affairs at the University of Washington.[30] They described their approach as follows:

> To achieve personal and managerial goals, you need a mind's eye map of the political environment in which you are operating. Political environments are characterized by complex and interconnected centers of power and authority, which convey resources and support for your organization, as well as opposition to your mission and organization. Operating within these complexities requires constant attention to a dynamic authorizing environment in order to maintain the viability of your organization. Mapping can become the tool by which you identify the important factors and forces within your environment that may help or hinder the achievement of your mission. A map possesses the advantage of a quick visual reference that can convey a lot of information quickly. There is no single best way to map an organizational environment, but the most effective maps are constructed with a given issue or scenario in mind.[31]

Further, they note that a well-constructed map places actors in the context of their pressures, interests, and relationships; permits the actors to understand the political and institutional interdependencies of their organization and mission; precedes strategic action and evolves as the actors encounter new and different scenarios; and reminds the actors to focus on building the human and institutional relationships that sustain organizational competence and generate the authority needed to convert good ideas and intent into effective strategic action.

Although Dobel and Day acknowledge that maps will take many different forms, they do provide a sample map that can become a point of departure for an analyst. Thus, figure 6.1 includes actors that are policymakers/legislators, resource controllers, media, clients served, staff and contractors, interest groups, constituents, and courts.

Figure 6.1   Map of the Political Environment

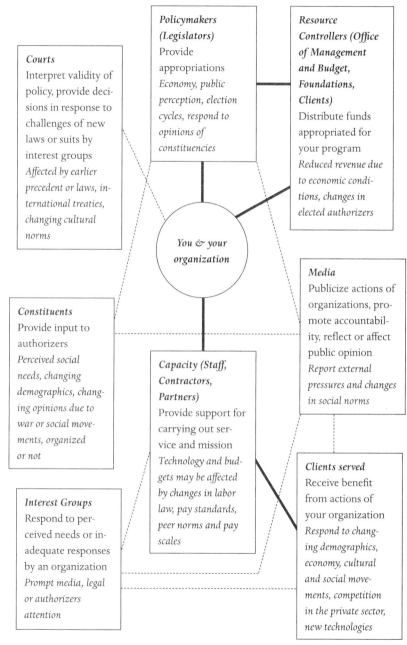

Source: J. Patrick Dobel and Angela Day, "A Note on Mapping: Understanding Who Can Influence Your Success," The Electronic Hallway, Evans School of Public Affairs, University of Washington, Seattle, 2005. Reprinted by permission.

Criteria Analysis

The technique of criteria analysis is particularly useful to a policy analyst when he or she is attempting to choose between alternatives but acknowledges that the criteria that would be used to make that choice are multiple, different from one another in terms of values, and difficult to quantify. However, this technique does allow the analyst to confront the trade-offs that must be made between four different categories of criteria: cost, effectiveness, political feasibility, and implementability. The process requires the analyst to examine each proposed alternative or option separately by determining how well it achieves each of the criteria elements.

Criteria are most effectively defined in specific terms and when the preferred state is made explicit. For example, cost criteria might include who bears the cost, direct or indirect costs, or short-term or long-term costs. Effectiveness criteria would be defined in terms of achieving the goals of the effort. Political feasibility would determine the relevant actors, as well as their motivations, strategies, resources, and arguments. And implementability would focus on the actor with the responsibility and authority to implement, the relationship between new responsibilities and existing work, staff capacity, resources available, the time frame, and leadership potential.

Analysts are challenged to nominate criteria and then to determine weights for each. These weights would represent the perspective of the analyst's client. Similarly, the process requires analysts to define options or alternatives that are appropriate for the client and make sure that all the options represent the client's views. Figure 6.2 represents a model grid that might be used to organize the information in such a situation.

Figure 6.2   Criteria Analysis Format

FAMILES OF CRITERIA	OPTION 1	OPTION 2	OPTION 3
Cost			
Effectiveness			
Political Feasibility			
Implementability			

The Development of Policy Evaluation

As was noted in chapter 2, policy evaluation and policy analysis became closely interrelated in the 1970s. Although evaluation as a field of practice predated the policy analysis field, it came from a different intellectual tradition than the economics-based world of the policy analyst. Evaluators were at work in the late 1930s and early 1940s, looking at the impact of educational programs on student performance.[32] During this period, evaluations also were conducted of programs in health, organizational sociology, industrial psychology, and educational testing and measurement. These efforts reflected the developments in the behavioral and social sciences, with important breakthroughs in research design, data collection, and data analysis. They were embedded in the positivist tradition and sought to replicate the logic and methods of the natural sciences to understand human behavior. The laboratory model and the development of controlled experiments allowed an analyst/evaluator to test the truth or falsity of a hypothesis. Like the original application of the cost-benefit technique, early evaluations were focused on specific interventions or projects rather than broad policy approaches.

By the 1960s and 1970s, however, there was increased interest in determining whether the new national programs that had been created in almost every domestic policy area were effective. Some programs were constructed around ideas of action research where evaluator/researchers were expected to operate hand in glove with program managers, providing regular feedback to the managers about the effectiveness of their efforts.[33] Congress built evaluation requirements into several large federal programs, and funds were allocated to conduct these evaluations. However, while calling for "evaluation," the legislative body did not specify what type of evaluation would be performed. At the Department of Health, Education, and Welfare, for example, 1 percent of funds for some programs (largely health programs) were set aside to support evaluation, but many types of studies were included under that umbrella.[34] Broadening the focus of evaluation away from projects to policy spawned an incredible growth in what some have called the *evaluation industry*. The funds that were available provided many social scientists with the opportunity to test their theories of human behavior.

Although evaluation took place after programs were in operation (postanalysis) and policy analysis focused on analysis of programs before they were created (preanalysis), the two worlds meshed by the 1970s. This merging was reinforced by the shifts in the policy analysis field away from the creation of new programs to the analysis of existing programs. Policy analysis offices, such as the Office of the Assistant Secretary for Planning and

Evaluation in the US Department of Health and Human Services, included both types of staff working side by side. The large-scale demonstration efforts that had begun in the Office of Economic Opportunity were devised to test models and theories of normative economists by using classic social science methodologies.

By the 1980s, however, the bloom was off the classic social science evaluation rose. Increasingly, evaluators were finding that decision makers were not responding to their findings. Indeed, Harold Wilensky termed the response to evaluation "Wilensky's Law" and posed it as "the more evaluation, the less program development; the more demonstration projects, the less follow-through."[35] Concern about utilization preoccupied the field for some time in what could be seen as the evaluator's variation on the clash between the cultures of politics and analysis. As funds became tighter, they found that it was important to fine-tune evaluations in ways that could meet the day-to-day needs of the decision makers. In some areas, particularly education, Congress actually built in evaluation requirements as part of the reauthorization process. These requirements were timed to match a natural life-cycle stage when legislation expires and programs must be reauthorized in order to continue. This part of the legislative process creates the closest thing to a feedback loop in the policy process.[36]

Techniques such as evaluability assessment were devised to determine whether full-blown evaluations of program outcomes were warranted.[37] There was a move away from techniques drawn from classic social science to focus on more modest efforts that might be helpful to program administrators or legislators. The shift was away from evaluation approaches that sought to answer broad-impact questions to evaluation efforts that met the concerns of program managers.

Indeed, by 1989 the evaluation field had migrated quite far away from its origins. In what was called fourth-generation evaluation, evaluation was treated not as a scientific process but as a social, political, and value-oriented enterprise.[38] Egon Cuba and Yvonna Lincoln argued that measurement activities characterized the first generation of the field, description the second, and judgment the third. Though they believed that each succeeding generation represented a step forward, they found that the evaluation activity continued to be disempowering, unfair, and disenfranchising to those who must use the results of the evaluation work.[39]

This is not to suggest, however, that there is agreement about the dimensions and directions of the policy evaluation field. Dale Krane has described two categories of current controversies in policy evaluation: (1) methods wars (quantitative vs. qualitative data, internal vs. external validity, and experimental vs. statistical control), and (2) contests over purpose (the function of evaluation, the choice of evaluative criteria, and evaluation and accountability).[40]

Lisbeth Schorr characterized the problem as a polarization of two camps: the experimentalists and the inclusionists. The experimentalists focus only on evidence that comes out of experimental evaluations, whereas the inclusionists look to evidence that is drawn from both practice and nonevaluation research. She seeks to find ways for the two camps to come to an agreement around four principles: Begin with a results framework, match evaluation methods to their purposes, draw on evidence from multiple sources, and identify core components of successful interventions.[41]

The question of evaluation and accountability has become more salient as members of the public and politicians have called for the production of information that assesses program performance. This requires evaluators to move away from approaches that emphasize the processes of program management and toward data that focus on the outcomes of these program efforts. To some extent, the current interest in performance measurement represents a return to the performance budgeting agenda of the early PPBS effort. It suggests that—at least rhetorically—decision makers are willing to cede their assessment of the effectiveness of programs to analysts and evaluators.

Other Tools

The range of tools now available to the policy analyst is very eclectic. One set of tools has developed from the technological advances that have been made over the past thirty years. The accessibility of computers has meant that analysts who in the past had to rely on others for data can now create their own data systems. Similarly, raw data from organizations such as the Census Bureau are now easily available.

As was described in chapter 4, both public and private organizations now have modeling capacities that allow them to be self-reliant and develop microsimulations. The technological developments have allowed this to occur without huge investments. Both the California Legislative Analysts' Office and the Congressional Research Service are now able to develop their own data systems and produce analysis that does not rely on data from the executive branch. The Heritage Foundation also has its own data system that allows it to be analytically independent. The Center on Budget and Policy Research has not created its own primary data sources, but it has commissioned survey research that addresses policy issues defined by its perspective.

Although primary data have become more accessible, policy analysts have also learned that information can be found in other places as well. Eugene Bardach has noted that the methods of data collection for policy analysts should not be "entirely coincident with those used in the social sciences."[42] Bardach suggested that the appropriate techniques for the policy analyst are closer to those of the journalist than they are to social science research. Skills involving interviewing, use of the telephone, use of the internet, and analysis of secondary data can be the most useful set of tools.

Policy analysts are thus challenged to be creative in the ways they look for information. To some extent, they become information brokers, who find ways to exchange information from diverse sources and identify what may have been nontraditional sources of data. As analysts have become more attuned to issues of policy and program implementation, they have found that the data attached to the implementation process have become more useful. Implementation information has been utilized by the Congressional Research Service, the California Legislative Analyst's Office, the Center on Budget and Policy Priorities, and the Office of the Assistant Secretary for Planning and Evaluation in the US Department of Health and Human Services.

The "Classic" Policy Analysis Framework and Its Critics

Whatever the analytic tool chosen, policy analysts have tended to follow a logical model that defines the analytic process. To some degree, this process is a variation of the classic rational planning framework that provides a structure for examining an issue. Bardach has termed this classic process "the eight-step path" and has defined its steps as follows:[43]

- Define the problem.
- Assemble some evidence.
- Construct the alternatives.
- Select the criteria.
- Project the outcomes.
- Confront the trade-offs.
- Decide.
- Tell your story.

Bardach and others have defined substeps within this framework. For example, many analysts have found that the definition of the policy problem is a very tricky enterprise, requiring individuals to acknowledge that problem definition is rarely an objective entity in its own right.[44] In addition, attention to the dimensions of the policy environment and its history is often viewed as an important aspect of the process. Often, analysts are encouraged to spend time thinking about the organizational and conceptual "map" that surrounds an issue.

However, analysts have circumvented or terminated the process at one or another step. Some analysts do not move beyond the mapping of the issues for the client. Others do not believe that it is appropriate for them to craft detailed options or to make recommendations for a decision. When a policy analysis organization such as the Congressional Research Service or the California Legislative Analyst's Office operates in a highly charged partisan political setting, it is not expected to move to the recommendation stage. It tends to avoid pushing the process to the decision process or what others may view as its next logical step.

Resistance to traveling the entire eight-step path comes from several sources. It may stem from the analytic abilities of the analyst, the intractability of the policy issue under scrutiny, or the expectations of the client. But perhaps the most basic resistance to this approach stems from those who have quite different ways of conceptualizing the intellectual framework of the policy analysis task. Perhaps the most compelling approach has come from Giandomenico Majone, who has substituted the idea of argument and evidence for the approach that has its roots in an applied social science frame. For some who see themselves as applied social scientists, the term "applied" relates to the subject of the analysis, not to the role played by the analyst. Majone and others call on the analyst to play the role of participant and mediator rather than objective scientist. Majone writes: "Argumentation is the key process through which citizens and policymakers arrive at moral judgments and policy choices. Public discussion mobilizes the knowledge, experience, and interest of many people, while focusing their attention on a limited range of issues. Each participant is encouraged to adjust his view of reality, and even to change his values, as a result of the process of reciprocal persuasion. In this way, discussion can produce results that are beyond the capabilities of authoritarian or technocratic methods of policymaking."[45]

Yet it is not always clear where this approach leads. Does it move toward a legal or judicial advocacy posture, or does it push analysts to acknowledge that other participants have different views on the issue?

Other formulations have also been offered that challenge the applied social science approach. Richard Neustadt and Ernest May have emphasized the importance of history in the analytic process, and Thomas Kaplan and others have employed the use of a narrative or story to present and explain a complex situation over time.[46] Both approaches are viewed as a way of providing a sense of the richness of meaning and detail involved that it is not possible to provide with other analytical forms. The critics of these approaches are concerned about the lack of standards in these types of analyses and the inability to determine that one interpretation is better than another.

But perhaps the most sweeping attack on the origins of the policy analysis field has come from the group of theorists who are a part of the critical theory tradition and emphasize interpretive approaches. The proponents of the interpretive approach argue that the rational analytical (or positivist) approach to the field "should be replaced with studies of the meanings that different persons bring to the policy process, the arguments used to legitimate policies, and the hidden assumptions or implications of the policy."[47] Few of these proponents have actually done analysis themselves or recognize the day-to-day demands of the profession. These individuals, such as Robert Denhardt, have rested their critique of the policy analysis field on the construct of the early period and have ignored the developments that have occurred since that time. Denhardt, for example, wrote that "policy analysis depends solely upon those 'value-free' techniques common to mainstream social science, the results inevitably support the existing 'facts' of political and administrative life, including existing patterns of control."[48] This set of concerns tends to limit the field to the model of activity found in DoD in the 1960s and ignores the variety of analytic organizations and practices that are found today. Some of these critics have emphasized what they believe to be antidemocratic or politically biased approaches that rely on the statements of experts.

There have been attempts to develop a middle course dealing with these criticisms. For example, while Duncan MacRae Jr. has acknowledged some of the criticisms of the postmodernists and critical theory proponents, he has sought what he calls a "middle ground between notions of a completely autonomous science and one that is malleable and undemocratic—by granting the claims of science where they seem justified, and acknowledging bias and rhetoric where they play a larger part."[49]

Defining Success

Whereas some analysts continued to define their success in terms of the impact of their analytic work on specific societal problems, others have clearly developed different goals for their work. Analysts valued their ability to influence decision makers and to sustain that influence over time.[50] Goals thus became more modest in scope and, at the same time, reflected an awareness of the multiplicity of subgoals contained in programs. Analysts often recognized the complexities involved in the implementation of their recommendations and moved to rethink the way they structured problems and thought about policy design.[51] Overall, few analysts held the simple, optimistic view of the achievement of an applied social science that was both scientifically rigorous and practical.

As Wildavsky noted in a retrospective look at policy analysis, the "macromacho" view of the endeavor, highlighting microeconomics and operations research, did not deliver on its promises. For analysts, he commented, "the real loss was innocence."[52] Another commentator noted that the metaphors of science and disinterested research have given way to "the metaphor of the market and its corollaries of promotion, advocacy, and intellectual combat."[53]

A Variety of Skills

Recruitment patterns over the years broadened the methodological approaches used by analysts; an early reliance on models and paradigms associated with economics training and operations research was complemented by other approaches. Many analysts found that their specific program knowledge was the most valued skill. Others emphasized implementation analysis, organizational analysis, and methods associated with policy evaluation tasks.[54]

As the field of policy analysis and policy studies developed, students and practitioners of the profession became more sophisticated in the way they described and understood the dimensions of the policymaking process. Whether they were optimistic or pessimistic about the long-term impact of policy analysis in the federal bureaucracy, there was a growing consensus that a model based on an assumption that decision making actually followed the formal hierarchical structure of the organization chart had limited applicability (indeed, to some, was naive). The accumulation of experience taught the analysts that the process needed to be understood in the complex context of multiple actors, levels of meaning, and external pressures that created policy systems.[55] When one realizes the constraints that emerge from these policy systems, it spawns a form of intellectual modesty that places the role of the analyst in perspective. Meaning thus comes as much from the process of searching for "truth" as from the answer that emerges from the search.

Martin Rein also reminded us that much of what is accomplished by policy analysts has a distinctly personal overlay:

It is useful to distinguish between matters of style and questions of substance. Style affects the content of analysis and its mode of presentation.
Two policy analysts who share a very similar value perspective may nevertheless interpret events quite differently because their styles diverge. The
matter of style is personal and idiosyncratic. . . . Some analysts are opti-
mists; they enjoy calling attention to what is possible. They seek to identify
the constraints which can be modified and the areas where accord about
ethical disagreements can be reached. By contrast, others are attracted to
the kind of analysis which exposes weakness in institutions. They enjoy
documenting the failure to achieve shared goals and displaying the underlying contradictions and conflicting interests that inhibit agreement. It is
through style that perversity or disagreeableness, graciousness or consideration, cynicism, scepticism, optimism, and other dimensions of personal-
ity, temperament and belief find expression.[56]

As Meltsner's early work on policy analysts in government indicated, analysts were expected to draw on both technical and political skills. However,
Meltsner found that during those early years most analysts were likely to fall
back on technical skills.[57] By the 1990s, however, the list of skill areas that
were relevant to a skilled policy analyst had become much more extensive.
Policy analysts—or at least teams of policy analysts—could be expected to
have facility in the following:

- case study methods
- cost-benefit analysis
- ethical analysis
- evaluation
- futures analysis
- historical analysis
- implementation analysis
- interviewing
- legal analysis
- microeconomics
- negotiation, mediation
- operations research
- organizational analysis
- political feasibility analysis
- public speaking
- small-group facilitation
- specific program knowledge

- statistics
- survey research methods
- systems analysis

Robert Nelson, a longtime staff member in the policy office of the Department of the Interior, has noted that in his experience "the mathematical econometric, and other more sophisticated techniques of the social sciences are frequently out of place and inapplicable in the world of government policymaking. . . . It is possible for many people to obtain an intellectual understanding of the key concepts of policy analysis in a few short courses; it nevertheless may take years to become a committed economist or policy analyst in the full professional sense."[58]

At the same time, there is increased interest in what has been termed "evidence based" policymaking. This is an effort to combine quantitative and formal information with information from the world of practice. It highlights what has been called the "promise" of data-driven policymaking.[59] It is described as a way to meet demands that agencies use the best information available. Jennings and Hall have noted that "amid ongoing demands for government accountability and performance, there is strong pressure to use practices based on effectiveness evidence."[60] They observe, however, that there is disagreement on what constitutes evidence across policymakers and administrators.

As policy analysts have become increasingly specialized in particular policy areas, specific program knowledge has become even more important. More than half of both the past and present policy analysts in the Office of the Assistant Secretary for Planning and Evaluation have indicated that specific program knowledge was the most essential skill for a policy analyst.[61] Most of the policy analysis organizations are organized on the basis of subject-area specialty, not on the basis of technique or approach to analytic problems. Policy analysts also learned that it was important for them to understand the processes of government (how decisions are made) as well as the substantive content of the decisions. There appears to be a shift in the field of practice from recruitment of individuals with knowledge of analytical techniques to individuals who begin with knowledge of a particular sector and then discover analytic approaches.

The Work Environment

Though the subject is rarely discussed, one gets the sense that in the early phases of the profession, it was assumed that policy analysts would spend much of their time working alone, as they would have done working for a research or academic organization. Though they might be assigned to work teams, the work they accomplished in the privacy of their offices would be transmitted through written reports first to the work group and then to decision makers, who would draw on the skills of the policy analyst as technician. This image does not describe the practice today, although some policy analysts would prefer the cloistered think-tank model.

Most policy analysts work in teams, either in interdisciplinary groups drawn from staff with various skills located in the policy analysis institution or in task forces that involve individuals beyond the policy analysis organization. Thus individuals are required to have interactive skills, know how to work in a group setting, engender trust and collaboration among the participants, and deal with multiple perspectives on a problem. Analysts who work in organizations such as the Twentieth Century Fund find that they must be able to convene groups that will work on a policy issue. Their role is one of facilitator rather than expert.

Because these teams often include individuals who are concerned about the details of operating a program, policy analysts are placed in situations where knowledge of the implementation details of a program becomes extremely valuable. Organizations such as the California Legislative Analyst's Office, the Center on Budget and Policy Priorities, and the Congressional Research Service have instituted hiring patterns that accentuate the importance of staff members who have knowledge of implementation realities.

In addition, policy analysts in multiple settings increasingly transmit their work in oral as well as in simple written forms. Skills in public speaking and oral presentations are valued, and analysts are required to present their findings in short, pithy formats to busy decision makers. It is an art form to be able to develop briefing materials that highlight the essential issues without reducing the findings to simplistic dimensions. Rarely does a decision maker want to see the detailed analysis that provided the backdrop for the presentation.

Policy analysis institutions clearly value the ability of analysts to write without jargon and present complex ideas clearly. Organizations such as the Center on Budget and Policy Priorities and the Heritage Foundation see themselves as bridges between policymakers, their specific constituencies, and the research community. Organizations that have to deal with highly politicized client settings (e.g., the Congressional Research Service and the California Legislative Analyst's Office) are especially conscious of the importance of using language in a way that minimizes bias. David Lyon, the president of the California Policy Institute and for many years a top official of the RAND Corporation, has noted that jobs in the field are increasingly for "people to write pithy, ideologically slanted briefs to sell a partisan position."[62]

Policy analysis organizations appear to recognize that the socialization of staff is important and have invested in this process. Though valuing the rigorous training of graduates of public policy schools in economics and quantitative analysis, some organizations (e.g., the Congressional Research Service) assume that younger staff members have to learn to be more attentive to the biases that are implicit in normative economics training. Dealing with clients with many different political agendas requires a policy analyst to be particularly careful in presenting a balanced perspective on an issue without consciously or unconsciously projecting a preferred alternative.

A Repertoire of Tools

Because policy analysts today play so many different roles, they are required to have a wide repertoire of tools to use or purchase as they practice their profession. Wildavsky wrote that analysis has many different faces—it is descriptive, prescriptive, selective, objective, argumentative, retrospective, inventive, prospective, and subjective:

> Analysis is *descriptive* in that it is designed to explain how a difficulty has come about. Analysis is *prescriptive* in that it aims to give advice on what should be done. Analysis must be *selective*, therefore, in that it is oriented to particular people (in specific slots within locatable levels of an organization) who have the authority, money, and other resources required to do what is recommended. Analysis may be *objective* by getting people to agree on the consequences of a variety of alternatives. Insofar as it is relevant to future choices, however, analysis inevitably is *argumentative*, leaning toward this view and rejecting that other one. The ability to rationalize is not to be rejected once it is recognized that the capacity to convince is essential for social support. Analysis is *retrospective* because it involves establishing a view of the past (this is why we need change) that will justify a desired future. But . . . analysis is *inventive*, representing a creative juxtaposition between resources and objectives. Analysis is *prospective*, seeking its rewards

in the future, which is always in doubt. Analysis must also be subjective, therefore, in that the choice of problems to be solved, as well as the alternatives considered, is not specified but must be worked out by particular people with individual interests [emphasis in the original].[63]

Wildavsky constantly reminded us that policy analysis is more than the technical ability to use formal analytic tools. He argued that the strengths of the field lie in its ability to "make a little knowledge go a long way by combining an understanding of the constraints of the situation with the ability to explore the environment constructively."[64] It is, indeed, an art form that makes incredible demands on its practitioners.

Klein and Marmor have commented that there is a case for eclecticism. They note: "In practice, no public policy analyst can use all the tools of the trade all the time: a rational choice analyst in the morning, a psycho-biographer in the afternoon, a historian in the evening, and a political theorist in the hours when sleep does not come. . . . Trying to understand and explain public policy as a whole—making sense of what governments do, rather than analysing specific election results or policy outputs—has to be, in our view, an exercise in synthesis."[65]

Notes

1. Aidan R. Vining and David L. Weimer, "Policy Analysis," in *The Foundations of Public Administration, Public Administrative Review* (2010): 1–2.

2. See Norma M. Riccucci, *Public Administration: Traditions of Inquiry and Philosophies of Knowledge* (Washington, DC: Georgetown University Press, 2010), 50.

3. David L. Weimer, "Institutionalizing Neutrally Competent Policy Analysis: Resources for Promoting Objectivity and Balance in Consolidating Democracies," *Policy Studies Journal* 33, no. 2 (2005): 132.

4. Yehezkel Dror, *Ventures in Policy Sciences* (New York: Elsevier, 1971), 228.

5. Aaron Wildavsky, "Rescuing Policy Analysis from PPBS," in *Classics of Public Administration*, 3rd ed., edited by Jay M. Shafritz and Albert C. Hyde (Belmont, CA: Wadsworth, 1968), 320–31.

6. Ibid., 320.

7. Henry J. Aaron, *Politics and the Professors: The Great Society in Perspective* (Washington, DC: Brookings Institution Press, 1989).

8. See American Academy of Political and Social Science, *Integration of the Social Sciences through Policy Analysis*, Monograph 14 (Philadelphia: American Academy of Political and Social Science, 1972).

9. John Dewey, *The Public and Its Problems* (Chicago: Swallow Press, 1927), 179.

10. Aaron Wildavsky, *Speaking Truth to Power: The Art and Craft of Policy Analysis* (Boston: Little, Brown, 1979), 393.

11. E. A. Shils, "Social Science and Social Policy," *Philosophy of Science* 16 (1949): 222, quoted by Laurence E. Lynn Jr., "Policy Analysis in the Bureaucracy: How New? How Effective?" *Journal of Policy Analysis and Management* 8, no. 3 (1989): 374.

12. Ralph Turvey, quoted by Wildavsky, *Speaking Truth to Power*, 180.

13. Peter J. May, "Policy Analysis: Past, Present, and Future," *International journal of Public Administration* 21, nos. 6–8 (1998): 1093.

14. Arnold J. Meltsner, *Policy Analysts in the Bureaucracy* (Berkeley: University of California Press, 1986).

15. Robert A. Heineman, William T. Bluhm, Steven A. Peterson, and Edward N. Kearny, *The World of the Policy Analysis: Rationality, Values and Politics* (Chatham, NJ: Chatham House, 1990), 45.

16. An extremely useful summary of these problems is given by David L. Weimer and Aidan R. Vining, *Policy Analysis: Concepts and Practice*, 2nd ed. (Englewood Cliffs, N.J.: Prentice Hall, 1992), chap. 9.

17. Daniel A. Mazmanian and Jeanne Nienaber, *Can Organizations Change? Environmental Protection, Citizen Participation, and the Corps of Engineers* (Washington, DC: Brookings Institution Press, 1979).

18. Ibid., 15.

19. Lynn, "Policy Analysis," 375.

20. Quoted by Wildavsky, "Rescuing Policy Analysis," 325–26.

21. These values are expressed by Edith Stokey and Richard Zeckhauser, *A Primer for Policy Analysis* (New York: W. W. Norton, 1978), perhaps the earliest of the policy analysis textbooks used in policy analysis introductory classes.

22. Hank C. Jenkins-Smith, *Democratic Politics and Policy Analysis* (Pacific Grove, CA: Brooks/Cole, 1990), 28.

23. Aidan Vining and David L. Weimer, "An Assessment of Important Issues Concerning the Application of Benefit-Cost Analysis to Social Policy," *Journal of Benefit-Cost Analysis* 1, no. 1 (2010), article 6.

24. Lucian Pugliaresi and Diane T. Berliner, "Policy Analysis at the Department of State: The Policy Planning Staff," *Journal of Policy Analysis and Management* 8, no. 3 (1989): 391.

25. Jeffrey H. Howard and Linda E. Benfield, "Rulemaking in the Shadows: The Rise of OMB and Cost-Benefit Analysis in Environmental Decisionmaking," *Columbia Journal of Environmental Law* 16 (1971): 143–77.

26. Ibid., 145.

27. US Department of Defense, *The Report of the Department of Defense on Base Realignment and Closure*, Required by Section 2824 of National Defense Authorization Act for Fiscal Year 1998, Public Law 105–85 (Washington, DC: US Government Printing Office, 1998), 109.

28. The base closing analytic approach has been suggested as a model for other decisions but has yet to move beyond its origins.

29. Donald A. Schon, "The Blindness System," *The Public Interest*, issue 18 (Winter 1970): 25–38.

30. J. Patrick Dobel and Angela Day, "A Note on Mapping: Understanding Who Can Influence Your Success," Electronic Hallway, Evans School of Public Affairs, University of Washington, Seattle, 2005. Another example of a mapping strategy was written by Douglas A. Johnson and Nancy L. Pearson, "Tactical Mapping: How Nonprofits Can Identify the Leers of Change," *NonProfit Quarterly*, Summer 2009, 92–99.

31. Dobel and Day, "Note on Mapping," 1.

32. This discussion draws on Dale Krane, "Disorderly Progress on the Frontiers of Policy Evaluation," *International Journal of Public Administration* 24, no. 1 (2001): 95–123.

33. Some of these efforts predated the Community Action Program of the War on Poverty.

34. The 1 percent set-aside continues to be available in some health program areas.

35. Harold L. Wilensky, *Social Science and the Public Agenda: Reflections on the Relation of Knowledge to Policy in the United States and Abroad*, Working Paper 96–15 (Berkeley: Institute of Governmental Studies, University of California, 1996), 6.

36. See Beryl A. Radin, "Evaluation on Demand: Two Congressionally Mandated Education Evaluations," in *Making and Managing Policy*, edited by Ron Gilbert (New York: Marcel Dekker, 1984), 239–56.

37. Evaluability assessment first clarifies the program design or theory and, if that process is appropriate, then collects information from the range of actors involved with the program. See discussion in Carol H. Weiss, *Evaluation: Methods for Studying Programs and Policies*, 2nd ed. (Upper Saddle River, NJ: Prentice Hall, 1998), 73–74.

38. See Egon G. Cuba and Yvonna S. Lincoln, *Fourth Generation Evaluation* (Newbury Park, CA: Sage, 1989).

39. Ibid., 22–33.

40. See Krane, "Disorderly Progress."

41. Lisbeth B. Schorr, "Broader Evidence for Bigger Impact," *Stanford Social Innovation Review* (Fall 2012): 50–55.

42. Eugene Bardach, "Gathering Data for Policy Research," originally published in *Urban Analysts 2* (1974), reprinted by Eugene Bardach, *A Practical Guide for Policy Analysis: The Eightfold Path to More Effective Problem Solving,* fourth edition. (Washington, DC: Sage/CQ Press).

43. Ibid.

44. See David Dery, *Problem Definition in Policy Analysis* (Lawrence: University Press of Kansas, 1984), 15.

45. Giandomenico Majone, *Evidence, Argument, and Persuasion in the Policy Process* (New Haven, CT: Yale University Press, 1989), 2. See also Frank Fischer and John Forester, eds., *The Argumentative Turn in Policy Analysis and Planning* (Durham, NC: Duke University Press, 1993).

46. Richard E. Neustadt and Ernest R. May, *Thinking in Time* (New York: Basic Books, 1986);Thomas J. Kaplan, "The Narrative Structure of Policy Analysis," *Journal of Policy Analysis and Management* 5, no. 4 (1986): 761–78. See also Emery Roe, *Narrative Policy Analysis: Theory and Practice* (Durham, NC: Duke University Press, 1994).

47. This is as characterized by Anne Larason Schneider and Helen Ingram, *Policy Design for Democracy* (Lawrence: University Press of Kansas, 1997), 37.

48. Robert Denhardt, "Towards a Critical Theory of Public Organization," *Public Administration Review* 41, no. 6 (November–December 1981): 633.

49. Duncan MacRae Jr., "Post-Modernism and Evidence in Public Policy Analysis," revised version of a paper presented at annual meeting of Association for Public Policy Analysis and Management, Pittsburgh, November 1, 1996.

50. Lucian Pugliaresi and Diane T. Berliner, "Policy Analysis at the Department of State: The Policy Planning Staff," *Journal of Policy Analysis and Management* 8, no. 3 (1989): 379–94.

51. Patricia W. Ingraham, "Toward More Systematic Consideration of Policy Design," *Policy Studies Journal* 15, no. 4 (June 1978): 611–28.

52. Aaron Wildavsky, "The Once and Future School of Public Policy," *The Public Interest* 79 (Spring 1985): 28.

53. James Allen Smith, *The Idea Brokers: Think Tanks and the Rise of the New Policy Elite* (New York: Free Press, 1991), 195.

54. Beryl A. Radin, "Policy Analysis in the Office of the Assistant Secretary for Planning and Evaluation in HEW/HHS: Institutionalization and the Second Generation," in *Organizations for Policy Analysis: Helping Government Think*, edited by Carol H. Weiss (Newbury Park, CA: Sage, 1992), 153.

55. See, e.g., Murray Edelman, *The Symbolic Uses of Politics* (Urbana: University of Illinois Press, 1964); and John W. Kingdon, *Agendas, Alternatives, and Public Policies* (Boston: Little, Brown, 1984).

56. Martin Rein, *Social Science and Public Policy* (London: Penguin Books, 1976), 81.

57. Meltsner, *Policy Analysts*.

58. Robert H. Nelson, "The Office of Policy Analysis in the Department of the Interior," *Journal of Policy Analysis and Management* 8, no. 3 (1989): 408.

59. Daniel Esty and Reece Rushing, "The Promise of Data-Driven Policymaking," *Issues in Science and Technology*, Summer 2007.

60. Edward T. Jennings Jr. and Jeremy L. Hall, "Evidence-Based Practice and the Use of Information in State Agency Decision Making," *Journal of Public Administration Research and Theory*, July 2011, 1.

61. Radin, "Policy Analysis," 152.

62. Quoted by Walter Williams, *Honest Numbers and Democracy* (Washington, DC: Georgetown University Press, 1998), 36–37.

63. Wildavsky, *Speaking Truth to Power*, 14–15.

64. Ibid., 16.

65. Rudolf Klein and Theodore R. Marmor, "Reflections on Policy Analysis: Putting It Together Again," in *The Oxford Handbook of Public Policy* (Oxford: Oxford University Press), 905–6.

Chapter 7

Information—Just Give Me the Facts?

John Nelson was fairly comfortable with the information that was available to him when he was in the Department of Defense (DoD). Although he sometimes felt that he did not have the right information at the right time, it was accessible and in a form that answered most of the analytical questions that were a part of his assignments. During those years, there appeared to be a fairly clear sense both inside DoD and in the general society that increasing a range of weapons programs would provide the means to achieving a well-defended country. The policy problems were defined in an explicit manner. Because the Planning, Programming, and Budgeting System process was focused on the relationship between programs and the budget, Nelson could link the budget information with the department's goals. His training as an economist had provided him with a belief that he would be able to package information that would be adequate for analyses of weapons prices and effects. And DoD's experience supported that assumption.

But when he moved to the Department of Health, Education, and Welfare, he found quite a different situation. He was faced with an array of programs with agreement on neither goals nor the causes of problems. This lack of agreement was found not only in the general society but within the administration itself. There were programs that not only did not produce data about their implementation but also did not have categories and typologies to use even if they wanted to collect data. He thought that some of DoD's program units did have information about their activities, but he did not have enough time during the day to establish contacts with these individuals involved. He noted that the bureaucratic split between planning and the budget office—despite the use of the Planning, Programming, and Budgeting System—meant that some information was in the hands of the budget office that was difficult for him to access.

While he sought clarity and data to help devise the range of new programs that were promised by the White House, he witnessed a decision process that was very different from the one he had expected as these policies were being designed. The information that was used was produced by interest groups that were advocates for particular policy solutions. Members of Congress created large-scale programs based on what seemed to him to be policy hunches and not on analytical data. This wasn't the world that he expected or to which he had been accustomed at the RAND Corporation and DoD.

When she was in graduate school, Rita Stone remembered that one of the faculty members for her program had a cartoon on the door clipped from The New Yorker *magazine. That cartoon—which showed a file cabinet with draw-ers labeled "our facts," "their facts," "neutral facts," "disputed facts," "absolute facts," "bare facts," "undisputed facts," and "unsubstantiated facts"—seemed to capture the information problem as Stone perceived it. When she worked at the Children's Defense Fund (CDF), she witnessed a series of policy dis-putes that were based on arguments constructed from very different informa-tion sources who viewed issues from different value perspectives. CDF had invested in its own research capacity because the organization did not trust the information that was produced by the Republican administration.*

During her summer internship at the Department of Health and Human Ser-vices (HHS) in the Office of the Assistant Secretary for Planning and Evalu-ation, Stone observed another situation. That office—one of the largest and most respected policy analysis shops in the federal government—seemed to be issuing a series of research reports that did not appear to be informing the decision process either inside or outside the department. The analysts as-signed to work on the child care issue were focused on the problems related to the lack of agreement on the goals of any intervention. As a result, that work did not appear to meet decision needs.

So when she had to decide where she would begin her Presidential Man-agement Interns placement, she decided that it was more important to her to find a way to infuse her analytical capabilities directly into the decision-making process. HHS's budget office seemed to provide that setting. Even if there was not agreement on goals, HHS would produce an annual budget and resources would be requested for child care programs.

Over the past few years, Stone has realized that the information that is help-ful to her has come from many different sources. Sitting in the budget office, she has regular contact with HHS child care program staff members. Her involvement in a range of meetings and conferences with interest groups in the field has given her access to current developments in programs across the country. She regularly checks in with the various groups that are a part of the child care issue network, either on the telephone or through e-mail. As she looks to the future, she is aware of lessons from the past. Although HHS dealt with child care separately from Head Start, she knows that the Head Start controversies of the past shouldn't be forgotten.

Early in her career, Veronica Lopez recognized that the information essential to a medical clinician was not always available in the formal data sets produced by insurance companies and others who focused on the financial aspects of medicine. And when she embarked on her master's in public health with a specialization in epidemiology, she saw yet another disparity between formal data and clinical information. She was often uncomfortable with the use of aggregate and formal data sets in the construction of practice guidelines. The norms that emerged from those practice guidelines were translated into requirements that seemed to her to be more appropriate for a factory than a medical practice. Dr. Lopez was interested in improving the way that medical services were delivered, but she saw medicine as a field that required practitioners to use their discretion and recognize the unique aspects of the clients whom they were treating. Although it may have been overstated, she resonated with the characterization of medicine as an art.

As Dr. Lopez's career developed and she moved to the Pan American Health Organization (PAHO), she became aware of still another user of information beyond the clinician and the constructor of practice guidelines. As she worked with staff members from a range of Latin American countries, she confronted the policy sector. Her colleagues were individuals who had moved beyond the treatment of individuals and had learned to operate within complex systems that reflected a country's broad social and economic aspects. Many PAHO member countries saw health care as a political issue, particularly those places where medical services were unavailable to the poor, to indigenous peoples, and individuals who lived in remote locations. Her earlier discomfort with aggregate information sources took on an additional aspect when she was not able to find disaggregated information that described the needs of individuals in specific locations.

Her current job with the Bill & Melinda Gates Foundation drew on all her past views about information sources. In addition to her earlier perspectives, she became more aware of the failure of drug trials to include children in their clinical trial groups. Thus the information that was available did not differentiate reactions of adults from those of children. And her work at Gates exposed her to an even wider range of information users than she had experienced in the past.

This chapter examines a series of topics that deal with information questions. It attempts to answer the question "What is information?" It discusses the dimensions of decision making that define the need for information, the functions of information, and sources of information, and it presents a checklist of information concerns that are relevant for policy analysts. It concludes with a discussion of information in the future and the possibility of developing an alternative to academic social science.

Approaches to Information

During the early stages of the policy analysis profession, faith in the methodologies of the analyst rested on an unarticulated assumption that information was available and appropriate. Though few analysts would have made this argument explicitly, they tended to rely on approaches that assumed information was out there, waiting to be plucked like low-hanging fruit on a tree. Not only was the information ready to be picked, but there was also an unarticulated belief that it would be easy to find "objective information" and that one could disentangle fact from value.

To some extent it is unfair to describe this attitude as naive. The views about information were not made explicit; rather, they were implicit in the conceptual paradigms that informed the work of early policy analysts. The twin frameworks of normative economics and positivist social science each had its own particular spins on this issue. For the economist, if one assumed that the market operated on the basis of perfect information, then it was not a great leap to assume that the marketplace of ideas also rested on such information. For the social scientist, reliance on the scientific method assumed that information could be objective, value free, and available for all to use to further test hypotheses. Neither group questioned its ability to differentiate the true from the false and to provide advice to decision makers based on that confidence.

These approaches to the information task did not appear to be influenced by the experience of others whose perspectives were less technical. It is interesting that one of the earliest policy advisers, Kautilya, thought about information in a highly strategic fashion. In the fourth century BC Kautilya devised an intelligence system whereby spies who had been trained and organized by the institute of espionage were posted throughout the realm in India: "Living as students, housewives, monks, farmers, beggars, prostitutes, and in hundreds of other roles, they penetrated every cranny of the state, as well as engaging in foreign operations. Orphans, having no family loyalties, were often favored recruits for the espionage system. These spies, unknown to each other, reported to the institute of espionage that transmitted their information to higher levels after checking its validity. When information from three different sources coincided, it was held to be reliable, but if the three sources frequently differed, the spies were punished or dismissed."[1]

Max Weber considered information an instrument of power that should be treated as such. Weber argued that, as an important resource, information was to be guarded and held closely: "Every bureaucracy seeks to increase the superiority of the professionally informed by keeping their knowledge and intentions secret. Bureaucratic administration always tends to be an administration of 'secret missions': Insofar as it can, it hides its knowledge and action from criticism. . . . The concept of the 'official secret' is the specific invention of bureaucracy, and nothing is so fanatically defended by the bureaucracy as this attitude."[2]

This approach was quite different from the one that valued scientific openness and information sharing that was assumed by some of the early policy analysts, particularly those who were rooted in the professional norms of the behavioral social sciences. Others did understand the differences between the experience of more traditional academics and those of individuals who focused on policy analysis as advising but did not seem to influence the early phase of practice. Both Aaron Wildavsky and Charles Lindblom acknowledged the limits of the academic approach.[3] As Martin Rein has suggested, we should recognize that concern about an issue and action forces an analysis; it is not the other way around.[4]

Attitudes about information have become much more complex in the several decades that have elapsed since the practice of policy analysis began. We have given attention to the definition of information, the kinds of information that are appropriate, sources of information, and the need for it, as well as its functions and uses. We have become much more sophisticated about the limits of the original views that were embedded in the conceptual paradigms and analytic approaches used by the early analysts. Though it is not clear that we have agreed on an alternative approach that would replace the academically based social science framework, we are increasingly moving to an approach that emphasizes the interrelationship between information and social interaction.

Defining Information

The question "What is information?" would have seemed trivial when the policy analysis field was emerging. There were obvious answers to the question, depending on the framework that the analyst brought to the task at hand. When information is defined by an experimental mode with roots in the controlled laboratory setting, the imperatives of the scientific method make it clear which information is appropriate and what should be collected and analyzed. Similarly, those who operate from an economic paradigm, based on the imperatives of a market, would seek other kinds of information. Stone describes this information as of two varieties: "objective" information about the price and quality of alternatives, and "subjective" information about personal preferences.[5]

Harold Wilensky has suggested that the information relevant to policy—what he calls "intelligence"—includes questions, insights, hypotheses, and evidence. He notes that it "includes both scientific knowledge and political or ideological information, scientific or not."[6] He defines a set of criteria that allow information to become intelligence: clear, timely, reliable, valid, adequate, and wide ranging.[7] Charles Lindblom and David Cohen have created a term to describe the approach to information that emerges from academic social science: Professional Social Inquiry. According to them, this set of activities can include the following:

- Sustained, systematic, and professional classification, conceptualization, development, and testing of nomothetic and other substantial generalizations, development and testing of theories (defined as logically interlocked sets of generalizations).
- Highly systematic data gathering and reporting (e.g., a census, much though not all survey research, and ethnological fieldwork).
- Statistical manipulation and analysis of social data.
- Mathematical and other modeling of social processes.[8]

As the years have elapsed, both the intellectual framework of the positivist social scientist and that of the normative economist have been the subject of criticisms within the policy literature. Majone and others have focused on the limitations of what he called the "uncritical acceptance of the 'scientific method' (or what is thought to be the scientific method.)"[9] He noted that individuals in the policy analysis field have overlooked "some important differences between the natural sciences and policy analysis":[10]

For if it is true that neither descriptive nor theoretical natural sciences require highly developed skills in testing evidence, beyond those already involved in producing information, this is for good reasons. In the natural sciences one usually has either a rich and reliable body of information with a relatively simple argument, or a complex theoretical argument needing evidence at only a few points. Such situations are rather exceptional in policy analysis, where one typically deals with large amounts of data of doubtful reliability or relevance. It is likely that the lack of suitable rules of evidence has contributed to the mounting level of dissatisfaction with certain applications of policy analysis.[11]

Rein has written that one of the key requirements in the positivist social science tradition has been the requirement that one would separate one's own ideological bias from the analysis.[12] Rein's critique of the positivist approach leads him to turn the traditional requirements upside down. He suggests that policy analysts, rather than avoiding a discussion of values, must approach their information collection task by announcing their values. He notes that we can prevent our personal values and ideologies from distorting our understanding: "No one can claim privileged exception from distortion; the problem is how to guard against it."[13]

The positivist belief in the ability to separate fact from value has become increasingly difficult to defend in the policy field. Carol Weiss has provided an extremely useful way to think about the information problem. She has characterized the information task as the three "I's"—information, ideology, and interests—and has argued that "the public policy positions taken by policy actors are the resultant of three sets of forces: their *ideologies*, their *interests* (e.g. in power, reputation, financial reward), and the *information* they have" (emphasis in the original).[14] She writes: "Observers who expect the subcategory of information that is social science research to have immediate and independent power in the policy process, and who bitterly complain about the intrusion of 'polities' (i.e., interests and ideologies) into the use of research, implicitly hold a distorted view of how decisions are made. Moreover, their normative view—that research *should* have direct effects on policy—proposes an imagery of appropriate policymaking that I believe is untenable and (if it should ever be realized) dangerous."[15]

Deborah Stone has focused on the differences between the views of economists and those of persons who emphasize what she terms "the polis"—the political community that includes diverse cultural communities.[16] She describes the market as a social system in which individuals pursue their own welfare by exchanging things with others whenever trades are mutually beneficial. Economists often begin their discussions of the market by conjuring up the Robinson Crusoe society, where two people on a lush tropical island swap coconuts and small game animals. They trade to make each person better off, but since each person always has the option of producing everything for himself, trading is never an absolute necessity for either one. . . . In the ideal market, information is 'perfect,' meaning it is accurate, complete and available to everyone at no cost. In the polis, by contrast, information is interpretive, incomplete, and strategically withheld.[17]

All these complications have made it more difficult to actually define policy-relevant information. Rein has written that "policymakers and administrators are therefore likely to discount what is said by social scientists who cannot agree among themselves. . . . I believe that, given the present state of social science knowledge, it is probably better to recognize how conflicting and uncertain its interpretations are than to assign a very high value to a particular orientation."[18]

Eugene Bardach emphasizes the need to turn data into information that in turn can be converted into evidence.[19] Similarly, Majone highlights the problems of producing and interpreting data at the problem-setting stage. He suggests that the distinction between facts and artifacts is a tricky one when social and economic data are involved.[20] He warns that the transformation of data into information involves three basic judgments: the possible loss of important details, the fit between the model used and the data available, and transformation of the data to the metrics of the problem.[21] Kathleen Hale addresses the use of information in networks and the complexity of the information sources that emerge from a wide range of network players.[22]

Dimensions of Decision Making That Define the Need for Information

As a number of students of the policy field have suggested, there are many ways to think about the decision-making process. Graham Allison's classic study of the Cuban Missile Crisis defined three analytical approaches that not only resulted in different policy recommendations but also generated very different types of information in the process. Allison's analysis indicated that participants in the policymaking process define issues in very different ways, depending on the lens they use in the process.[23]

In the case of the Cuban Missile Crisis, when participants viewed the problem as a situation defined by the rational actor paradigm, they sought evidence about details of behavior, statements of government officials, and government papers. This evidence was "then marshaled in such a way that a coherent picture of the value-maximizing choice . . . emerges."[24] The organizational process paradigm, the second of Allison's lenses, called for evidence that provides information about standard operating procedures and governmental routines.[25] Allison notes that the third paradigm, the governmental bureaucratic approach, created difficulties in information collection because it entails looking for details of differences in perceptions and priorities among the decision makers involved in the bargaining situation.[26] The information required by the second and third models, according to Allison, dwarfs the information needed by the analyst assuming the rational actor model.[27] The information that is viewed as important to each of these settings was distinct from that required by others.

Martha Feldman's study of information use in the Department of Energy contrasts three different models used in decision making. She writes that in the rational and bounded rational models, "information provides the means of choosing the optimal or satisfactory solution. The information needed is a function of the specified goals."[28] Incremental models of decision call for information that provides feedback on past action as well as new solutions; "the type of information gathered tends to be guided by the focus of the procedure with which it is associated."[29] By further contrast, the garbage can model of decision making is helpful in exploring problems and solutions, discovering preferences, maintaining lines of communication, and establishing the legitimacy of the decision processes.[30] Both these examples suggest that it is not possible to think about information without paying attention to the context in which it will be used.

The Functions of Information

Once we acknowledge that information is defined by very different approaches to decision making as well as the type of problem and decision to be made, it is not surprising to find that information serves many functions in the policy process. Although we tend to think about information use in an almost mechanistic fashion (the input that is "fed" to decision makers), in reality it serves a wide range of functions that go beyond the direct relationship between analyst and client. Analysts not only need to predict the likely outcomes of various options but also need to decide what information is essential to perform that prediction.

Majone describes this machinelike process as "grossly misleading" and argues that analysts of this "persuasion would like to project the image of technical, nonpartisan problem solvers who map out the alternatives open to the policymaker and evaluate their consequences by means of mathematical models or other objective techniques of analysis."[31] Rather, he states, "the policy analyst is a producer of policy arguments, more similar to a lawyer— a specialist in legal arguments—than to an engineer or a scientist. His basic skills are not algorithmical but argumentative: the ability to probe assumptions critically, to produce and evaluate evidence, to keep many threads in hand, to draw for an argument from many disparate sources, to communicate effectively."[32] Further, according to Majone, evidence is "information selected from the available stock and introduced at a specific point on an argument to persuade the mind that a given factual proposition is true or false."[33]

Rein puts it somewhat differently: "Knowledge is not used simply to influence policy actively. The process is more complex; as policy evolves, knowledge is used selectively to justify actions reached on other grounds. Moreover, knowledge and policy are interactive, being as much influenced by as influencing the current agenda for reform."[34]

In her work on the use of information in Congress, Weiss has differentiated among three categories of information: policy information, political intelligence, and analytic work. She argues that analytic information serves four main functions for members of Congress. First, it provides support for members' existing policy positions, allowing them to mobilize support from other members and strengthen their coalitions. Second, it serves as a warning system, signaling that something should be done. Third, it provides guidance that allows staff and members to design strategies and procedures or fine-tune existing procedures. Fourth, it offers a source of what Weiss calls "enlightenment," which helps staff and members reconceptualize issues, modify their thinking, and offer new ways of thinking about issues.[35]

Weiss has depicted the functions of information in a legislative context as support for a preexisting position, warning, guidance, and enlightenment. She has described the uses to which it is put as political ammunition, reordering the agenda, design of activities, and modification in thinking; see table 7.1.

Information in the policy process serves other functions as well. It can reduce conflict in a situation. Even when it does not resolve the conflicts between competing values and agendas, it can help to minimize the range of issues that are in dispute. As in the legal process of stipulation (where both parties to the case agree on specific information regarding the situation), the presence of information can act as a constraint on the issues under contention. This function of information production and collection is best understood as a process of interactive problem solving and social learning.[36]

Table 7.1   Legislative Uses of Analytic Information

Function That Information Serves	Use to Which It Is Put
Support for preexisting position	*Political ammunition*
Certifies that the position is right	Reinforces advocates' confidence in their stand; strengthens coalition
	Persuades undecided members
	Weakens opponents' case and support
Warning	*Reordering the agenda*
Signals that a problem is (or is not) severe	Moves the problem up (or down) on the policy agenda
Guidance	*Design of activities*
Indicates better alternatives	Leads to legislative provisions, amendments, and further queries
Enlightenment	*Modification in thinking*
Offers new constructs, new ways of thinking about issue	Reconceptualizes issues
	Raises level of discussion

Source: Carol H. Weiss, "Congressional Committees as Users of Analysis," *Journal of Policy Analysis and Management* 8, no. 3 (1989): 425. Reprinted by permission.

In some cases the presence of information can be used to demythologize public views about an issue. The Century Fund, for example, has produced a number of publications designed to challenge widely held myths about social policy issues. This may be the first stage in a public education campaign whereby various policy actors seek to change views about the dimensions of a problem or about a possible solution. The Center on Budget and Policy Priorities highlights the need for information in its outreach campaigns to inform the public about specific program opportunities and policy needs. Similarly, the strategy of the Heritage Foundation accentuates the use of information as an organizing device.

Feldman has also suggested that information production may be used to resolve uncertainty or reduce ambiguity. She notes that uncertainty can be resolved by obtaining certain pieces of information but that it may be costly or even extremely difficult to obtain those data. By contrast, she notes that ambiguity cannot be resolved simply by gathering information because "ambiguity is the state of having many ways of thinking about the same circumstances or phenomena."[37]

In some cases policy analysts find that they are tasked with gathering information that simply rationalizes a decision that has already been made. These situations are particularly troubling to individuals who have been trained in use of the scientific method, and thus want to search to differentiate the true from the false. This process is somewhat akin to the writing of legal briefs for a particular position, but it is often done without the formal rules of evidence that constrain the legal process. Though some would argue that social science rules also act as a constraint, they are not codified in the way that legal evidence operates.

Machiavelli focused on a different aspect of the information process and accentuated the qualities of the prince that lead to different types of information needs. He wrote that "there are three types of intelligence: one understands on its own, the second discerns what others understand, the third neither understands by itself nor through the intelligence of others; that first kind is most excellent, the second excellent, the third useless."[38]

Others have focused on the need for information or evidence for different purposes. Bardach suggests that policy analysts need evidence for three principal purposes:

> One purpose is to assess the nature and extent of the problem(s) you are trying to define. The second is to assess the particular features of the concrete policy situation you are engaged in studying. For instance, you may need to know—or guess—about agency workloads, recent budget figures, demographic changes in a service area, the political ideology of the agency chief, the competency of the middle-level managers in the agency, and the current attitudes of some other agency which nominally cooperates with this one on some problem. The third purpose is to assess policies that have been thought, by at least some people, to have worked effectively in situations apparently similar to your own, in other jurisdictions, perhaps, or at other times. All three purposes are relevant to the goal of producing realistic projections of possible policy outcomes.[39]

Sources of Information

The traditional researcher operates with a set of shared assumptions about the sources of appropriate information. As was suggested in chapter 6, the choice of tools or analytic method can predetermine the information source. But experience suggests that the sources of policy information are much less predictable. Several of the policy analysis organizations analyzed in chapter 4 describe their approach to information as extremely eclectic (e.g., see the California Legislative Analyst's Office). For them, information comes in many shapes and forms.

Majone has argued that "in policy analysis data are often 'found' rather than 'manufactured'; that is, they are obtained by unplanned observations . . . rather than by planned experiments."[40] In addition, these data have to be molded and refined into quite different forms before they can be used in the decision-making process. This involves refining the data into information, a task that calls on the policy analyst to exert a wide range of personal judgments.

In their critique of Professional Social Inquiry (i.e., the reliance on the tools and techniques of the traditional social scientists), Lindblom and Cohen note that too many policy analysts and researchers greatly underestimate the use of what they call "ordinary knowledge":

> We mean knowledge that does not owe its origin, testing, degree of verification, truth status, or currency to distinctive PSI [Professional Social Inquiry] professional techniques but rather to common sense, casual empiricism, or thoughtful speculation and analysis. . . . For social problem solving, we suggest, people will always depend heavily on ordinary knowledge. Ordinary knowledge tells us that legislatures make laws and perform certain other functions, some public officials take bribes, most families in industrial societies are nuclear rather than extended, wheat farmers will restrict production if paid to do so, children become angry when thwarted, and so on. . . . It is ordinary knowledge that tells us so fundamental *a* fact as that the moving forms we see about us displaying shape and movement like ours are human beings much like ourselves.[41]

The idea of ordinary knowledge has an implicit open and democratic bias to it. It does not give the individual with an advanced degree a monopoly on the production of information. Rather, it indicates that relevant information can be found from "journalists, civil servants, businessmen, interest-group leaders, public opinion leaders, and elected officials."[42]

Bardach's suggestion that the appropriate techniques for the policy analyst are more like those of the journalist than the social scientist offers another way of thinking about the potential richness of information sources.[43] He emphasizes that policy information is "derivative rather than original" and suggests that information for the analyst is found in two classes: documents and people.[44] He compares the search for information to branches on the tree of knowledge and reminds analysts that people lead to people, people lead to documents, documents lead to documents, and documents lead to people.[45]

In her study of policy analysts in the Department of Energy, Martha Feldman emphasizes that information is often found in unexpected places or gathered in unconventional ways.[46] She also notes that analysts have the ability to actually create information: "They gather data, analyze them, and write information reports. These reports have a dual role: They are negotiated agreements, subject to the same constraints as other papers, but they also make new information available for future use."[47]

The wide array of possible sources of information is both a resource and a challenge. It is very easy for the policy analyst to be overwhelmed with the potentialities of information. Bardach counsels the policy analyst to "think before you collect," and he offers some suggestions for self-control in this task. He notes that the cost of data collection "often leads good and experienced policy analysts to make do with 'back of the envelope' estimates."[48]

A Checklist of Information Concerns

As the discussion above has suggested, policy analysts should be attentive to the traps that are involved in the process of finding, defining, and using information. Several areas are especially problematic.

The Structures of Different Programs and Policies

Information definition and collection are much easier when they involve programs that are directly implemented by one level of government. When programs are devolved to other levels of government (e.g., federal programs implemented by state governments; or state programs administered by local government), then the process of information definition and collection becomes extremely difficult. It involves touchy relationships in which other levels of government are charged with collecting information that they may not believe to be important. Or, more problematically, they may believe that the information they have collected will be used to control or punish them in the future. To further complicate this picture, in this age of contracting out and privatization, the information required to assess program effectiveness or plan for policy modifications may be the property of nongovernmental bodies.

The Levels of Targeting in Program Design

Many public programs are designed to benefit specific elements within the population. Targeting of benefits may be focused on specific population groups—defined by race, ethnicity, gender, age, or other variables. Yet many information sources are available only as aggregate analyses and do not provide appropriate data that would allow an analyst to estimate how a proposed program might affect a particular population group.

The Source of the Information

As has been discussed, it is extremely difficult for policy analysts to find information that is truly objective or neutral. In one way or another (implicitly through choice of methodology or problem definition, or explicitly when it is attached to a policy agenda) the information that is both available and appropriate has values embedded within it.

Though analysts cannot avoid this set of problems, they can find ways to minimize the negative effects of information bias. Several of the case studies presented in chapter 4 provide useful examples for how to deal with this situation. Both the California Legislative Analyst's Office and the Congressional Research Service operate in highly charged political environments. And AARP's lobbying activities put its information directly in a political environment. Though the analysts may not have their own policy agenda, they know that their clients look for information from the interest groups that share their values. The challenge for the analyst is to present a balanced picture, defining objectivity and nonpartisanship as "fairness" rather than the clear differentiation between truth and falsity. Or, as the Center on Budget and Policy Priorities puts it, there is a need to establish quality-control checks that produce credible information even when it is presented with a point of view.

The Form of the Information

After many years, it has become obvious that policy analysts cannot expect their clients to pore over academic treatises that analyze and describe the minute details of policy alternatives. Busy decision makers are not likely to read much more than an executive summary, if that. Analysts have learned to recognize that many decision processes do not rely on the written word at all but rather on the oral tradition.[49]

Concern about the form of information production has led to very different packaging approaches. Inside government, policy analysts have learned how to make presentations that are interesting and yet substantive. Policy organizations (e.g., the Heritage Foundation and the Century Foundation) have used magazines, speeches, op-ed columns, pamphlets, and books to communicate their findings. The challenge to the analyst is to find a way to present complex issues simply without becoming simplistic.

Dealing with Secrecy and Proprietary Information

As Weber told us, because information is power, it is not surprising that those who hold information do not always want to share it. The world is far from an open marketplace of information. This is as true for individuals in the policy world as for those in the competitive business market. Policy analysts must deal with two aspects of this problem. They may search for information that they know exists but that is not made available to others by those who hold it. Information holders may stonewall the analyst (e.g., fail to return phone calls, break appointments, or actually state that they will not provide it). Conversely, analysts may find that they are the information holders and believe that they will serve their clients most effectively by withholding that information when others request it.

Both aspects of this problem are rarely discussed—particularly when analysts are trained in the norms of social science research.[50] The advent of new computer technologies has minimized some elements of this problem. Both the accessibility of computer hardware and access to the internet have meant that individuals are less likely to hold a monopoly over some forms of data.

Issues of Confidentiality

Given that policy analysts are increasingly tending to specialize in a particular policy area, they are likely to develop relationships of trust with their important information sources. Their involvement with a particular issue leads them to become integral parts of the issue networks with which they are dealing. Though these relationships are extremely helpful and important, they may also introduce complications in terms of questions of confidentiality. Information may be available to the policy analyst that is not meant to be shared widely. Indeed, client confidentiality may sometimes be a barrier to creating good information systems. Though there are few explicit norms to guide the analyst confronting this situation, the problem is much like that of the journalist who wants to protect sources.

The Mistaken Pursuit of Authoritativeness

Lindblom and Cohen warn against what they call "the mistaken pursuit of authoritativeness"—the tendency for policy analysts to believe that they can arrive at answers that are scientifically definitive or conclusive.[51] They note that there are two kinds of authoritativeness: one in which the degree of scientific conclusiveness is high, and another in which scientific conclusiveness is less high but its conclusions are confirmed by ordinary knowledge.[52] The experience within the field during the past three decades clearly leads one to define answers and approach recommendations with a strong sense of modesty. It is not surprising that this is likely to lead to incremental rather than broad, comprehensive approaches to change.

The Problem of Timeliness

Even when policy analysts have confidence that they will be able to collect and analyze information that is appropriate and useful for the decision process, they are faced with the limits of time. Research time and policy time are rarely the same. As Bardach has noted, "'Time pressure' is as dangerous an enemy of high-quality policy analysis as politically motivated bias."[53]

To some degree the seriousness of the timeliness issue depends on the type of policy analysis that is being done. If the work is being driven by an externally imposed deadline, the policy analyst must learn to live with the reality that there is not enough time to accomplish the "ideal" piece of work as defined by some platonic ideal. If the work accomplished on the "back of the envelope" is completed in time to influence the decision process, then it deserves high marks. At the same time, it needs to be fair and reasonably valid.

Feldman has observed that policy analysts often find that their assignments require much more time than they originally estimated.[54] This is attributable to the complexity not only of finding information but also of obtaining agreement from the relevant players on the information and analysis that is to be accomplished.

Information Overload

Whether or not policy information is actually used to influence decision making, it is clear that the availability and diversity of information often have led to an information overload. The challenge for the policy analyst is to avoid the cynicism that seems to accompany what is sometimes described as a flood of analysis. Alice Rivlin has suggested that "the information overload is frustrating and intimidating and it affects people in different ways, making some extremely cautious, others impatient. In the face of this overload, there is an attraction to simple organizing principles or ideologies that will sort everything into convenient categories."[55] This situation has been described as "information fatigue syndrome."

The Lack of Investment in Information Collection

During the past decade or so, governments have become increasingly reluctant to invest in data collection systems that would provide useful information to the policy analyst. As one individual has put it, "we are in a situation where data is disappearing from under us." This erosion of historic systems is attributable to at least two causes. The first is the general budget crunch and efforts by governments to eliminate what they view as expendable costs. A number of long-standing data systems in federal departments involving housing, education, and health were either eliminated or scaled back during the 1980s. Other information systems have been the victims of efforts to reduce paperwork requirements imposed on other governments, businesses, and the general citizenry. The Paperwork Reduction Act in the United States created a process that gave authority over the collection of certain forms of information to the Office of Management and Budget. That act was intended to reduce the amount of paperwork handled by the US government and the general public.

As a result of these limited information resources, policy analysts are forced to make recommendations based on what they know is extremely incomplete and perhaps misleading information. To some extent, the congressional reluctance to adopt sampling techniques for the 2000 census is an expression of this problem. Though the public arguments that have been used to oppose sampling have little to do with the potential uses of the information, they point to the fear that the new data might cost them loss in influence and congressional seats. This reflects the reluctance by some in society to provide information sources that might lead to more effective policies and programs.

Policy Information in the Future

We have traveled far from the picture of the policy analyst as an academic living in an ivory tower who produces and analyzes information. Although some people want to return to that role, it is not obvious that there is an alternative formulation that has replaced that image. Feldman has observed that policy analysts continue to operate with "a professional ideal of objectivity."[56]

In her study of policy analysts in the Department of Energy, she found analysts who do not actually value what they do because that activity does not fit their image of the field.

At the same time, analysts are moving into a set of tasks and roles that bring them into the mainstream of the decision-making process. They have learned how to work with individuals who do not share either their intellectual or personal values and approaches. They have developed negotiating and bargaining skills that allow them to create alternative approaches. They have become a part of broader issue networks and value their interaction with others who are in organizational settings beyond their own. Though information does not drive these interactions, it is clearly an important resource.

Yet one is still confronted with the idealized picture of the past. Wildavsky offered an explanation for the disparity between the assumptions of the field's founders and the experience of practicing policy analysts: "The relative objectivity of analysis depends on people living together in reasonable trust within a common culture. The cultural conditions within which analysis takes place—the sort of social structure thought desirable, the values to be obtained—guide and shape what is done. If trust declines the framework of facts that can be taken for granted declines with it. Without agreement on a starting place, there is no end to debate. Theories harden into dogma, and assertion replaces evidence. Policies then are judged not by their merits but by the motives of their proposers."[57]

Despite this, policy analysts have learned to be more creative about developing new information sources. The internet has provided analysts with an important resource. Agencies that support research and evaluation are increasingly requiring contractors to deliver their data as well as analytical reports to the funding agency. Data sources have been placed on the internet, which allows researchers, advocacy groups, and decision makers across the country to access them. This approach, which has been called the "democratization of data," responds to the expansion and diversity of the policy analysis profession. These efforts to "democratize data" have been described as ones that "enable the entire research and policy community to participate in the analysis of federal programs by first creating costly data bases . . . and then by making them available to the community."[58]

Notes

1. Herbert Goldhamer, *The Adviser* (New York: Elsevier, 1978), 14.

2. H. H. Gerth and C. Wright Mills, *From Max Weber: Essays in Sociology* (New York: Oxford University Press, 1946), 233.

3. See, e.g., Charles Lindblom, *The Policy-Making Process* (Englewood Cliffs, NJ: Prentice Hall, 1968); and Aaron Wildavsky, *Speaking Truth to Power: The Art and Craft of Policy Analysis* (Boston: Little, Brown, 1979).

4. Martin Rein, *Social Science and Public Policy* (New York: Penguin Books, 1976), 32.

5. Deborah Stone, *Policy Paradox: The Art of Political Decision Making* (New York: W. W. Norton, 1997), 68.

6. Harold L. Wilensky, *Organizational Intelligence: Knowledge and Policy in Government and Industry* (New York: Basic Books, 1967), viii.

7. Ibid.

8. Charles E. Lindblom and David K. Cohen, *Usable Knowledge: Social Science and Social Problem Solving* (New Haven, CT: Yale University Press, 1979), 8.

9. Giandomenico Majone, *Evidence, Argument, and Persuasion in the Policy Process* (New Haven, CT: Yale University Press, 1989), 50.

10. Ibid.

11. Ibid.

12. Rein, *Social Science*, 80.

13. Ibid., 85.

14. Carol H. Weiss, "Ideology, Interests, and Information: The Basis of Policy Positions," in *Ethics, the Social Sciences, and Policy Analysis,* edited by D. Callahan and B. Jennings (New York: Plenum Press, 1983), 221.

15. Ibid., 221–22.

16. Stone, *Policy Paradox*, 19.

17. Ibid., 17, 27–28.

18. Rein, *Social Science*, 33.

19. Eugene Bardach, *A Practical Guide for Policy Analysis: The Eightfold Path to More Effective Problem Solving,* fourth edition (Washington, DC: Sage/CQ Press).

20. Majone, *Evidence*, 58.

21. Ibid., 60–61.

22. Kathleen Hale, *How Information Matters: Networks and Public Policy Innovation* (Washington, DC: Georgetown University Press, 2011).

23. Graham Allison, *Essence of Decision* (Boston: Little, Brown, 1971).

24. Ibid., 35.

25. Ibid., 96.

26. Ibid., 181.

27. Ibid., 252.

28. Martha Feldman, *Order without Design: Information Production and Policy Making* (Stanford, CA: Stanford University Press, 1989), 20–21.

29. Ibid., 21.

30. Ibid.

31. Majone, *Evidence*, 21.

32. Ibid., 21–22.

33. Ibid., 48.

34. Rein, *Social Science*, 34.

35. Carol H. Weiss, "Congressional Committees as Users of Analysis," *Journal of Policy Analysis and Management* 8, no. 3 (1989): 424–25.

36. See Lindblom and Cohen, *Usable Knowledge*.

37. Feldman, *Order without Design*, 4–5.

38. Peter Bondanella and Mark Musa, eds. and trans., *The Portable Machiavelli* (New York: Penguin Books, 1979), 154.

39. Bardach, *Practical Guide for Policy Analysis*.

40. Majone, *Evidence,* 46. A similar argument is made by Lisbeth B. Schorr, "Broader Evidence for Bigger Impact," *Stanford Social Innovation Review*, Fall 2012, 50–55.

41. Ibid., 12–13.

42. Ibid., 13.

43. Eugene Bardach, "Gathering Data for Policy Research," originally published in *Urban Analysts* 2 (1974), reprinted by Bardach, *Practical Guide for Policy Analysis*.

44. Ibid..

45. Ibid..

46. Feldman, *Order without Design*, 62.

47. Ibid.

48. Bardach, *Practical Guide for Policy Analysis*.

49. Weiss describes the oral tradition of the Congress as a constraint on the use of analysis; Weiss, "Congressional Committees," 414.

50. Bardach discusses this set of problems extensively; Bardach, *Practical Guide for Policy Analysis*.

51. Lindblom and Cohen, *Usable Knowledge*, 40.

52. Ibid., 42–43.

53. Bardach, *Practical Guide for Policy Analysis*.

54. Feldman, *Order without Design*, 85.

55. Alice Rivlin, "Out of the Trenches: A Public Policy Paradox," *Journal of Policy Analysis and Management* 4, no. 1 (1984): 19.

56. Feldman, *Order without Design*, 117.

57. Wildavsky, *Speaking Truth to Power*, 7.

58. Michael Stegman, "Foreword," in *Development and Analysis of the National Low-Income Tax Credit Database*, edited by Office of Policy Development and Research, US Department of Housing and Urban Development (Washington, DC: US Government Printing Office, 1996).

Chapter 8

The Policy Task

When John Nelson arrived at the Department of Defense (DoD), there were many similarities between the day-to-day tasks he was assigned in that federal department and his assignments as a staff member at the RAND Corporation. Defense Secretary Robert McNamara was quite familiar with both the techniques Nelson used and the potential contribution of analysts in a bureaucracy. McNamara created an atmosphere in the department that placed the analysts working on the Planning, Programming, and Budgeting System (PPBS) effort in an elevated role.

Nelson felt that there was a general deference to analytical expertise at DoD that gave him and his colleagues the ability to influence the top decision makers. Staff members enjoyed a monopoly over the analytic role and could be assured that their memos and papers would be read carefully by the secretary. There was a shared belief that if recommendations were based on intellectually rigorous analysis, they would lead to action. There were few constraints of any kind that could not be overcome by good analysis. It was assumed that resources would be available to put these recommendations in place, and it was relatively easy to be optimistic about the future.

The PPBS structure offered a framework that linked budget and programmatic decisions. Although DoD's traditional budget office tried to bypass the influence of the policy analysts and maintain its tried-and-true relationships with the individual military services, it could not ignore the growing importance of the Office of the Secretary in the decision process. But Nelson did know that the budget office actually prepared a line-item budget for Congress that met the traditional expectations of the legislators.

Their centralized perch at DoD gave the analysts the opportunity to move from issue to issue in that very large agency. The diversity of issues was *intellectually challenging, and if he needed supplemental analysis, Nelson could call on resources both inside and outside the department.*

When Nelson moved to the Department of Health, Education, and Welfare, he was faced with analytic assignments aimed at developing a range of new programs. He felt he was all over the place and was truly a generalist analyst. As at DoD, he had access to the top decision makers in the department and was able to provide them with analyses that were new to them. His office had a monopoly on such work, and others in the department weren't quite sure how to deal with the sophisticated reports that emerged from it.

But after he worked there for some time, he began to realize that it was becoming increasingly difficult for society to produce what President Johnson labeled "guns and butter." By 1967, the Vietnam War was beginning to erode confidence that adequate public-sector resources could be found to solve the nation's social problems. Although he had not been aware of it when he was at DoD, it appeared that the expertise he represented did not help decision makers decide where to invest increasingly limited government budget resources.

Early in her career, Rita Stone decided that she would be advantaged by developing a policy specialization; given her personal values and interests, child care issues seemed to be that logical focus. When she began her first job in the federal government, she described herself as a child care specialist, not as a policy analyst. Although she identified with the professional policy analysis field and regularly attended the research conferences sponsored by the Association of Public Policy Analysis and Management, she decided to give herself the label "child care specialist."

As her career developed, she came to believe that she was being rewarded for her detailed knowledge of the programs and possibilities in the child care area. She was familiar with the implementation of fine points of programs and the various policy alternatives that had been floated at the federal level over the years. She was well known in the field and was frequently called upon to advise others ranging from staff in the White House to advocates in various interest groups. She often felt that she provided the institutional memory for an ever-changing field.

Even though she was still quite young, there were times when she felt that she was replaying the same script over and over. Her tenure in the federal government paralleled very pointed changes in attitudes toward social policy that developed as a result of the shift in power in the US Congress. At the beginning of the Clinton administration, she believed that chances were very good for the passage of a large-scale federal child care program. But when the Republicans took control of Congress in 1994, that sense of possibility eroded.

She found that she constantly confronted two sets of constraints: budget limitations in an environment of fiscal scarcity, and strong ideological differences between administration officials and the congressional leadership.

Every year or so she found herself giving an introductory "course" in child care policy to a new group of decision makers. Stone became somewhat bored with those basic lectures and felt that neither she nor the field was making much progress. The budget constraints that structured the decision process did not provide much leeway for the substantive discussion of alternative strategies or thinking about developing a perspective on the issue that included more than annual budgets. Even though the department was expected to submit plans along with the budget to Congress and the White House that met the requirements of the Government Performance and Results Act, the requirements for a strategic plan and annual performance plans seemed to be compliance exercises rather than substantive planning processes. Though she agreed with the premise of the legislation—that it is important to focus on outcomes and performance—she was somewhat skeptical about the ability of government-wide requirements to pick up the nuances of specific program areas. She had read about the experiences in the federal government under PPBS and zero-based budgeting and thought that both of these earlier requirements had been much too broad-brush in their application to deal with significant differences between agencies and programs.

Stone's personal expertise in the child care policy field gave her whatever influence she had in the process. Sitting in the budget office of the Department of Health, Education, and Welfare provided her with a role that seemed to give her some clout, but she thought it was her expertise, not her organizational role, that was the most important. Her positive personal relationships with the program staff in the department stood her in good stead because the department's style of decision making was being increasingly decentralized to the program units. Although she met frequently with the secretary, those sessions were usually fairly large meetings with individuals from a range of program and staff units.

Because she started her career as a clinician, Veronica Lopez did not think about the policy or decision-making processes that defined the context for health care service delivery until she moved to the Centers for Disease Control and Prevention (CDC). While she was still dealing with other health care practitioners at the CDC, she became more aware of the structure of the federal decision-making process involving health policy. When she was asked about accountability relationships before coming to the CDC, she immediately thought about the point of interacting with her patients and what her colleagues and mentors had taught her about professional norms and expectations. But when she joined the CDC, she found herself in situations where her clinical perspective had to be integrated with a different world. She became aware of the complex structure of federal health policy decision making and the roles of the executive branch and Congress in defining the world where she was now living.

Dr. Lopez learned a new vocabulary and began to read the daily newspapers with much more interest. She recognized that many of the clinical issues that had been a part of her earlier professional experience were determined by non-MDs who focused on budget issues and questions related to regulation and the appropriate role of government. Up to that point she was an observer rather than a participant in the policy process. But when she interacted with state and local health officials concerned about services for children, she realized that she would be much more effective if she understood the constraints that kept those individuals from achieving their shared goals.

By the time she joined the Pan-American Health Organization (PAHO), she saw her role as one of bridging the multiple worlds within the health system. When she tried to explain her role to others, she found that the image of a juggler was the most appropriate one. Whether working in the United States or in one of the Latin American countries, she faced a wide range of individuals and groups who had legitimate but varied perspectives on health care issues. She had to deal with individuals who were involved in funding decisions. These included both political actors and health professionals. The programs that were developed not only included funding decisions but also substantive determinations that might encompass areas where the government would regulate how those funds were spent. And after programs were designed and funded, there were always difficult issues involved in their implementation. Whether in Washington or in Brasília, the expectations of the national government did not always match the needs and reality of local populations. She didn't think that one-size-fits-all approaches made sense in large, federal systems or even in smaller but diverse settings. As she became more familiar with the individuals around the globe who shared her concerns, she developed a wide range of contacts involving government officials who could help her access the appropriate decision-making system.

Her years at PAHO also made her very aware of the role of nongovernmental organizations in the delivery of services. Sometimes these organizations represented the health providers—doctors, hospitals, and other medical groups. But increasingly she learned that community-based organizations were essential players in the health care system; they were not only able to communicate with populations that required services but also provided links to health education efforts. And when she moved to the Bill & Melinda Gates Foundation, she developed relationships with other foundations and advocates for improved health care.

Dr. Lopez saw her challenge as balancing her clinical sensitivities with the policy reality. That was not always easy to accomplish. She still tended to think about health issues in terms of individual problems and needs. She admitted that whenever a specific health problem emerged in the policy debate, her physician's mind immediately went to an individual whom she had treated. She quickly remembered this individual, even by name. But she knew that the policy task was much broader than that.

This chapter sketches the changes that have taken place in the policymaking environment of the policy analysis profession that have affected its practice. It discusses the impact of fiscal scarcity, the impact of the proliferation of policy analysis activities, shifts in government structure and operations, and a sense that the space for action is more limited today than it was in the 1960s. It also reviews the impact of increased specialization, the structure of policy analysis offices in government, and current demands on analysts, including increased attention to performance.

Policy Tasks

During the early years of the policy analysis field, the challenge for analysts was to come up with new programs and policies, drawing on resources and a sense of optimism about government action. The task of the analyst in this environment was to give policymakers options for new action, and thus to choose among various approaches to achieve what were seen to be agreed-upon goals. As Alice Rivlin described it, during that period "the bureaucracy was both energized and overwhelmed by the magnitude of the new challenges. The job of our fledgling ASPE office [Office of the Assistant Secretary for Planning and Evaluation in the US Department of Health and Human Services] was to bring analysis and systematic thinking to bear on planning and priority setting and to try to evaluate the new programs so as to make them work as effectively as possible."[1] There is now a much more eclectic approach to the forms that policy takes; unlike in the 1960s, when the field highlighted analysis for new programs, policy is now seen to be expressed in budget allocations, organizational structure, and standard operating procedures.

The set of policy tasks that is a part of the world of the policy analyst in the twenty-first century is much different than it was when the field took form in the 1960s. It is not exaggerating to characterize the environment of policymaking that structures the contemporary world of the policy analyst as a transformed world. It has moved from a US domestic focus to one that includes global players and issues. At the most macro level, society has shifted from a mood of optimism to a sense of skepticism about the role of government. Despite some evidence that analysts have been involved in interesting policy initiatives, this sense of gloom has characterized at least some in the policy analysis community.[2] At the least, the public has raised a series of questions about government action, ranging from queries about whether the public sector should be involved at all in a particular policy area, to attempts to sort out what government can do well, to doubt about the ability of government to handle the goals with which it has been charged.

In addition, changes in public perceptions about the causes and possible solutions of policy problems have led to challenges in what might be described as "framing" problems. For example, violence issues are no longer viewed as the sole purview of the criminal justice system but, increasingly, are also viewed as public health and education issues. Environmental issues cannot be defined only within the borders of the United States but need to include global behaviors as well.

One is struck by the structural changes in the role of government at all levels. At the federal level, policies have been increasingly devolved to other levels of government, particularly the states. At all levels of government, some tasks that were previously carried out by government officials have been contracted out to others, often private-sector organizations. Given these new forms of relationships, the roles of the public and private sectors have changed, and the boundaries between the two institutional settings have become increasingly blurred. Yet the new players in the process do not always have the expertise or analytical skill necessary to handle these new responsibilities. At the same time, the availability of information on the Web has provided these players with access to information that had not been widely available.

Policy analysts also confront a policy environment that to many is highly polarized. There is conflict about the role of government per se, both in the United States and in many other countries. Divisions in society make reaching agreement on policy goals much more difficult. Increasingly divided government is the reality, whether at the national level with a president of one party and a Congress of the other party or at the state level with a governor of one party and one or both legislative chambers of the other one. Though partisan differences do not always have to lead to polarization and conflict, the relationships are made more difficult by increasingly ideological political parties.

To some extent the behavior of elected officials is tied to their relationships with interest groups. Whether as a result of these officials' dependence on these groups for campaign contributions or of the growing sophistication in how groups seek to influence the policy process, many elected officials are perceived to be and define themselves as representatives of particular economic, social, or religious interests. For example, the Heritage Foundation has developed relationships with identifiable members of Congress who share the organization's values. Similarly, the AARP policy group works closely with the organization's lobbyists. Though the close relationship between interest groups and members of Congress is clearly not new, interest groups' resources—both money and expertise—have become more prominent. It is somewhat ironic that the language of analysis has become more widespread at the same time that the values of openness and intellectual fairness have become harder to find when they play out in the political environment.

The World of Scarcity

For the past several decades both decision makers and policy analysts have perceived their parameters of action to be limited by very scarce resources. During the early 1990s the presence of a huge federal budget deficit defined the scope of action. New ideas could not be developed unless they were budget-neutral; that is, whatever modifications were made in programs could not lead to increases in the federal budget for that program area. Though some argued that concern about decreasing the budget deficit was really a trap laid by those who argued for less government action (particularly involving policies with redistributional goals), the deficit clearly defined action.

Given the focus on the budget, more decisions were made in the budget than in the program. The budget constraints made it difficult to argue for the most effective policy intervention or even to focus on the details of implementation that would determine whether a program could operate effectively or whether the effort would be able to reach its targeted clientele. It is not surprising that block grant programs became more attractive, which reflected the definition of programs in fiscal rather than substantive terms. It is easier to construct programs that are simply transfers of funds rather than national designs for policy interventions, especially when the decision makers are wed to the ideology of giving responsibility for decisions to the lowest possible governmental level. As a result, rather than being close to the top decision makers, policy analysis and planning offices have sometimes found themselves at the fringes of influence when they have sought to analyze the substantive details or possibilities of proposed programs. In some cases the policy analysis offices have been engaged in the debate on issues when they treat the budget offices as their clients.

The End of the Monopoly

As was noted, policy analysis is a field of practice found in almost all the US institutions and organizations involved in the policy process. And as chapter 3 explains, the US model has been modified as the field has moved around the world. Policy analysts are found in the executive branch bureaucracy, in the legislative branch, in interest groups, and in free-standing think tanks. The proliferation of analytic capacity has led to a shift in how the profession both perceives itself and operates. The original policy analysts in the federal government effectively had a monopoly on the practice. Not only were they located at the top of the agency's structure, but there also were few others who were trained to submit competing analyses to the decision makers.

Within federal agencies, policy analysts are now found at multiple levels; as a result, analysts need to assume that their work will be scrutinized by others who have the ability to produce comparable accomplishments. It is thus harder for analysts to adopt a posture that calls on deference to technical expertise as the mode of operation; no single right answer emerges from the application of analytic tools and techniques. Analysts who focus on implementation issues, for example, are likely to focus on operational details and impacts of program recommendations on other existing activities. By contrast, analysts who focus on fiscal effects are likely to develop options that downplay the implementation questions.

The presence of competing sources of advice has led to a shift in how analysts think about their role. Sometimes the most effective way to accomplish desired ends is to plant the seeds of an approach with others who might be working on the issue. When these ideas are suggested by others, then they take on a life of their own and develop momentum for gaining support. Good relationships with other analysts are necessary to accomplish this. These shifts suggest that analysts who adopt the technician's role, sitting in a bureaucratic ivory tower, are not likely to influence others.

The end of the monopoly on analysis has been an extremely important development in the field. Not only does it call for the development of skills that were not traditionally a part of the analytic role, but it also supports a modest, incremental approach to policy options. At the same time, in an era of ideological conflict, this stance is hard to maintain as policy conflicts are turned into debates between analysts. One could view these developments as the democratization of the policy analysis function, providing access to analysis and effectively leveling the decision playing field. To the extent that policy analyses are available to all parties, this access has the effect of leveling the playing field. Increasingly (although still not commonly) information is viewed as a public good where the multiple players involved have access to it.

Shifts in Government Structure and Operations

Since the end of the twentieth century, policy analysts inside government have had to deal with a new set of expectations about the way that agencies operate. Beginning with the pronouncements issued by Osborne and Gaebler in their book *Reinventing Government* (which highlighted shifts in local government) and continuing on to the National Performance Review in the federal government, there have been a number of changes in views of appropriate and effective ways to organize government agencies.[3] Vice President Al Gore's efforts in the National Performance Review represented what became the norm for the reinventing government initiative during the Clinton administration. In addition to a focus on budget reductions, this effort included attention to reorganization, empowering line managers, improving customer service, and changing decision systems.[4] The impact of these changes has been to flatten organizational structures and to decentralize many responsibilities to operating components that were previously located in centralized governmental units. These changes have not always been institutionalized from one administration to another. Indeed, many of them were overturned during the George W. Bush administration.

The Policy Space

Many of these developments in the policy environment have contributed to a sense that the space for action is much more limited than it was in the 1960s. At the macro level budget limitations and skepticism about government action have led to a diminished sense of program possibilities. The new programs that have emerged have not always been based on analysis; indeed, many decisions are made without analyses at all—if the decisions can get beyond ideological or partisan battles. As a result, there are many fewer recommendations for new programs emerging from the policy analyst's portfolio. Those new initiatives that are devised are often the result of political calculations and thus spring from the White House, the congressional leadership, or other overtly political agendas aimed at elections or satisfying specific constituency groups. Though policy analysts in the bureaucracy may be assigned to work on the development of these initiatives, the criteria that guide their efforts emphasize the political dimensions of the issues. For example, the health care reform proposal that emerged from the White House during the first Clinton term involved a number of policy analysts from the Department of Health and Human Services who were assigned to work directly with the White House staff on a day-to-day basis. Analysts learn that the political spin on an issue often becomes an important focus and that the questions raised by public affairs staff members become the sole source of criteria.

This contraction of the policy space has also reinforced an increased interest in analyzing the implementation details of existing programs. If it is difficult to propose new programs that have a possibility of enactment, then it makes more sense to focus on fine-tuning and modifying existing programs. Evaluation studies and research might be expected to be of particular interest to an approach that accentuates marginal change. However, at the same time the implementation focus has increased, both staff and fiscal resources for evaluation activities have decreased.

Increased Specialization

With the exception of the earliest days of the practice of the policy analysis profession, analysts have tended to focus on a relatively narrow set of issues. The rationale for their career development centers on interest in a few policy problems and programs. This is not surprising, given the fragmented organization and structure of policymaking in the United States that follows issue dimensions. The assumption that the policy analyst would be an analytical generalist, applying expertise through an array of analytical techniques to a range of issues, has been turned on its head. Analysts not only have become a part of specific issue networks, but many of them have also moved among various organizations and institutions within those networks. Thus, during their careers, it is not unusual for analysts to move among executive branch agencies, congressional committees, and even interest groups. This career progression mirrors the tendency for specialization within society at large.

Specialization has both positive and negative effects on policy analysts. It allows analysts to develop close relationships with other players in the policy process and to become highly expert in the details of the programs. Their longevity in the process provides them with the ability to serve as the institutional memory in a policy environment characterized by a high turnover of appointed and elected officials. Robert Nelson suggests that the policy analysis office in the Department of the Interior provided a very useful function as the institutional memory during periods of changes of administration and when new officials came into office.[5] At the same time, he notes that changes of administration can be "trying times" for a policy office.[6] Though term limits may not be formally required in all settings, the careers of elected officials at all levels of government have become shorter and shorter.

However, specialization may also contribute to a number of problems that affect the policy analyst. When an individual analyst has been around for many years, participants in the policy process may find his or her contribution to be predictable. In such a circumstance, it is difficult for the analyst to move out of expected policy behavior. When an analyst is around for many years working on the same set of policy issues, he or she may suffer from a form of professional burnout, which breeds a sense of cynicism and exhaustion. This can have the effect of turning analysts into technocrats.

Specialization also may make it difficult for analysts to think about issues in new ways. Although many policy issues are now defined in ways that accentuate crosscutting relationships among separate programs, highly specialized analysts (as well as decision makers) may resist the need to conceptualize a broader range of actors than those who have been traditionally involved in an issue. Issues such as drug abuse, for example, cut across a range of health and social services, criminal justice and education agencies, and issue networks. The focus on networks also may increasingly mean the elimination of traditional boundaries between policy sectors.

The Structure of Policy Analysis Offices in the Government

At the same time that policy analysis capacity has spread into various parts of government agencies and is found in both program and staff offices, the centralized policy analysis offices in the federal government have changed in both function and structure. The PPBS inheritance of the federal offices emphasized a *prospective* approach to policy development, and these units were often described as the planning offices in government. The identification with planning in the 1960s had three main related attributes. First, this approach sought to move beyond annual proposals that were constrained by the yearly budget. Second, its posture strove for the ideal and emphasized maximizing rather than satisficing goals (as economists would put it). And third, the analysis that was performed was viewed as significantly different from that done by other staff offices (especially traditional budget offices).

However, as the years progressed, the planning orientation of the policy analysis offices tended to diminish. Some policy areas that were dominated by analysts trained as economists continued to strive for the ideal and to take a multiyear perspective. However, these analysts had decreasing influence over policy decisions. In addition, not only was the analyst function found in program units, but it also became more difficult to differentiate individuals who had the job titles "management analyst" or "budget analyst" from the people who were staffing the official policy analysis offices.

Generally, the numbers of analysts in federal agencies decreased over the years, although there were irregular increases at particular times (particularly when the White House was occupied by a Democratic president). Thus a smaller number of analysts operated with competition from more bureaucratic staff and, at the same time, increased specialization in the policy analysis unit. In addition, the formal policy analysis units also compete with analyses done by nongovernmental organizations and interest groups. It is increasingly common for individuals who occupy top positions in policy analysis units to be chosen for their knowledge of particular policy issues rather than for generic analytic expertise. Though individual analysts might have influence over the design of policy initiatives, whatever power they had did not come from their bureaucratic location in the policy analysis office but from their personal expertise and reputation.

Broadening the Definition of Client

As has been discussed in earlier chapters, policy analysts today do not only advise the prince or the top decision maker. The clients for policy analysts are very diverse and reflect the proliferation of the function both inside and outside government. Decision making involving networks cuts across traditional boundaries between government and the private sector. As a result, they include not only individual decision makers at multiple levels of government organizations but also the ongoing decision processes that have been institutionalized within government agencies. Policy analysts are likely to be participants in special task forces or interagency efforts to devise program modifications or to define new initiatives. In some cases the analyst may actually serve as the staff person for these assignments, and then the task force or interagency group effectively becomes the client. The policy analysis office in the Department of the Interior, for example, organized and managed the internal budget process, reviewing correspondence and legislative proposals, and regulations.[7]

The profiles provided in chapter 4 also indicate that policy analysts found outside executive branch government agencies work for a range of clients. Policy analysts operating in the legislative branch have many different clients because the legislative institutions are made up of multiple actors. For instance, both the California Legislative Analyst's Office and the Congressional Research Service balance a client pool that is segmented by political affiliation, level of knowledge of an issue, and assumptions about appropriate action. Analysts need to deal with clients that have well-defined interests, organizational needs, and values.

There are also instances when the policy analyst completes an assignment without actually knowing who has requested the work. Indeed, as the analyst becomes more specialized and reaches seniority in an organization, the work could have been self-defined. The assignment may be given by the top policy analyst, who does not let the analyst know why the work has been requested. It is hard for an analyst to be sensitive to a client's values and interests when he or she is far removed from contact with the client. Under these circumstances, analysts who have worked on a policy issue over the years may be ready to pull out a piece of work completed in the past and repackage it for current use.

Functions of Policy Analysts Today

Unlike the policy analysts of the 1960s, when PPBS defined and structured their work, today's analysts spend their time on a range of functions. Some offices do continue to work on longer-term planning projects that are assigned to them to meet specific organizational needs. Most policy analysis offices support longer-term research efforts; though there are many fewer resources available for these research projects, they continue to be a part of the work. Evaluation activities of various sorts are also a part of the policy analysis portfolio; some are longer-term evaluation research activities, whereas others are shorter-term evaluations that attempt to provide information to individuals who implement programs. Still another function is found in the policy analysis units; what are often called quick-and-dirty analyses seek to provide immediate advice to decision makers on issues that are topical or constitute a response to bad press.

This mix of functions calls on contemporary policy analysts to be able to perform a number of tasks. They are encouraged to think outside the box. They must understand the context (especially the players in a network), know the details of programs, and be familiar with a number of analytical techniques. They must understand the budget and legislation process cycles that define the venue for their work. Research and evaluation activities are increasingly performed through contracts or grants with outside research or consulting organizations. The work that is done by these outside groups is viewed as a direct extension of the responsibilities of the internal analysis office. Thus the in-house policy analyst is called on to manage these contractual arrangements and to ensure that the work being performed is available in a useful and timely fashion.

Analysts also find themselves continuing to play the role of research and evaluation translators—a role that was described as one of the early attributes of the field. They are called upon to interpret or restate the technical findings of researchers in language that is appropriate and understandable to decision makers. They are required to find ways to infuse the research findings into the discussion. Sometimes this may take the form of summaries of these findings; at other times the findings may emerge as a part of an issue brief and evidence for a recommended position.

Over the years, many policy analysts have become much less reliant on traditional written documents to communicate their work to decision makers. Analysts are required to make short, pithy oral briefings to capture the interest of busy decision makers. Computer-generated briefing formats (e.g., PowerPoint) have become increasingly common. Often analysts find that they are most effective when they participate in meetings and conferences organized by issue networks and are able to infuse their expertise into the discussion of alternative approaches. The information that is available on websites speeds up the process, and analysts are often asked for work in real time.

The Focus on Performance

If there is a single theme that has characterized the public sector since the 1990s, it is the demand for performance. A mantra has emerged, heard at all levels of government, that calls for documentation of performance and explicit outcomes of government action. Although this demand has also emerged from governors' offices, state legislatures, and city and county governments, perhaps no activity better embodies this request than the federal Government Performance and Results Act (GPRA) of 1993, the legislation that has structured expectations for performance-based management in the federal government.[8]

The GPRA requirements are built around several processes. The first, a strategic plan, is expected to include a comprehensive mission statement for the agency, a specification of general goals and objectives (including outcome-related goals and objectives) as well as how they will be achieved, the relationship between the goals and objectives and performance goals, identification of key factors that could affect the achievement of the goals and objectives, and a description of the program evaluations used in establishing or revising the goals and objectives. The five-year time frame for the strategic plan provides an opportunity for agencies to adopt a planning mode and look at their mission and goals beyond an annual budget process. Agencies are required to consult with Congress and others interested in or affected by the plan.

The second set of requirements focuses on the specification of annual performance plans that would include each program activity set in the budget. These plans include performance goals that define the level of performance to be achieved by a program activity; articulate specific goals in objective, quantifiable, and measurable form; indicate the operational processes, skills, technology, and resources required; provide performance indicators to be used in measuring relevant outputs, service levels, and outcomes; establish a basis for comparing actual program results with the established performance goals; and specify the means to be used to verify and validate measured values. Although not discussed explicitly, there is an assumption embedded in the requirement that data are already available and agreed upon to make these assessments.

The third set of requirements calls for annual program performance reports that will compare the actual performance for each program activity with the performance goals in the plan for that fiscal year. These requirements ask agencies to explain why performance has not been met and to provide plans for achieving the performance goal in the future.

On its face, it is both important and appropriate for agencies to be required to define their goals (and the measures for achieving them) in terms of concrete outcomes. This set of requirements has put new demands on the traditional process of measuring performance by the amount of money spent, the level of staff deployed, or the number of tasks completed. The focus on outcomes is meant to be a way to focus on the differences that government programs make in the economy or in the lives of program participants.

In many ways, the GPRA requirements hark back to the rational planning assumptions embedded in the PPBS process of the 1960s. In many federal agencies, policy analysts have been involved in preparing the submissions required by the legislation, especially the requirement for a strategic plan. Because the annual performance plans are viewed as a part of budget submissions, however, the budget offices—rather than the policy analysis offices—may assume the major role in developing these submissions. In addition, the effort received strong support from some advocates of policy and program evaluation, who saw this as an opportunity to bring evaluation data to the decision-making table. In at least one federal agency, however, the policy analysis/evaluation staff found that very few of the evaluation studies that had been commissioned assisted the organization in its effort to find data that described performance outcomes.

The GPRA process has also made it clear that it is difficult to measure performance when there are very limited resources for policy analysis and research. It is increasingly difficult to justify large-scale data collection approaches. Resistance to information collection demands compounds the problem. Despite the rhetoric focusing on performance, it has become more and more problematic to find ways to convince the recipients of government funds that they should provide useful data on their accomplishments. Stories of gaming information and difficulties supporting information collection abound.

Failure to Evaluate the Investment

After more than fifty years, one would assume that there has been an attempt by policy analysis practitioners to systematically evaluate the impact of their field. There has been a considerable investment in analytic activity, both inside and outside government, in terms of people, money, and effort. Although we may acknowledge that the field has been modified considerably during these years—reflecting a world of political pressures, ambiguity, and messiness—there have been very few attempts to take stock of the impact of the profession. Those few attempts that have been made to develop a self-critical stance have been largely impressionistic. For example, a panel during the 1997 research conference of the Association for Public Policy Analysis and Management attempted to review the impact of policy analysis activity involving welfare policy over the years.[9] Though the discussion was extremely interesting, there was no attempt to explore the issues further after the panel session was over.

Dealing with Realities

The policy analysis task is much more complex today than it was in the 1960s or even at the end of the twentieth century. Analysts must deal with the complexity of the decision-making process, with its multiple avenues for intervention. The experience of more than three decades and the attendant changes in society accentuate the constraints in the policy environment. As a result, analysts are more modest in what they expect from their activities, in terms of both their role and the scope of possible action. According to James Smith, a student of think tanks, analysts now deal with the realities "of promotion, advocacy, and intellectual combat."[10] At the same time, they struggle to maintain norms of fairness and accuracy within this environment.

Notes

1. Alice M. Rivlin, "Does Good Policy Analysis Matter?" Remarks at the Dedication of the Alice Mitchell Rivlin Conference Room, Office of the Assistant Secretary for Planning and Evaluation, Department of Health and Human Services, Washington, February 17, 1998.

2. See David R. Beam, "If Public Ideas Are So Important Now, Why Are Policy Analysts So Depressed?" *Journal of Policy Analysis and Management* 15, no. 3 (1996): 430–37.

3. See David Osborne and Ted Gaebler, *Reinventing Government: How the Entrepreneurial Spirit Is Transforming the Public Sector* (Reading, MA: Addison-Wesley, 1992).

4. Beryl A. Radin, "Varieties of Reinvention: Six NPR 'Success Stories,'" in *Inside the Reinvention Machine,* edited by John DiIulio and Donald Kettl (Washington, DC: Brookings Institution Press, 1995).

5. See Robert H. Nelson, "The Office of Policy Analysis in the Department of the Interior," *Journal of Policy Analysis and Management* 8, no. 3 (1989): 408.

6. Ibid., 400.

7. Ibid., 408.

8. The Bush administration's Program Assessment Rating Tool (PART) and a revised GPRA added to the original GPRA legislation. In December 2010 Congress amended GPRA and slightly pulled back some of the centralization found in PART. See Beryl A. Radin, *Challenging the Performance Movement: Accountability, Complexity and Democratic Values* (Washington, DC: Georgetown University Press, 2006). See also Beryl A. Radin, "The Government Performance and Results Act (GPRA): Hydra-Headed Monster or Effective Policy Tool?" *Public Administration Review* (July–August 1998): 307–15.

9. The review took place in a panel titled "Do Clients Use Policy Analysis?" Annual Research Conference, Association for Public Policy Analysis and Management, Washington, November 1997. The panel was chaired by Larry Mead of New York University and included individuals who had experience with analytic activity in the welfare policy field inside government and as staff members in Congress as well as researchers.

10. James Allen Smith, *The Idea Brokers: Think Tanks and the Rise of the New Policy Elite* (New York: Free Press, 1991), 194.

Chapter 9

Where Are We? And Where Are We Going? Has Policy Analysis Reached Middle Age?

Rita Stone and Veronica Lopez found themselves sitting next to one another as panelists at a children's issues conference sponsored by the National Academy of Sciences. Each one's interests and areas of contribution were quite different. Stone spoke about child care issues, whereas Lopez focused on pediatric infectious diseases. One was a federal staff member who had started as a careerist but had moved to a political position, whereas the other was a former federal official who was currently working for the Bill & Melinda Gates Foundation in both the United States and abroad. After they gave their presentations, however, they were both fascinated about the views that they seemed to share in common.

Despite their differences in background, both women were very committed to policy change involving children. Lopez was intrigued that Stone was both an advocate for children as well as an individual trained as a policy analyst. Although Lopez always described herself as a physician, she found that she increasingly identified herself by using the word "policy" in her explanation of her role and interests. Stone was also intrigued by Lopez. She was amazed that a physician not only saw herself as an advocate concerned about policy but also maintained her identity as a medical clinician. After the conference ended, both of them wanted to continue their conversation, so they whipped out their calendars and found a time to have lunch.

After leaving the meeting, Stone was reminded of the conversation she had nearly fifteen years earlier with John Nelson, a former staff member in the policy analysis office of the Department of Health, Education, and Welfare (HEW).

Their accidental meeting took place on an airplane when they were both return-
ing from work assignments in Paris. The long flight from Paris gave them time to
compare their experiences as policy analysts during two very different eras of
development in the field. Stone had been so interested in that comparison that
she actually wrote a somewhat fictionalized version of the conversation that
appeared in a book on policy analysis. She decided that Lopez might find this
account of interest and sent her a copy of the book before their lunch meeting.

When Lopez received the book containing Stone's essay, she immediately
sat down and read it. Although her work put her in the midst of the policy-
making world, she had not thought about herself as a policy analyst. And she
certainly did not know much about the details of the development of that field.
Here is what she read:

"Rita Stone was sitting on an airplane on her way back from an international
meeting of the Organization for Economic Cooperation and Development
(OECD) in Paris. The meeting had provided an opportunity for her to see how
other governments were approaching the child care issue and had given her
many new ideas to bring back to Washington. During her spare time, she had
had a chance to visit with the people she had worked with when she had one of
her rotational assignments at the OECD [as a Presidential Management Intern].

"Stone wasn't sure how she was going to spend the seven hours of the
flight. She had already seen the movie that was being shown, and she did have
a lot of reading to do for work that should be finished when she came back to
the office. She began to read the papers from her briefcase but wasn't really
concentrating on them.

"Sitting next to her was a man in his sixties who was reading Robert McNamara's memoirs. He noticed that she was plowing through a stack of papers,
many of which contained the letterhead Office of the Assistant Secretary for
Planning and Evaluation [ASPE], Department of Health and Human Services.
When the flight attendant came around to serve drinks, the man—John Nelson—decided that he would begin a conversation with the young woman.

'Excuse me, but I couldn't help noticing that you are reading memos from
ASPE. Do you work there? I actually was in that office when it first opened.
I'm now a partner in a consulting firm in California that does work for DoD [the
Department of Defense] and have been in Europe working on a study for the
base-closing commission. I'm curious to know what has happened to that office. When I was there, it was an incredible place to work—exhausting but very
stimulating.'

"Stone told him that she did not work in ASPE now but was a budget analyst in the Office of the Assistant Secretary for Management and Budget at

the Department of Health and Human Services. She noted that she worked very closely with ASPE staff. She commented, 'Although I work in the budget office, I am a graduate of a public policy program and, in many ways, identify myself as a policy analyst. I have a feeling that the ASPE office today is very different from the office that you worked in. I'd love to hear your impressions of the early ASPE.'

"Stone was intrigued to hear about the early days of ASPE because she had learned about its origins when she attended a lecture given by Alice Rivlin just a few months earlier: 'You know, it is an amazing coincidence that I am sitting next to someone who had been in that office during a time that many old-time department hands viewed as its prime.' She told Nelson a little bit about her background and what she was doing now. He told her that he had started his Washington career at DoD in the 1960s and was very interested to read McNamara's account of that period. Although he had been back in California since the late 1960s, he had tried to keep apprised of the developments in the field that he called policy analysis.

"The flight turned out to be an excellent opportunity for Stone and Nelson to compare their experiences and to talk about the future of the field. Stone asked Nelson, 'What could you tell me about the staff members in the policy office in what was then called HEW?' As he described the staff, he noted that a number of them had come from DoD, he among them: 'Some of the staff members were systems analysts, but most were economists.' Stone was very surprised to hear that some of the people he recalled had stayed in ASPE throughout its life. Indeed, one of the earliest staff members had just retired, having been in ASPE from the 1960s to the late 1990s. Nelson had thought that the pattern of staffing followed his experience of staying in the federal government for a few years and then moving on.

"Nelson had assumed that the staff would continue to be systems analysts and economists and that most of them would have PhDs. When Stone described the current staff, however, they both realized that there were very few PhDs or economists in the office. She noted, 'Most of the people who joined the staff came from graduate schools of public policy, arriving with master's degrees in what was an interdisciplinary field. Few characterized themselves as researchers but rather as individuals who were able to apply a range of techniques and approaches to policy analysis and sought to be a part of the decision process in the department.'

"Stone had heard that ASPE's early staff members had emphasized the use of the cost-benefit technique in their work. She asked Nelson about this. As he recalled, he was quite ambivalent about the use of cost-benefit analysis: 'I was sold on the technique when I was in DoD, finding that it was a powerful analytic *approach to sorting out trade-offs among program elements. But when I came to HEW, I found that it was of limited utility. It was extremely difficult to quantify some of the anticipated benefits and to find a way to compare programs across different sector and client groups.' But he was amazed to learn that very few—if any—cost-benefit analyses were being done in the domestic social policy agencies today. If they were done at all, they were contracted out to consulting firms.*

"He asked Stone about what analytical models were currently being used in the department to develop alternatives and recommendations. He told her about the analytical models that were being developed in DoD to come up with recommendations for base closings: 'I think that those models are analytically rigorous and quite elegant.' But Stone was somewhat stymied by this question because—at least in her work—it was hard for her to think about an analytical framework that captured the complexities of the programs that were a part of her portfolio. As she tried to answer his question, he recognized that Stone was focusing on the operational and implementation details of programs, not simply on achieving the broad parameters of program goals.

"When she recounted the approach that she was using to gather information about alternative child care options, she described her relationships with other analysts in the department, in interest groups, and in Congress. Nelson kept shaking his head as she went through the litany of colleagues. 'Isn't it difficult to deal with all those individuals with so many agendas?' he asked. 'How can you arrive at the best policy option when you have to spend your time bargaining and negotiating with them?' Stone realized that it had been a long time since she had thought about the best option; she was more concerned with developing an option that was likely to attain the broadest range of support: 'I don't really separate the analysis process from the decision-making process since so many decisions in the department are made on the basis of personal interaction between players and few documents describing options are actually advanced in the process.'

"As he reminisced, Nelson described his encounters with the department secretary and undersecretary. Although she had had many conversations with the secretary and the deputy secretary, Stone had quite a different attitude about the top officials in the department. She listened to Nelson's account. 'During my time,' he commented, 'decisions were made by the top officials, not by a collaborative group of officials ranging from the secretary to middle-level staff.' Both Nelson and Stone were aware that much of what they did depended on the interests and style of the sitting president as well as the secretary of the department.

"Nelson told of walking into the secretary's office with a short executive summary accompanying a detailed analysis of options for a new health program: 'The analysis emphasized two elements: alternative cost estimates for different options and estimates of coverage of the target population.' Stone asked, 'Didn't you ask anything about the implementation of the proposed option? And did you try to calculate the level of political reaction to the proposal? Didn't the analysts from the health programs bring up these issues? And what did the White House say about them?'

"Nelson realized that he didn't have to deal with those issues. It was a good thing that he could avoid them because he did not know the answers to the questions and didn't have the time to find them. There were no other analysts attached to the program units. And the White House seemed to be willing to defer to the proposals from the department: 'When I briefed the secretary, I knew that this proposal was just one of a number of new programs being suggested and that the top officials in the department had very little time to focus on the details of implementation. The window of opportunity was open wide, and it seemed more appropriate to take advantage of it with a program proposal before it slammed shut.'

"'But didn't you worry that you were coming up with programs that really couldn't achieve the anticipated goals?' Stone was appalled that the analysts hadn't focused on the problems that were subsequently described as 'unanticipated problems' because she felt that attention to the implementation details would have minimized the serious difficulties with many of the programs of the mid-1960s.

"Stone was also intrigued with Nelson's ability to separate the political dimensions from program design. When she asked him about it, he realized that he hadn't given that problem much thought. He described the early process at DoD, where Secretary McNamara sought to control what he viewed as runaway military services. Although he didn't impose a control agenda with a similarly heavy hand, Secretary John Gardner at HEW also sought to find ways to centralize authority in the department and to identify areas where programs could reinforce and support one another. As Nelson thought about it now, it was quite amazing that no one at either DoD or HEW had spent a lot of time thinking about potential resistance from a wide range of interest groups. Although there was evidence of this problem later, it did not become a part of the analyst's agenda.

"When Stone talked about the ideological resistance to many of the programs at the Department of Health and Human Services today, Nelson was overwhelmed: 'I felt privileged to be in Washington during an era when *government activity was viewed in positive terms by most people in society. Not only was there a close relationship between the executive branch and Congress during that period, but there was also a sense that the nation had adequate resources to meet defined needs.' He did remember that the advent of the Vietnam War marked a changed view about resource availability. But it seemed minor compared with what Stone described.*

"Stone had read about the PPBS process in several of her courses in graduate school, so she queried Nelson about the experience: 'I'm especially interested in the belief that planning and budgeting could be closely linked since my experience is so very different from the rhetoric of PPBS.' She noted that in her experience budget conversations were almost in code, with specific dollar allocations used as surrogates for program substance. Nelson speculated about the reasons for these differences: 'Perhaps it was because a system that was devised in the Defense Department carried the assumption that programs (particularly weapons systems) had multiyear time frames. Even though the budget proposals were submitted to Congress on an annual basis, they were constructed on multiyear plans for development.' In addition, he recognized that it did not seem so unrealistic in the early 1960s to think about five-year time frames because society seemed to be relatively stable.

"Nelson had known a little bit about the Government Performance and Results Act but, until Stone started describing the implementation process, he hadn't recognized some of the ways in which it paralleled PPBS. In an era of divided government and rapid change, he did wonder whether the requirement for a five-year strategic plan made much sense. He thought it was important to think about the goals and outcomes of programs and the strategies employed to achieve them, but he shared Stone's skepticism about the ability of the current budget process to 'listen' to that approach.

"As they were finishing up their lunch on the plane, Nelson asked Stone to describe how she spent her days: 'What is a typical day like for you?' Stone laughed because she was also thinking about what she had to do tomorrow when she returned to the office. 'Well, here is what usually happens. I come into the office early in the morning and read the e-mails that have been sent since I last checked. They include a number of canned messages from the secretary, the deputy secretary, the assistant secretary for management and budget, the deputy assistant secretary for budget, and the executive secretariat. I also am on several listservs in the child care issue field. Though they aren't written specifically for me, it's important that I know what is going on. There will also be a number of messages for me personally from others in the department who are working on the child care issue. I'll probably be asked a

number of questions in those messages but will also be invited to participate in several meetings that day.

"'Once I read the e-mails, I look very quickly at the paper that has piled up in my in-box. There are likely to be several requests for information from members of Congress and the White House. I may need to give assignments to my staff to respond to these requests or write a short note outlining a response to them. In addition, there are probably a number of phone calls that I have to return from various people in interest groups, other parts of the department, and the White House.

"'Though I try to respond to all forms of communication (e-mail, written mail, and phone messages) by the next day, sometimes I find that isn't possible. During a typical day, I'm likely to have between four and six meetings scheduled; most of them are an hour long. If the meetings are held outside my building, I have to allow time to take the subway or a taxi to arrive there. And if the meetings come to some conclusion, they are likely to spin off additional sessions. When I return, I have to brief my boss on the outcomes.

"'Probably the analysts who work on child care in ASPE have a similar schedule. If they have an assignment to write a report, they are likely to work with an outside contractor to do the first draft. For all of us, face-to-face meetings provide the setting for most information exchange. Does this resemble the way that you spent your time when you were in ASPE?'

"Stone's description of her typical day was not what Nelson had expected. He could not see any difference between what she did with her time and traditional bureaucratic behavior. He tried to reconstruct a typical day at ASPE, realizing that many years had elapsed and that his memory of the details might be somewhat faulty: 'I remember life at ASPE as a pattern that was much less responsive to other people's agendas or their time. I was given assignments by the assistant secretary, worked on them behind a closed office door, developed drafts that I shared with others at ASPE, and then eventually had the opportunity to brief the secretary or the undersecretary. I regularly kept up with articles on methodology that were published in the academic journals. And I had a small network of other researchers and analysts in academia and in think tanks and would occasionally share drafts of reports with them. They all knew, however, that I was responding to my client—the secretary. I really didn't have the opportunity to develop close relationships with others beyond ASPE either inside or outside the department because my assignments changed so often in terms of their substantive focus.'

"As they told their stories, each of them felt envy for the other's life to some degree. Stone realized that she had no opportunity to write, even though she *had many ideas that she thought ought to be documented. Nelson realized that his life at ASPE had been quite circumscribed and hadn't given him the opportunity to see his ideas come to completion.*

"As the pilot announced that the plane was beginning its descent into Dulles Airport, Stone and Nelson exchanged business cards. Both knew that they would leave the plane with some disquieting thoughts about the policy analysis field. Before this conversation, Nelson had painted a picture for himself of a time of incredible possibilities, when analysts were advisers to the top decision makers, were insulated from partisan political debates, had confidence in their methodologies and information sources, and believed that decisions were likely to be better as a result of their work. After his conversation with Stone, he recognized that this picture was overly optimistic, painted in black and white, with few colors used to describe that world. Indeed, he felt that technician analysts like himself had to take some of the responsibility for the programs of the 1960s that suffered severe implementation problems. And he was somewhat uncomfortable with the elitism that seemed to be intrinsic to the group that had a monopoly on analytic advice.

"By contrast, Stone realized that her analytic world was incredibly messy, that policy advisers were strewn around the policy landscape, and that it was difficult to escape from the pressures and demands of partisan and ideologically driven debates. She rarely had an opportunity to step back and think about the best possible solutions to the problems with which she dealt. She knew that analysts were questioning their methodologies and acknowledging the limits of their information. In many instances, the analysts were marginal to many decision-making processes. It was hard to argue that the system produced better decisions as a result of their work. At the same time, she did feel some competence in a specialized policy area and believed that the policy world contained many people like her who really cared about a particular issue. Even though she agreed with Nelson that to some degree policy analysts had become "traditional" bureaucrats, they still were able to bring some level of rigor and logic to the messy world of decision making. And she was very comfortable with what she saw as the "democratization" of the field, with analytic capacities found both inside and outside government.

"Stone went back to work the next day, facing a huge pile of e-mails, messages, and papers. Nelson went to the Pentagon to report on his European visit and then caught a plane to Los Angeles. Both thought that they had been the beneficiary of serendipity and that their plane conversation had been a special experience."

After she finished reading the account of the conversation between Stone and Nelson, Lopez was struck by how much things had changed in the fifteen years since that exchange. Although she had met analysts who resembled Nel-son and were trained as economists, most of the health economists with whom she had contact had moved far away from identification as generic economists and instead worked only on the specifics of the health field. Given her focus on health services for poor children, actually most of those individuals were concerned about questions of access to health services. She also found that the reliance on written work exhibited by both Stone and Nelson wasn't what she had experienced. Rather, she dealt with clients largely in an interactive set-ting, providing clients with on-the-spot advice to help them deal with emergent and often immediate problems. She wasn't sure whether individuals in other fields experienced that fluid work environment, but the demands of health care policymaking around the globe were usually fast-moving and often politicized.

Lopez also felt that the information sources that both Stone and Nelson used in their work tended to be developed either inside of the government or in traditional academic settings. She had found real limits to that information and usually sought sources in nongovernmental organizations, interest groups, or in face-to-face encounters with individuals affected by the policy problem. She sometimes thought that Google had become her Bible; when faced with a new issue, she sat down at her computer and found information readily avail-able by going to the Google website. She was interested to learn that Nelson's early reliance on the use of traditional cost-benefit analyses had already been replaced; Stone seemed to be more comfortable with analytic approaches that allowed her to look at issues from the perspective of specific actors involved in an issue. Although improving efficiency was important, it was not the only thing that she and her clients valued. They were also concerned about effectiveness of programs as well as their equity aspects.

Lopez resonated with Stone's description of the demands of her job. Keep-ing in contact with a wide range of players in a policy area was really time con-suming, and she too felt that she could not keep up with the constant flow of e-mails. She thought that both analysts and clients were less sanguine about the ability of decision makers to think about issues without confronting major political and ideological differences in the years that had elapsed since the conversation between Stone and Nelson on the airplane. And the fiscal issues attached to the budget deficit just provided another setting for ideological con-flict and antigovernment sentiments.

Dr. Lopez looked forward to her lunch with Rita Stone. She found the ac-count of the conversation between the two analysts very informative, and she really appreciated learning about the differences in the perspectives of those two generations of policy analysts. She wondered whether Stone's views about her own job had changed over the years and whether they shared perspectives about the current demands on them. She wasn't sure whether the views of a Hispanic woman from Texas who was also a physician could be generalized beyond her unique experience. But she did have the feeling that both she and Stone were attempting to balance advocacy and analytical perspectives.

After more than fifty years, the policy analysis field has taken its place in the contemporary world of decision making. But it is also clear that the original view of policy analysis as a process of advising a prince or ruler—harking back to Machiavelli—does not capture the complexity of the field today. Indeed, it is difficult to characterize the field as a two-person advising process that is like a simple conversation.

Policy analysis is now a field both in the United States and around the globe that encompasses multiple languages, values, and forms, and has many types of individuals and groups as clients. Its conversations take place across the policy landscape. Though its diversity is frustrating and dissonant to some, it also mirrors American society itself. Instead of being a profession controlled by an elite few, it is now democratized with an eclectic set of practices and people who represent very different interests. As the field has become more complex, however, it has become increasingly difficult to establish a clear sense of professional norms and a definition of success.

Defining Success

As the policy analysis profession has changed over time, policy analysts have struggled to figure out what criteria they should use to evaluate their own work. They have fewer opportunities to point to new programs and take pride in the role they played in bringing them to life. More frequently than not, analysts circumscribe their activity to small-scale issues and to working at the margins of policy debates. Given the range of actors and analysts involved in policy discussions, it is difficult to point to one's individual contribution to the process.

Analysts continue to confront the balancing act that has been a part of the profession since its early days: the conflict between being responsive to the client and hewing to the values of rigor and fairness. Although few analysts would wrap themselves around abstract concepts of neutrality and objectivity, recognizing that values and interests are implicit in most policy discussions, they do want to produce work and advice that are as complete and balanced as possible. The norms established for the academic expression of the field are not always sensitive to the real world of decision making.

Though this has been a challenge for analysts since the early days of the profession, in recent years the blurring of the boundary lines between analysis and advocacy have made this task more difficult.

There seems to be a disconnect between the analyst's perception of self-worth, which is often drawn from the rational-actor model, and the real contribution that the individual makes in the nooks and crannies of the policy process. Many analysts seem to believe that formal studies or reports are the only types of products that are noteworthy. They seem to need a language to describe what they do and to convince themselves—as well as others—that they contribute to the process. They are challenged to think about ways of developing standards for their work that reflect their diverse experiences: What are the standards against which work should be measured? Should it be drawn from a peer review model? Should accountability revolve around questions of utilization? How should one deal with the perception that this is an elitist profession? Also, there has not been a commitment to encourage self-reflection on the part of seasoned professionals and to give them the tools to think about their contributions.

This situation calls for a renewed commitment by schools of public policy to think about a curriculum that will best meet contemporary needs. A number of schools have effectively continued course offerings that were put in place when the schools opened in the 1970s. Some schools are beginning to reexamine this curriculum and to consider the changes that have taken place since then. Also, these academic programs are increasingly being staffed by faculty members without much experience advising decision makers.[1]

Also, very little attention has been given by these professional schools to patterns of career development in the field, to the kinds of skills that are now appropriate for the profession, and to expectations about packaging or marketing the results of the analytic process. Students should be familiar with techniques such as organizing and running focus groups; they will need to figure out ways to gauge the intensity level for certain issues, assessing not only classic political feasibility factors but also the level of venom around some policy areas. They are required to be sensitive to the demands of making presentations to busy clients and to acknowledge that many clients participate in networks with multiple players and diverse perspectives. The experiences of organizations like the Heritage Foundation and the Center on Budget and Policy Priorities are instructive for thinking about the various ways to effectively present analytic findings. Good packaging can take many different forms. For instance, several projects sponsored by the World Bank have published the results of evaluation studies by posting them on the walls of village clinics and community centers. These simple wall charts are understandable by village residents and create a set of accountability expectations for service delivery.

Future Changes in the Policy Environment

In coming years policy analysts can expect to deal with several shifts in the policy environment. These might include the constant presence of budget deficits, globalization, devolution of policy implementation to lower levels of government, and political conflict—all of which challenge the current framework that has been developed in the profession. For many years analysts operated within the confines of budget deficits, and they thus were forced to restrain the parameters of policy possibilities because of very limited resources. In the short run the decision rules that have been adopted for creating budgets will continue to constrain activity at the national level and largely to emphasize short-term proposals.

Globalization

As discussed in chapter 3, policy issues increasingly have global dimensions, and analysts will be required to think about how policy decisions framed in the context of the US system will affect policies in other countries. Conversely, when thinking about policy issues in the United States, analysts will be challenged to think about the effects of international perspectives on domestic policy. The interrelationship between domestic and foreign issues has become fairly obvious in economic issues, particularly those related to trade and domestic production. But as the welfare policy experience has indicated, many issues are affected by changing immigration patterns and related demographic developments in other countries.

At the same time that there is increased recognition of globalization in the policy field, there is also a growing interest in policy analysis in other countries. As the field develops around the globe, it is becoming clear that it is not the uniquely American phenomenon that we once believed it to be. Increased interest in federal systems and other forms of decentralization, the growth of the European Union, and the end of the Soviet Union have all created complex political and social systems that share some attributes with the United States. These developments seem to have contributed to interest in analytic and advising processes that had not been contemplated in traditional parliamentary or centrally controlled systems.

Devolution

During the past several decades, the trends toward increasing devolution of responsibilities to state and local governments and reliance on contracting in the private sector have shifted the points of leverage for policy change away from Washington. Though there has been some interest over the years among state governments in the policy analysis function, only a minority of the states have invested in analytic capacity such as that found in the California Legislative Analyst's Office. Few of the decisions that are made in the process of budget cutting are made with the assistance of analysis; rather, they reflect raw politics in action.

Devolution of policies to state and local levels has also created new opportunities and interest in policy analysis among nongovernmental groups. Interest groups that are focused on particular policy issues have found that it is important to develop evaluation and monitoring capacities at the state and local levels. The kinds of activities and investment in analytic networks that have been undertaken by the Center on Budget and Policy Priorities involving welfare and social redistribution programs may be expected to increase in other policy areas, providing expanded opportunities for policy analysts in the nonprofit community.

Political and Ideological Conflict

It appears that the current environment of ideological and partisan conflict is likely to continue into the future. Given the intensity of the conflict in the contemporary setting, it is likely that—at least in the short run—policy analysts will continue to confront the pressures of ideological and partisan debates.

The experiences of the Congressional Research Service and the California Legislative Analyst's Office are particularly instructive for those who must think about plying their craft in such an environment. Analysts will continue to expect a range of clients with very different experiences, values, and policy agendas. They will seek to acknowledge the diverse demands of these clients, but at the same time they will try to produce analyses that are as complete and fair as possible.

A Commitment to Democratic Values

This book has indicated that there have been commentators throughout the evolution of the policy analysis field who have expressed fears about the elite and antidemocratic nature of the profession as it was originally designed. Many developments during the field's history have moved away from the elements that supported those fears. The monopoly on analysis found in the early years of practice has been broken, and analysts are now attached to a pluralistic and fragmented policy world. Though this has opened up the profession, it has also made it more difficult to define in rigorous terms the attributes that make up good policy analysis or to find effective ways of dealing with networks.

More people are now aware of the limitations of focusing only on efficiency values as they establish criteria for assessing policy options. Technological developments and a commitment to open information have eroded a tendency for analysts to hold information close at hand. Efforts to democratize data have increased the ability of various players to have information available to them. Indeed, the problem is sometimes a surplus of information and an inability to distinguish the important from the trivial. Concern about transparency has become stronger and has had an impact on the work of policy analysts.

In addition, the field has explored new ways to put into practice Aaron Wildavsky's belief that policy analysis involves social interaction. Analysts are increasingly involved with the decision makers themselves and participate in issue networks. Efforts such as participatory policy analysis have been devised to allow analysts to involve stakeholders in the process of problem definition and exploring options.

Conclusion

As this book has argued, the field of policy analysis is very different than it was when it first took shape in the 1960s or even when the first edition of this book was published in 2000. Although some observers would argue that these developments constitute a decline, I believe that the opposite is true. Policy analysis could be a richer, more interesting field than it was in its infancy. Yet there are some disturbing signs that the field has retreated into the ivory tower or assumed technocratic postures that limit its use by decision makers. At the least, instead of characterizing the policy analysis field as speaking truth to power, it would be more accurate to describe the activity as speaking truths to multiple powers. Instead of a field that focuses on a single conversation between the adviser and the ruler, it is a field in which multiple conversations are needed that take place at once. It is now a profession with many different voices that reflect the diversity and complexity of American society. We can expect these conversations to continue to develop in new ways in the future. Indeed, we can see that the field of policy analysis has reached middle age.

Note

1. Earlier faculty members often had experience as practitioners and were able to deal with both theory and practice.

Index